D1617562

FOREIGN POLICY DECISION-MAKING

FOREIGN POLICY DECISION-MAKING

A Qualitative and Quantitative Analysis of Political Argumentation

IRMTRAUD N. GALLHOFER
and WILLEM E. SARIS

PRAEGER

Westport, Connecticut
London

Library of Congress Cataloging-in-Publication Data

Gallhofer, Irmtraud N.
    Foreign policy decision-making : a qualitative and quantitative
analysis of political argumentation / Irmtraud N. Gallhofer and
Willem E. Saris.
        p.   cm.
    Includes bibliographical references and index.
    ISBN 0–275–95433–1 (alk. paper)
    1. International relations—Decision making.   I. Saris, Willem E.
II. Title.
JX1308.G35   1996
327.1′01′9—dc20   95–37652

British Library Cataloguing in Publication Data is available.

Library of Congress Catalog Card Number: 95–37652
ISBN: 0–275–95433–1

First published in 1996

Praeger Publishers, 88 Post Road West, Westport, CT 06881
An imprint of Greenwood Publishing Group, Inc.

Printed in the United States of America

The paper used in this book complies with the
Permanent Paper Standard issued by the National
Information Standards Organization (Z39.48–1984)

10 9 8 7 6 5 4 3 2 1

Contents

Preface

Our interest in the study of political decision-making originated a long time ago, when one of the authors of this book (Gallhofer 1968) wrote her Ph.D. thesis on negotiations to bring about a peace treaty between the king of France and Emperor Charles V of the Habsburg empire in the sixteenth century. The study was carried out as a historical case study, and was not capable of summarizing in a comprehensive way the detailed arguments encountered in the documents with respect to the chances of success of the various strategies considered by the decision-makers.

Not satisfied with this description, the first author consulted the second author of this book about further possibilities for studying the decision-making arguments. The second author had recently taken a course on mathematical decision-making at the Mathematical Centre in Amsterdam. Given the social science tradition of carrying out systematic empirical research based on theoretical grounds, he suggested applying decision theoretical concepts to the study of documents on political decision-making. The idea was that such theoretical notions should apply to foreign policy decisions if to any decisions, since the decision-makers have to consider different strategies and their possible consequences.

Before a long-term study was started, a test of the approach using decision theoretical concepts and models was carried out on the sixteenth century historical data concerning the decision-making of Charles V (Saris and Gallhofer 1975). This study was very illuminating, and offered considerable insights into how one would have to conduct further systematic research in this field. It was clear from this study that the decision-makers were speaking in terms of strategies, consequences, values, and probabilities. This means that the basic concepts turned out to be very useful. We were even overoptimistic about the application of rational choice models to describe people's political decision-making. In this case study, the evaluative statements and the probability statements were quantified and no distinction was drawn between individual decision-makers and the collective process. Under these conditions, the information aggregated across documents and across decision-makers showed that the decisions made were in agreement with the Subjective Expected Utility model (SEU model) often suggested (Savage 1954) and equally often attacked, for example, by Simon (1957), and Baybrooke and Lindblom (1963). In this respect, our approach was similar to that of Gross-Stein and Tanter (1980), of which we were unaware at the time. At present, we no longer analyze data across persons and documents. Nor do we quantify evaluative statements. We have even lost the conviction that we are studying the decision-making process of individual decision-makers, as we thought in the beginning.

Nevertheless, this first test of decision theory on empirical documents was very encouraging for us, as it illustrated the timeless character of the decision theory concepts. As a result, we started a long-term research project, the results of which are summarized in this book.

Our ideas about political decision-making have gradually developed over the years of this research since 1968 and can be followed in our publications. In this book we present in a systematic manner our present thinking about political decision-making. It should be made clear that we will make a distinction between arguments conducted by individual politicians to convince their colleagues and the decision-making that occurs when a group of politicians convenes. In this book we describe the results of our research on the arguments of individual politicians, based on the empirical research we have carried out over many years. In a separate volume, we will present our empirical findings with respect to the way decisions are made by groups of politicians.

Since we wanted to conduct empirical research on political argumentation with decision theory as the starting point, we had to solve a number of problems: which documents to use, how to analyze these documents, how to study the decision rules used, how to evaluate the correctness of our approach, why different people formulate decision problems differently, and so on. All these problems will be discussed in this book, but let us mention one point in advance. We used as basic documents for the quantitative study a sample of documents concerning decisions of the Dutch government in this century. We made this choice for convenience; both authors were living in the Netherlands and we could relatively easily obtain these documents. This does not mean that the conclusions drawn from this study are only applicable to the decision-making of the Dutch government. We have tried in our approach to study the features of argumentation that are common to politicians in the Western world. In order to demonstrate this point, we have added some studies to the original study where we show that the same procedures and models can be applied to such diverse decision-making processes as the decision of the Austro-Hungarian government to start World War I, the decision of the U.S. government to blockade Cuba during the missile crisis in 1962, and Hitler's decisions that led to World War II.

In this way we try to demonstrate that the findings of this book and the approach used are of more general significance than the mere generalization of our empirical evidence would formally allow.

ACKNOWLEDGMENTS

This book represents the efforts of many people. Many students have helped to gather the data, but it would not be practical to try to thank by name everyone who has contributed by coding, if only for fear of inadvertently omitting some of the coders. To all of them, our thanks. Special thanks go to Maarten Schellekens, who, together with the authors of this book, carried out the validation study of individual decision rules. Additional thanks go to the department of Methods and Techniques for Social Sciences of the Free University of Amsterdam, who in the 1970s provided funds for the development of the content analysis approach. We would also like to thank the Dutch Organization for the Advancement of Pure Research (NWO, formerly ZWO) for financing part of this research (grant nr. 43-114). We are also grateful for valuable information on substantive matters and comment on some case studies from the late prime minister, Willem Drees, Sr., and the late minister of foreign affairs, Eelco Van Kleffens. Since most of the documents under investigation were secret and unpublished, we needed to get access to the archives of the Council of Ministers, the Ministries of Foreign Affairs, Economics, and Defense, and to several collections in the State Archives. We therefore wish to express our gratitude to those officials who gave us access, and especially to Mr. M. de Graaff at the State Archives, who helped us on several occasions in the most pleasant way to find the required documents. Last but not least, we wish to thank Mr. M. Pearson for his efforts to correct our English.

Introduction

In October 1948, the Dutch government received the advice of its commander of the troops in Indonesia, at the time still a Dutch colony but seeking independence, not to continue negotiations under the auspices of a United Nations delegation with the self-proclaimed national government, but to restore law and order by military measures. He gave the following argument. If the negotiations were to continue, it would certainly lead to the loss of Indonesia. But if they were to send an ultimatum to the United Nations delegation and start military action at once should the Indonesian government fail to agree, which he considered almost certain, then there would be a fair chance of achieving positive and acceptable results. In this case he foresaw quick military success, only limited international sanctions, limited personal and material losses, and the possibility of holding on in Indonesia.

This is a typical example of the type of argument that we wish to study in this book. These arguments do not occur only in the Netherlands. Let us look at a more recent example from the United States. Then Secretary of State George Shultz's argument on May 16, 1988, for getting the military dictator Noriega out of Panama by negotiations was made during a recorded phone conversation with then Vice President Bush and later on in an Oval Office meeting in the presence of President Reagan (Shultz 1993, p. 1062). The secretary of state thought that if the United States did nothing, Noriega would remain in charge in Panama and his drug trafficking and support of Cuba would continue. If it tried to oust him by an invasion force, the risk of losing many lives, both American and Panamian, was quite high, but if they tried to continue to negotiate him out of Panama, even by dropping his drug trafficking indictment, the result would be to hold him in exile and out of Panama.

In these examples the arguments are made in order to signal a problem that arises with the perception of a discrepancy between the preferred situation and an existing situation and to convince other members of the decision-making group of the need to reach a collective decision.

This book presents a systematic empirical study of the arguments presented in the type of memoranda that we have just presented, arguments that are used as the basic material to start the discussion in a decision-making body like a ministers council. These texts are very important in the decision-making process. If they are convincing and all decision-makers agree, the decision is made immediately. If, however, the argument is not convincing, some other members of the cabinet will present alternative arguments and a lengthy process of decision-making will ensue. Given the importance of these memoranda, we will study their structure and evaluate the correctness of the arguments.

This book consists of two parts; Part 1 deals with qualitative studies of arguments of individual participants in decision-making processes, and Part 2 relates to quantitative studies of arguments.

In Chapter 1, we briefly review three different approaches to the analysis of arguments by individuals. The first set of theories deals with argumentation in the broad sense. We discuss in depth the approach suggested by Vedung (1982), who applied his theory to political science. Second, we discuss cognitive mapping theory, which was applied to political texts by Bonham and Shapiro (1986), in order to evaluate the kind of arguments we wish to study. Finally, we discuss a means-and-goals approach that comes close to the kind of analysis we use. After discussing these three different approaches, we indicate why we think that there is a need for a different approach based explicitly on decision theory concepts (Chapter 2).

We expected the concepts of decision theory to be useful in this analysis because we thought that decisions concerning foreign policy have to do with the evaluation of different possible strategies, possible outcomes of these strategies, the probabilities of these outcomes, and the evaluations (or utilities) of these outcomes. Beside these concepts, one also needs decision rules that determine what strategy should be chosen in a given situation.

In Chapter 3 we show how we have approached the study of individuals' arguments with the concepts and the rules of decision theory. Chapter 4 presents the individual arguments of Austro-Hungarian ministers as to whether or not to declare war on Serbia in July 1914, which is accepted as the beginning of World War I. Chapter 5 studies Hitler's arguments for initiating World War II. Chapter 6 presents the arguments of the members of President Kennedy's Executive Committee about how to proceed with Cuba during the missile crisis in October 1962, while Chapter 7 studies the arguments of Dutch officials and cabinet ministers over whether or not to restore law and order in Indonesia by military measures in the fall of 1948. These case studies from Austria-Hungary, Hitler's Germany, the United States, and the Netherlands demonstrate the general applicability of this approach.

Chapter 8 describes three different tests by which we have tried to demonstrate the universal character of this argumentation. Chapter 9 discusses the quality of the arguments found. Chapter 10 provides an overview of the characteristics of situation, organization, and personal and social contexts mentioned in the literature that might explain differences in the structuring of the argumentation, and then discusses the research methodology employed. The results of these later topics are presented subsequently in Chapters 11 through 13. Chapter 11 tries to explain differences in the generation of strategies. Chapter 12 deals with variations in the generation of consequences, and the last chapter (Chapter 13) offers an explanation for the differences in argumentation one can find in the data and between politicians.

FOREIGN POLICY DECISION-MAKING

Part 1

A Qualitative Analysis of the Argumentation of Individual Participants in Decision-Making Processes

As mentioned in the introduction, we discuss in this part the way arguments are constructed by individual participants in a decision process. We anticipated that the concepts of decision theory would be useful in this analysis since we believe that decisions concerning foreign policy have to do with the evaluation of different available alternatives, outcomes of these alternatives, and the probabilities and evaluations (or utilities) of these outcomes. Besides the use of these concepts, decision or argumentation rules are also required, and these determine what strategy must be chosen in a given situation.

In Chapter 2 we demonstrate our approach to the study of individuals' argumentation with the concepts and rules from decision theory. In Chapter 3 the methodology is discussed in detail and illustrated by a real-life example. Chapters 4 through 7 summarize case studies. But before we commit ourselves to our own approach, we shall discuss in the first chapter three different approaches that, although designed for the analysis of argumentation, as we shall demonstrate, do not satisfy our requirements.

Chapter 1

Argumentation in the Literature

In this chapter we will briefly review three different approaches to the analysis of arguments of individuals. The first set of theories deals with argumentation in the broad sense. We will discuss especially the approach suggested by Vedung (1982) who applied this approach to political science. Secondly, we discuss the cognitive mapping theory, which was applied to political texts by Bonham and Shapiro (1986) in order to evaluate the arguments of the authors of the text. Finally, we will discuss a means-and-goals approach that is close to the kind of analysis that we use. Following this survey, we will indicate why we think there is a need for a different approach, starting explicitly from the concepts of decision theory.

ARGUMENTATION THEORIES

The classical background of argumentation theories is logic, dialectic, and rhetoric. Modern logicians are mainly concerned with distinguishing between valid and invalid forms of argument in symbolic language.

Argumentation theories that study argumentation in natural language (e.g., Perelman and Olbrechts-Tyteca 1969; Toulmin, Rieke, and Janik 1979; Vedung 1982; Van Eemeren, Grootendorst, and Kruiger 1984, 1987) frequently combine descriptive and normative elements. In these theories, argumentation is defined as "a social, intellectual, verbal activity serving to justify or refute an opinion, consisting of a constellation of statements and directed toward obtaining the approbation of an audience" (Van Eemeren, Grootendorst, and Kruiger 1987, 7). An opinion may be an assertion, a preference, a view, a judgment, and so forth. The aim of these theories is to assess whether or not the content of the argumentation meets certain standards for good reasoning.

We will first illustrate what can be understood by an "argument" by giving a simple example:

Since the negotiations have not led to a satisfactory result, I would therefore recommend that military action be taken.

This argument consists of two parts: a premise, "Since the negotiations had not led to a satisfactory result" (also called the "reason" or "justifying statement" or "ground"), and a conclusion, "I would recommend that military action be taken" (also called the "claim" or "thesis" or "position"). The function of a premise is to support or refute a proposition. In this argument the premise supports the conclusion to take military action. Arguments that support a conclusion are called "pro arguments," and arguments that weaken or refute a proposition in order to arrive at another conclusion, which is the refutation, are called "counterarguments."

In practice, an argument consists of a set of statements that support or refute one or more propositions. We will illustrate the various steps in a potential argumentation analysis, using Vedung's method (Vedung 1982), as this author concentrates on political arguments. The following text fragment will be used:

In connection with the critical situation here in our colony, I would like to bring the following to your attention.

If the proposals of the Security Council were likely to bring about an improvement in the present untenable state of affairs here, I would be the first to recommend the acceptance of these proposals. But the contrary is true. Our ambassador has also mentioned that the measures proposed by the Security Council are inspired by "passion, fanaticism and prejudice." I therefore urge you to reject the new proposals and recommend that we take military action. It is generally recommended here and it can still lead to the destruction of the subversive local government. There might also be no sanctions imposed by the Security Council.

This text consists of premises, conclusions, and implicit rules which specify how to draw the conclusion. To analyze the text, the premises and conclusions must first be identified. Then their actual meaning must be worked out, since there is often ambiguity in texts. Thereafter, the premises and conclusions must be represented in "argumentation schemes."

Argumentation schemes are structures that contain a proposition and either the supporting premises or the refuting premises. If both kinds of premises are used in a particular argumentation, the supporting reasons and refuting premises must be represented separately. Figure 1.1 shows two argumentation schemes derived from the excerpted text. The figure displays an argumentation scheme representing the supporting reasons for the conclusion to "take military action" (Scheme 1). Scheme 2 relates to the refutation of the proposition to "accept the new proposals of the Security Council."

Given these schemes, one can proceed to establish the validity, correctness, or soundness of the argumentation. This is done by examining the conclusions and the premises in the light of some standards of rational reasoning, which consist of a set of rules (e.g., Vedung 1982, 31–39).

Figure 1.1:
Argumentation Schemes Supporting and Refuting Proposals

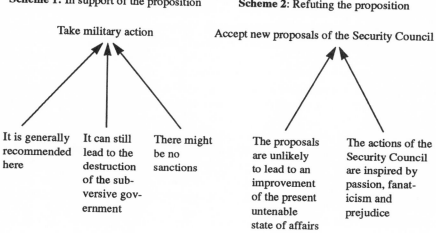

There are five important rules:

1. The argument must be consistent.

2. The argument must be clear.

3. The propositions must be supported or refuted by the premises.

4. The argument must be relevant to the subject matter.

5. The argument must be based on true premises.

Several tests can be applied to determine if these rules are followed.

The first of these rules deals with *consistency*. One can examine whether the inferences from premises to a conclusion are derived in a logically valid manner. In order to test this, one can transform each argument that consists of support for a conclusion into the following logically valid form:

Premise 1   : if p, then q

Premise 2   : p

Conclusion   : q

This form of the hypothetical syllogism is called the *modus ponens*. The analyst must establish whether each single argument can be transformed in this way. Here is one example:

Premise 1   : If military action can still lead to the destruction of the subversive
                government, then we have to take military action.

Premise 2   : It can still lead to the destruction of the subversive government.

Conclusion : Therefore we must take military action.

From the *modus ponens* it is clear that this argument is logically valid. The first premise was not stated literally in the text; it was tacit and we had to uncover it. Here the author has partially violated the rule that states that the conclusions must be supported by premises. The first premise clearly formulates the rule determining how to draw the conclusion, and the second premise states the fact. If we continued with this exercise, we could demonstrate that the other arguments in support of the conclusion are also logically valid.

An example of a logically valid form to test the refutation of a proposition is, for instance, the *modus tollens* of the hypothetical syllogism:

Premise 1   : if p, then q

Premise 2   : not q

Conclusion : not p

The logical validity of the refutation of the proposition to "accept new proposals of the Security Council" based on the premise that "the proposals are unlikely to lead to an improvement of the present untenable state of affairs" (Scheme 2) can be tested as follows :

Premise 1   : If we should accept the new proposals of the Security Council, then they
                should bring about the improvement in the present untenable situation
                here.

Premise 2   : They do not lead to an improvement in the present untenable situation
                here.

Conclusion : Therefore we cannot accept them.

This argument also is logically valid, the conclusions and premises having been stated literally in the text.

Another test for consistency relates to the detection of contradictions between premises and between conclusions. This would be the case if a person first asserted something and thereafter denied it. This is self-evidently an inconsistency since both statements cannot be true simultaneously. An inspection of the schemes (Figure 1.1) shows that no contradictions are present.

Another rule for the analysis of arguments relates to clarity. This means that conclusions and premises must not be formulated in such a way that they allow for multiple interpretations. With respect to the argument we are looking at here, this can be ruled out.

The third rule relates to relevance, that is, whether the arguments are relevant to the subject matter. Examining the premise "it is generally recommended here," employed to support the conclusion to "take military action," one gets the impression that this appeals to the prejudice that since many people support an action, it must be the right action, which is not necessarily true. Such a hidden premise is generally considered unsound, since it constitutes a stereotyped form that is irrelevant to this specific conclusion. Stereotyped forms of this kind are called "fallacies," and the one detected in the text is called an *argumentum ad populum*. A further inspection of the argument shows that the statement "the actions of the Security Council are inspired by passion, fanaticism and prejudice," which is used to argue against accepting the proposals of the Security Council, is also a stereotyped prejudice irrelevant to the specific conclusion. It is not concerned with the matter or the facts but with the motives of those who advance the proposals, and it attacks them directly. This fallacy is known as an *argumentum ad hominem*. The other premises seem to be relevant to the conclusions. As far as relevance is concerned, then, two violations have so far been detected.

But relevance also relates to the consideration of all important facts. Is there a biased selection of premises present? Has the person overlooked some facts? In the present context, for example, it can easily be shown that the person has failed to mention facts that would refute the military action, so here again some violations of the rule are detected .

The last rule states that the argument should be based on premises that are true. It is difficult to test this since there are different and conflicting criteria of truth. Vedung (1982, 165-179) summarizes some of these criteria. One conception of truth is that premises should correspond to existing facts. Another criterion is the coherence theory of truth, which means that they should be consistent with each other. Still another approach considers truth as "what is held as true." Given the difficulties with the operationalization of "truth," the argumentation under consideration will not be examined in this respect. To conclude the analysis of the soundness of the content of the argumentation, it can be stated that the argumentation in the example presented does not meet all standards of good reasoning because there are violations with respect to relevance, fallacies, and omission of premises.

This very brief introduction of argumentation theory illustrates the generality of this theory and shows that it can be applied to any kind of argument. It concentrates on the quality of these arguments, particularly considering whether the different statements support each other or contradict each other, on relevance of the premises, and so on. On the other hand, this theory is not directly aimed at the analysis of arguments in favor or against different strategies. A further analysis of this issue follows at the end of this chapter.

COGNITIVE MAPPING

Next, the possibilities of cognitive mapping (Shapiro and Bonham 1973; Axelrod 1976) are investigated. In this approach the argumentation of policy makers is studied in terms of their beliefs and values, which play a role in their

explanation of events. The cognitive structure of an individual, that is, his cognitive map, is construed as a causal diagram of beliefs. To be less abstract, we will
illustrate it with an example. The following fragment of text will be analyzed:

Our allies' intensified military activities against country X have increased tensions with
other nations, which has a negative effect on our relations with nonallies. If we explicitly
support our allies they will appreciate it. But it will damage our relations with nonallies,
who will consider us cowardly. If we do not support our allies it will lead to repercussions
in our relations with them.

In order to construct a cognitive map, first, statements in the text have to be
transformed into causal assertions. A causal assertion consists of a concept of
cause and a concept of effect linked by a causal relationship. A positive causal
link is obtained if the cause and effect concepts have the same direction, that is,
when the cause increases, the effect also increases, or when the cause decreases,
the effect also decreases. If one increases while the other decreases, the causal
link is negative. This can be depicted graphically as follows:

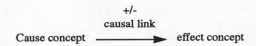

For example, the first sentence in the text contains the following causal assertion: "Our allies' intensified military activities" (cause concept) "have increased
tensions with other nations" (effect concept). The link between the two concepts
is "+" since the increase in the one leads to an increase in the other.

On the basis of the text, we have constructed a cognitive map (Figure 1.2).
The figure shows a cognitive map consisting of two values that are in effect
concepts, "the relations with nonallies" and "the relations with allies." Next to
the antecedent event of "the allies' intensified military activities against country
X" the map contains two policy alternatives, to support the allies or not to support them. It also contains three concepts relating to beliefs about the behavior or
intentions of other nations: "tensions with other nations," "nonallies consider us
cowardly" and "allies appreciate it."

A rule has been specified by which one can determine on the basis of a
cognitive map which policy alternative will be chosen (Bonham and Shapiro
1986). The rule states that one expects an alternative to be chosen only if the
total effect of the alternative has a positive overall sign. In order to determine
this, one has to calculate the total effect of each alternative on the values. The
computation of the total effect of "support of allies" on the two values consists
of taking into account the direct and indirect effects. In order to obtain the sign
of the indirect effects, the direct effects, consisting of "+" or "-" leading via
specific paths to V_1 and V_2, are multiplied. The total effect of each policy alternative is calculated by taking the sum of its effects.

However, in our example, "support of allies" produces one negative indirect

Figure 1.2:
Cognitive Map of the Argumentation

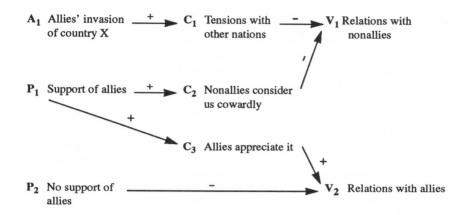

Abbreviations: A antecedent event; V value concept; C cognitive concept (beliefs about the behavior or intentions of others); P policy alternative.

effect $(P_1 * C_2 * V_1 = + * - = -)$ and the other indirect effect from P_1 on V_2 is positive $(P_1 * C_3 * V_2 = + * + = +)$. The total effect of P_1 on the values is thus not entirely positive. With the other option, "no support of allies," only a negative effect is obtained (direct effect P_2 on V_2 is negative). Since the effects of both policy alternatives on the values are mainly or partially negative, the conclusion would be that the decision-maker should search for another alternative.

This cognitive mapping analysis of the choice between alternatives comes fairly close to meeting the needs of our investigations, but the study of decision theory in Chapter 2 will show that the concepts of decision theory are more appropriate to the study of choice rules, or what we call "argumentation rules," making the rules simpler and easier to follow.

MEANS-AND-ENDS APPROACHES

Means-and-ends approaches are procedures more directed toward decision-making (e.g., Dunn 1981; Kuypers 1980; Biel and Montgomery 1989; Van de Graaf and Hoppe 1989). The argumentation of a policy maker is viewed in these approaches as a policy plan intended to improve a given situation in the long run. A policy maker is considered to have in mind a desirable situation for the future (a goal, objective, or end) and he selects available means to bring about this desirable situation. We will briefly illustrate this approach using the method developed by Kuypers (1980) and further developed by Van de Graaf and Hoppe (1989).

In the approach described here, a "goal" or "end" is defined more precisely as the situation desired by the policy maker, who must have the will to achieve it and the means to realize it, at least approximately (Van de Graaf and Hoppe 1989, 81-84). A "means" is an action or a course of actions the policy maker must be able and willing to carry out in order to achieve the ends. Means-and-end relations can be represented in a goal tree. There are various methods for deriving goal trees (e.g., Allen 1978; Von Winterfeldt and Edwards 1986; Biel and Montgomery 1989). Here, a goal tree is taken to consist of chains of final relations between means and goals. A final relation consists of terms that link means to means, ends to ends, or means to ends. The assumption behind arguments expressed in goals and means is that a means should be chosen if it leads to the desired end. Figure 1.3 displays a goal tree based on the following fragment of text:

We want to create a better image of our country abroad. In order to achieve this, our cultural attaches must organize more cultural manifestations promoting our country abroad. A prerequisite for these manifestations is to have sufficient funds. These funds must be created by stimulating businessmen to take part in these manifestations and by increasing the government subsidies.

The figure shows that such arguments consist of specifications of sequences of means to ends, from which subsequent means follow until the central goal is reached. According to this policy maker, the central end or main goal is to bring about "a better image of our country abroad." In order to approach this desired

Figure 1.3:
Goal Tree of a Means-and-Ends Analysis

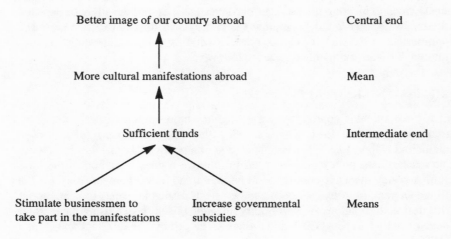

situation, he intends first to raise funds, which is considered an intermediate end. The means to achieve this subgoal are twofold: stimulate businessmen to take part in the cultural manifestations abroad, and increase government funding. By these two means, in the opinion of this policy maker, sufficient funds will be acquired. Once the funds are available, cultural manifestations can be organized abroad that will improve the country's image in the long run. The sequence indicates that the means lead to the end and therefore they should be implemented. When a plan exists in the form of a goal tree, it can be evaluated in terms of its expected effects and its acceptability, feasibility, efficiency, costs, and so forth. (Van de Graaf and Hoppe 1989, 115-116) before a decision is made about implementation.

Having studied the possibilities of means-and-ends approaches, we conclude that they have considerable overlap with decision theory (Gallhofer, Saris, and Van de Valk 1978) but that they relate to long-term policy planning in a time of noncrisis rather than to situations where a specific problem is signalled for which a solution must be sought in the immediate future. In the latter situations, which are the situations we intend to study, policy makers argue quite differently, as we will see.

CONCLUSIONS

This chapter introduced three different approaches to the analysis of argumentation. The more or less classical argumentation theory is very general and does not offer specific provisions for arguments concerning the selection of alternatives from a set of possibilities. This means that there are no rules that indicate which of the alternatives seems to be the best in any sense. For this reason, this argumentation theory is too general for our purposes.

The cognitive mapping approach is very useful for analysis of causal schemes in texts. Such causal arguments occur frequently in arguments pro or contra different alternatives. They indicate the likelihood that certain events will or will not occur. It maybe the case that some texts can be analyzed by this text analysis approach as well as by our decision theory approach (Bonham and Shapiro 1986). On the other hand, we think that cognitive mapping is less attractive where arguments pro or contra different alternatives are concerned, because the choice rule is too crude to take into account probabilities. It is also difficult to deal with conditional statements such as "if the Germans win the war, then — but if the allies win, then —." Since both features occur frequently in texts of decision-makers when they specify their preference for an alternative action, we did not choose cognitive mapping as the tool of text analysis.

The means-and-ends approach is one that comes very close to the type of instrument we were looking for. However, there is a difference between the type of text for which this approach is best suited and the one we want to analyze in this book. If decision-makers or agencies have a lot of time and want to elaborate the possibilities of realizing a certain aim, for example, a new rail connection between two towns, then a means-and-end approach will be most useful. If, however, a government is confronted with a problem that has to be solved, like an uprising in a colony or a proposal to join NATO, one does not have an explicit goal that one would like to realize but must evaluate two or more different possible alternatives: military action or not, joining or not. In such cases one has to evaluate the consequences of these options in order to determine which course of action is the best, taking into account the different side effects of the different options. It seems that in the latter case, the starting point is the choice of alternatives. In the means-and-ends approach, the starting point is the goal. Therefore the means-and-ends approach would seem to be a good instrument for a different kind of text than the texts we analyze in this book. Given that none of these approaches is satisfactory for our purposes, in the next chapter we will discuss the decision theory approach and show that this approach is better suited to the kind of texts in which foreign policy decision-makers specify their preferences.

Chapter 2

Argumentation from the Perspective of Decision Theory

Arguments in favor of one alternative above others can be formulated in very many different ways. In this chapter we will survey systematically the various arguments, but before doing so we will give as an illustration four different arguments for the same choice.

Example 1

If we take military action the chance is very high that we will be able to restore law and order. This is the most desirable outcome for us. However, there is also a very small chance that we will not be able to entirely restore law and order. This would, of course, be less satisfactory for us. If we do nothing we will certainly lose our colony. In my opinion this is the worst outcome. I think we must select the alternative for which we can expect the best results. Since this is certainly true for the choice of the military action, I recommend that we go ahead with it.

Example 2

If we take military action the chance is very high that we will restore law and order. But there is also a very small chance that we would lose our colony. If we do nothing, it is almost certain that we will lose our colony. I therefore suggest that we select the strategy with the highest probability of a positive outcome, which is to take military action.

Example 3

If we take military action, I am convinced that we will restore law and order and there will be no national unrest. If we do nothing, I am certain that law and order will not be restored, and there will be no national unrest either. Since the situation in our colony will be much better if we take military action than if we do nothing, and nationally the outcome, which is quite good, is the same for both strategies, I recommend that we take military action.

Example 4

If we do nothing, we will not restore law and order in our colony. If we take military action, it is not only possible that we will restore law and order but it is even possible that the self-proclaimed rebel government will cease to exist. We should choose the strategy which only leads to positive outcomes. Therefore I recommend that we take military action.

Each of these examples sets out an argument in favor of military action, while the rejected alternative action in each case is simply "doing nothing." This alternative is very common in this kind of text. These examples also have in common that the consequences of the possible actions are specified: the restoration of law and order, loss of the colony, national political unrest, and the liquidation of the rebel government.

Furthermore, we see that a rule is mentioned that indicates how a choice should be made. In the first example it is said, "We must select the alternative for which we can expect the best results." The second example states: "We select the strategy with the highest probability of a positive outcome." In the third example it is said, "Since the situation in our colony will be much better if we take military action than if we do nothing, and nationally the outcome is the same for both strategies, I recommend that we take military action." Finally, in the last example the following rule is mentioned: "We should choose the strategy which only leads to positive outcomes." It is clear that a different rule is suggested each time, but on the other hand, the suggested choice is always the same, namely, taking military action.

These rules are different since the texts also partially differ. The differences lie in the specified evaluations of the outcomes (or "utilities," as they are often called) and probabilities. We will make a distinction between statements about probabilities and utilities with intensity and those without intensity. Let us clarify what is meant by intensities. In Example 1, probabilities and utilities of the outcomes have been specified with intensities. This example mentions "If we take military action the chance is very high that . . . " and also, "However, there is also a very small chance that . . . " and finally: "If we do nothing we will certainly lose our colony." All these probability statements not only specify that something might happen but they also communicate in an imprecise way the extent of this probability (respectively: close to 1, close to 0, and exactly 1). If probability statements try to specify the extent or at least a rank order, then we speak of probability statements with intensity. In the same way, we treat the evaluations of the outcomes or utilities. In Example 1, it is said, "We will be able to restore law and order. This is the most desirable outcome for us" and later, "If we lose our colony, in my opinion this is the worst outcome." Here we see again that the statements try to communicate some order or degree, and therefore we speak of utilities with intensities. Example 1, therefore, is characterized by probabilities and utilities with intensities.

At the other extreme, Example 4 is characterized by probabilities and utilities without intensities. In this example it is said, "If we do nothing, we will not restore law and order in our colony. If we take military action, it is not only possible that we will restore law and order but it is even possible that the self-proclaimed rebel government will cease to exist." In these arguments only possibilities are mentioned, not probabilities with intensities. With respect to utilities, no information is explicitly given, but from the context it is clear that restoring law and order is something positive and that not restoring it is therefore negative. The liquidation of the rebel government is of course also positive, even though this has not been stated. Clearly, if no explicit statements exist, there is no indication of the intensity of the utilities. Thus the fourth example is characterized by probabilities and utilities without intensities.

The reader can check for himself that Example 2 is characterized by probability statements with intensities and utility statements without intensities, and that Example 3 is characterized by utility statements with intensities and probability statements without intensities.

This brief outline suggests that the arguments differ markedly depending on the way the probabilities and utilities are specified. This hypothesis is also summarized in Table 2.1, which suggests that, depending on whether utilities and probabilities are specified with or without intensity statements, we expect different rules to apply in order to predict the preferred choice. The table suggests that we expect four classes of decision rules to exist. The rules we expect to apply to the different situations can be obtained from decision theory. Therefore we shall first introduce some basic concepts and decision rules from decision theory, and then we will review the different arguments that we expect in the documents.

DECISION THEORY

Decision theory was originally developed by Von Neumann and Morgenstern (1947) and subsequently further elaborated through collaboration between stat-

Table 2.1:
Classification of Texts by the Precision of the Information about Utilities and Probabilities

	Utilities with intensities	Utilities without intensities
Probabilities with intensities	I	II
Probabilities without intensities	III	IV

isticians and experimental psychologists (e.g., Savage 1954; Edwards 1961; Fishburn 1964; Keeney and Raiffa 1976).

In the sections that follow, the concepts employed are first introduced, then decision trees and decision tables and the basic decision rules are discussed.

Concepts of Decision Theory

A strategy is a program or course of action that can be adopted. At its simplest, it can consist of only one "alternative" or "option," such as "accept the proposals of the Security Council." But it can also consist of a series of alternatives or options to be adopted under certain conditions, such as "continue to negotiate, and if this is unsuccessful, take military action."

When a decision-maker specifies the available or relevant alternatives, he must also take into account the "possible actions of the other nations" involved. The other nations, in pursuance of their own goals, might take measures that counteract the decision-maker's own. In order to exclude undesirable effects, a decision-maker is therefore required to review possible actions of other nations. The following example of a strategy illustrates the incorporation of actions that another nation might take: "Accept the proposals of the Security Council; if the others do not accept them, take military action."

Then again, events may occur that change the entire situation. These are called "new developments," since they are caused neither by the actions of the decision-maker himself nor by the actions of other nations, but by "nature." Before choosing a strategy, a decision-maker may also take into account the likely occurrences of new developments. An example of a new development would be, for instance, "If nobody wins the war" or "If the harvest turns out to be bad."

The choice of strategy is based on the likely outcomes or consequences or results. Since not all outcomes are desirable, a decision-maker should examine the entire set of relevant "possible outcomes for the decision-maker's own nation" before selecting a strategy. An example of a possible outcome might be "the loss of territory" or "the gain of territory." Outcomes do not necessarily coincide with goals, even when they are desirable, since they may represent only the partial realization of these goals. Outcomes can also be composed of several "aspects" or "dimensions," which are considered systematically across strategies. Decision-makers could, for instance, consider for each outcome the international, national, and legal aspects.

Since some outcomes or aspects of outcomes are more desirable than others, the choice of strategy is based also on the degree of desirability of the different outcomes or aspects. A decision-maker will therefore explicitly assign "subjective values" or "utilities" to the different outcomes or aspects of outcomes and new developments. They are considered subjective because they relate to the particular decision-maker.

The actions of other nations are uncertain. Whether new developments and outcomes or aspects of outcomes will occur is also uncertain. Which strategy, then, will most probably produce desirable outcomes? To answer this question, it is necessary to estimate subjectively the probabilities of occurrence of outcomes or aspects of outcomes, new developments, and actions of other nations. The argumentation of decision-makers in terms of these concepts can be represented in a decision tree, known also as a decision diagram.

Decision Trees

A decision tree consists of a chronological sequence of the alternatives (A) available to the decision-maker; the possible actions of other nations (AO), where appropriate; the possible new developments (ND), if specified; and the possible outcomes (O) for the decision-maker. The subjective values or utilities (U) of the possible outcomes (O) as well as the subjective probabilities (P) of the actions of the other nations, the new developments, and the outcomes are also included in the diagram. Figure 2.1 shows an example of a decision tree. The tree starts with a node or branching point specifying the available strategies.

In this example, two strategies, S_1 and S_2, are assumed to be available as far as the argumentation is concerned. If S_1 is adopted, the decision-maker has to start with action A_{11}. If A_{11} is taken, the decision-maker foresees two possible outcomes, O_{11} or O_{12}. For both outcomes, a subjective utility is indicated. For O_{11} it is $U(O_{11})$, and for O_{12} it is $U(O_{12})$. The likelihood of occurrence of the outcomes is also specified on the branches by subjective probabilities. Outcome O_{11} has probability p_{11}, and outcome O_{12} has probability p_{12} which is $(1-p_{11})$ since $(p_{11}+p_{12})=1$. The formulation of the probability statements indicates the assumption that subjective probabilities, relating to alternative outcomes deriving from the same node or branching point in the tree, also sum up to one.

Figure 2.1:
A Decision Tree

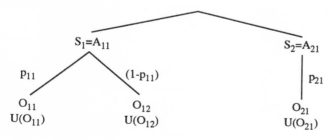

Symbols: S_i strategy i
          A_{ij} alternative j under strategy i
          O_{ij} outcome j under strategy i
          $U(O_{ij})$ subjective utility of outcome j under strategy i
          P_{ij} subjective probability of the O_{ij}'s

If the decision-maker adopts the second strategy (S_2), he would employ action A_{21}, and in this case he foresees only one outcome, O_{21}, with subjective utility $U(O_{21})$ and probability p_{21}. Since he has indicated only one outcome, p_{21} specifies a probability of one, which is certainty. Although this scheme represents a trivial argument, whereas the argumentation is generally more complex than this, as an illustration of the approach, it serves its purpose.

Figure 2.2:
A More Elaborate Decision Tree

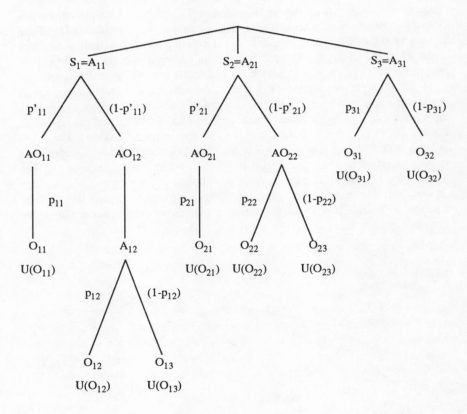

Symbols: S_i strategy i
A_{ij} alternative j under strategy i
AO_{ij} action of the opponent j under strategy i
O_{ij} outcome j under strategy i
$U(O_{ij})$ subjective utility of outcome j under strategy i
P_{ij} subjective probability of the O_{ij}'s
P'_{ij} subjective probability of the AO_{ij}'s

The method used to construct decision trees is taken from Fishburn (Fishburn 1964). It differs slightly from Raiffa's method (Raiffa 1968) in that the latter indicates with specific symbols whether nodes or branching points relate to decisions or to chance. The node leading either to A_{11} or A_{21} in Figure 2.1 would specify a decision node, according to Raiffa, since the decision-maker has two alternatives at his disposition, that he has himself generated. The node leading either to O_{11} or O_{12} would be a chance node, since the decision-maker can only indicate the likelihood of these events but has no influence on their occurrence. Furthermore, in Raiffa's approach there is no distinction made between the actions of opponents, new developments, and outcomes, which are all called events.

Figure 2.2 shows the scheme of a more elaborate decision tree. In this scheme the decision-maker considers three available strategies. If he employs Strategy 1, he starts with action A_{11}. Subsequently he is prepared for two possible reactions by his opponent. If his opponent employs AO_{11}, he is certain that O_{11} will occur. If the opponent takes AO_{12}, the decision-maker may choose action A_{12}, which could lead to either O_{12} or O_{13}. When employing Strategy 2, the decision-maker would start with A_{21}. Thereafter his opponent could react either with AO_{21} or AO_{22}. Outcome O_{21} would follow from AO_{21}, according to the decision-maker. If his opponent uses AO_{22}, either O_{22} or O_{23} could occur. Strategy 3 consists of only one action by the decision-maker, A_{31}, which could lead either to O_{31} or O_{32}. This slightly more elaborate example of a decision tree comes quite close to modelling the political argumentation that will be presented in the coming chapters.

A final example (Figure 2.3) illustrates a decision scheme where outcomes consist of multiple aspects. Figure 2.3 shows a decision tree consisting of three available strategies. For each possible outcome, the decision-maker considers the same three aspects. They differ only with respect to their subjective utilities.

The examples given show that a decision tree presents the structure of the decision problem in terms of the number of available strategies, the number of outcomes, and other foreseen events and indicates the evaluation of probabilities and utilities. Decision trees also give detailed descriptions of foreseen steps by which the outcomes are obtained. A less detailed representation of the same information is given in decision tables. These tables can be derived from the decision trees. Since these tables are frequently used in this text, we will introduce them here.

Decision Tables

A decision table is a matrix with the strategies in rows and the outcomes in columns, while in the cells is specified the utility and probability of the outcomes expected for each specific strategy (row) and outcome (column). An example of such a derived table is presented in Table 2.2, which is derived from the decision tree of Figure 2.1.

Figure 2.3:
A Decision Tree with Multiple Aspects

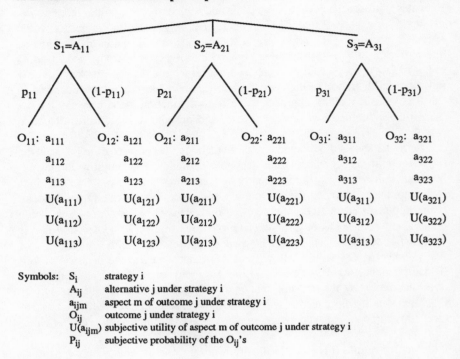

Symbols: S_i strategy i
          A_{ij} alternative j under strategy i
          a_{ijm} aspect m of outcome j under strategy i
          O_{ij} outcome j under strategy i
          $U(a_{ijm})$ subjective utility of aspect m of outcome j under strategy i
          P_{ij} subjective probability of the O_{ij}'s

Table 2.2:
The Decision Table Derived from Figure 2.1

Strategies	Outcomes		
	O_{11}	O_{12}	O_{21}
S_1	$U(O_{11})$	$U(O_{12})$	
	P_{11}	P_{12}	
S_2			$U(O_{21})$
			P_{21}

Table 2.3:
The Decision Table Derived from Figure 2.2

	O_{11}	O_{12}	O_{13}	O_{21}	O_{22}	O_{23}	O_{31}	O_{32}
S_1	Pt_{11}	Pt_{12}	Pt_{14}					
	$U(O_{11})$	$U(O_{12})$	$U(O_{13})$					
S_2				Pt_{21}	Pt_{22}	Pt_{23}		
				$U(O_{21})$	$U(O_{22})$	$U(O_{23})$		
S_3							Pt_{31}	Pt_{32}
							$U(O_{31})$	$U(O_{32})$

Symbols: p^t total subjective probability of the O_{ij}'s

This table contains exactly the same information as Figure 2.1. The information is simply presented in a different way. This is not always the case. If the decision tree consists of different stages, a reduction of the tree is necessary in order to represent the tree in a table. In that case the probability of obtaining an outcome for a strategy is the product of the probabilities along the path to the outcome in the tree.

Let us clarify this approach by an example. For illustrative purposes, we use the decision tree of Figure 2.2, where several stages are specified. Table 2.3 gives the representation of this tree in a table. If the construction of the table requires the calculation of the probability (P^t_{ij}) of the outcome O_{ij} for strategy S_i, these probabilities can be calculated as the products of the probabilities along the path from S_i to O_{ij} in the tree. This leads to the following results:

$P^t_{11} = p'_{11}*p_{11}$,

$P^t_{12} = (1-p'_{11})*p_{12}$,

$P^t_{13} = (1-p'_{11})*(1-p_{12})$,

$P^t_{21} = p'_{21}*p_{21}$,

$P^t_{22} = (1-p'_{21})*p_{22}$,

$P^t_{23} = (1-p'_{21})*(1-p_{22})$,

$P^t_{31} = p_{31}$,

$P^t_{32} = (1-p_{31})$.

After these calculations, this table contains all the information about the decision problem required to select a strategy. In order to select a strategy, one needs decision rules that specify how one should select a strategy, which is in some sense optimal. This will be the topic of the next section.

Decision Rules

Originally the only decision rules discussed were the Subjective Expected Utility, or SEU, model and the Multi-Attribute SEU, or MAUT-SEU, model (Von Neuman and Morgenstern 1947; Savage 1954). The SEU model prescribes that the decision-maker should choose the strategy with the highest subjective expected utility, which is defined as the sum over the products of the probabilities and the utilities for each strategy. For strategy S_i this would be:

$$SEU\ (S_i) = \sum_{j=1}^{k} p_{ij}\ U(O_{ij})$$

where SEU (S_i) indicates the subjective expected utility of strategy i, p_{ij} the subjective probability of the occurrence of outcome j under strategy i, and U_{ij} the subjective utility of outcome j under strategy i.

If the SEU for each strategy is calculated, these quantities can be compared and the strategy with the largest SEU can be chosen. If each outcome is characterized by different aspects, the definition of SEU (S_i) changes, but the rule remains the same. In that case the MAUT-SEU for strategy S_i is defined as:

$$SEU\ (S_i) = \sum_{j=1}^{k} p_{ij} \sum_{m=1}^{m} U(a_{ijm})$$

where SEU (S_i) indicates the subjective expected utility of strategy i, p_{ij} the subjective probability of the occurrence of outcome j under strategy i, and $U(a_{ijm})$ the subjective utility of the mth aspect of outcome j under strategy i.

These models specify that one should choose the strategy that, averaged over a number of occasions, would lead to the best result. It is questionable whether one would wish to apply this criterion for selection of a strategy if one could make a choice only once, as is often the case in political decision making.

It is also clear that the application of these rules requires very precise data and good calculation skills. In normal life neither requirement is often satisfied. Therefore, psychologists concerned with empirical research on decision-making have looked for alternative rules, or heuristics, which require less precise data and hardly any calculation, so that they are more plausible in practice (Tversky 1972; Svenson 1979; Von Winterfeldt and Edwards 1986). These decision rules can be classified according to the amount of information they require with respect to probabilities and utilities. Table 2.4 summarizes this classification.

Table 2.4:
Relationship between Decision Rules and the Precision of Information about Utilities and Probabilities

	Utilities with intensities	Utilities without intensities
Probabilities with intensities	SEU model MAUT-SEU model I	Risk-Avoidance Rules II

Probabilities without intensities	Minimax Rule
	MAUT Rules:
	  Dominance Rule
	  Lexicographic Rule
	  Addition-of-Utilities Rule, etc.
	III
		Simon's Rule
		Reversed Simon Rule
		
		IV

The table shows that there are decision models which require probabilities and utilities with intensities. There are also decision rules that require only utilities and probabilities without intensities, which means that the utilities need only be indicated as "good" or "bad" and the probabilities in terms of "certain" or "uncertain."

It is evident that this classification of decision models fits very well with the classification of the texts we gave in Table 2.1. This "coincidence" suggests that there are different decision rules available for each class of texts previously distinguished. Rather than discuss all the different decision models first in this section and later again in the section on argumentation, we shall discuss these different models in the course of reviewing the different argumentations for the four classes of problem descriptions we have distinguished.

FOUR CLASSES OF ARGUMENTATION

After the introduction of the basic concepts of decision theory, we now want to look at the use of these concepts and rules in argumentation. In this context, an argument consists of four components:

1. A description of the structure of the decision problem

2. A rule for deriving a conclusion: if a condition is satisfied, then S_i must be chosen

3. Information on whether the condition is satisfied in practice

4. The conclusion that follows

The structure of this type of argumentation is in principle always the same. The point of further research is to determine the relationship between the description of the structures of the decision problems and the rules that can be used for the derivation of conclusions with respect to the choice of a strategy.

We have concentrated in our approach on texts that describe the decision problem in terms of the different available alternatives, the possible outcomes, the probabilities, and the utilities of these outcomes. We have also mentioned that the descriptions can vary in the precision of the utility and probability statements. We have made the distinction between four different classes of descriptions depending on the precision of the utility and probability statements.

Given that the decision rules can be classified in the same classes with respect to the information required for the rule, we can formulate the prediction that the decision rules from a specific class should also be the rules used in the formulation of the conditions for the derivation of choices of strategies in these same classes. If this is the case, these decision rules applied to the description of the decision problem should lead to the conclusion that is also drawn in the text. In the rest of this chapter we shall outline the types of argumentation for the different classes starting with the Class I type of descriptions.

Argumentations in Class I

Cell 1 in Table 2.1 contains descriptions of decision problems specified with intensities for probabilities and utilities. Cell 1 of Table 2.4 contains models that require probabilities and utilities with intensities. One of the rules mentioned in Class I is the Subjective Expected Utility (SEU) model, according to which a decision-maker should choose the strategy with the highest subjective expected utility as again defined here:

$$SEU\ (S_i) = \sum_{j=1}^{k} p_{ij}\ U_{ij}$$

where SEU (S_i) indicates the subjective expected utility of strategy i, p_{ij} the subjective probability of the occurrence of outcome j under strategy i, and U_{ij} the subjective utility of outcome j under strategy i.

Argumentation that uses the SEU rule can be summarized formally in the following way:

1. Description : Utilities and probabilities indicated with intensities and no aspects of outcomes

2. Rule   : If SEU (S_i) > SEU (S_j) then S_i must be chosen

3. Condition : SEU (S_i) > SEU (S_j)

4. Conclusion : S_i must be chosen

The first component of the argument in this class should give a description of the problem in statements indicating, for each strategy, the possible outcomes without systematic aspects but with statements concerning probabilities and utilities that have been specified with intensities.

The second refers to the argumentation rule, which is the same as the decision rule in this class of problems. The third component refers to the factual situation: whether the specified condition is satisfied for one of the strategies. If this condition is satisfied, one can conclude that a particular strategy should be selected.

It is clear that the decision-maker must translate his evaluations of probabilities and utilities into numbers and then perform for each available strategy a computation by taking the products of the probabilities and utilities for each outcome and summing them. We have already mentioned that it is quite unlikely that decision-makers actually behave in this way. This does not mean, however, that arguments of this kind do not occur. An example of such an argument is given in Example 1 and repeated below:

If we take military action the chance is very high that we will be able to restore law and order. This is the most desirable outcome for us. However, there is also a very small chance that we will not be able to entirely restore law and order. This would, of course, be less satisfactory for us. If we do nothing we will certainly lose our colony. In my opinion this is the worst outcome. I think we must select the alternative for which we can expect the best results. Since this is certainly true for the choice of the military action, I recommend that we go ahead with it.

Figure 2.4:
Decision Tree for an Argument Using the SEU Model

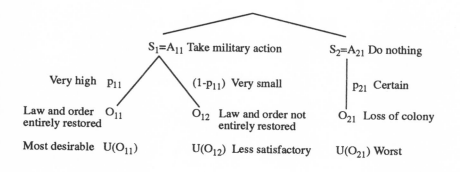

Symbols: S_i strategy i
           A_{ij} alternative j under strategy i
           O_{ij} outcome j under strategy i
           $U(O_{ij})$ subjective utility of outcome j under strategy i
           P_{ij} subjective probability of the O_{ij}'s

Figure 2.4 displays a decision tree for this argument. The decision tree shows that for each strategy, outcomes without aspects have been indicated, while the utilities and probabilities are rank-ordered, so that they are specified with intensities. The rule specified is a very weak formulation of the SEU Rule: "I think we must select the alternative for which we can expect the best results." One cannot expect more precise formulations of such a rule in a text. But if the rule is applied to this description, one can see that strategy S_1 will certainly lead to a more satisfactory outcome than S_2, as stated in the text, and that therefore even without calculations this rule leads to the choice of S_1, the strategy that is indeed proposed in the example.

It should be clear that this is an exceptional case. Normally a conclusion cannot be drawn without numerical information and calculation. This point is illustrated in the next example of this class.

The next decision rule mentioned in Cell I of Table 2.4 is the Multi-Attribute Subjective Utility (MAUT-SEU) model. This model also directs that a decision-maker should choose the strategy with the highest subjective expected utility. But it differs from SEU in so far as outcomes consist of several attributes or aspects or dimensions that have to be considered systematically across strategies and separately evaluated.

Argumentations that use the MAUT-SEU model can be summarized formally in the following way:

1. Description : Description of outcomes in terms of aspects, probabilities and utilities with intensities
2. Rule   : If MAUT-SEU (S_i) > MAUT-SEU (S_j) then S_i must be chosen
3. Condition   : MAUT-SEU (S_i) > MAUT-SEU (S_j)
4. Conclusion : S_i must be chosen

The decision-maker has an even harder task in this case than in the previous example. He is supposed to sum the subjective utilities assigned to each dimension of each outcome of a strategy before multiplying them with the probabilities, and again sum these products in order to obtain the MAUT-SEU score for each strategy. Although this argument is complicated, this does not mean that it cannot be formulated. The following example illustrates this:

If we take military action, the chance is very high that we will restore law and order in our colony and that there will be no international sanctions against us. This outcome would be very good for us at the colonial level as well as at the international level. However, there is also a very small chance that we will restore law and order in our colony but still attract some minor international sanctions. This would be very good at the colonial level, but less good at the international level. If we do nothing, we certainly cannot restore law and order in our colony, but there is no risk of sanctions at the international level. This would of course be very bad at the colonial level but quite good at the international level. I think we must select the strategy with the highest expectation of a favorable outcome, which is undoubtedly the military action. I therefore recommend that we take military action.

Figure 2.5 displays the decision tree based on this argument. The decision tree shows that for each outcome the decision-maker has systematically considered two aspects, a colonial and an international one. These aspects are evaluated separately in terms of rank order. The probabilities are also indicated by rank order. Both utilities and probabilities are thus indicated with intensities.

The decision rule mentioned is again a very simple one: "I think we must select the strategy with the highest expectation of a favorable outcome." Even though the decision-maker claims that military action satisfies this condition, it is hard to imagine how a decision-maker can expect others to be convinced by this argument without numerical values and calculation. S_1 can lead to O_{12}, which is very good with respect to the law and order aspect and "less good" with respect to the international aspect. On the other hand, S_2 will certainly lead to O_{21}, which is quite good with respect to the international aspect and very bad with respect to the law and order aspect. Only more precise numerical information about these utilities and the probabilities can show whether MAUT-SEU (S_1) is larger than MAUT-SEU (S_2) and therefore whether the conclusion to choose S_1 is correct.

Figure 2.5:
Decision Tree for an Argument Using the MAUT-SEU Model

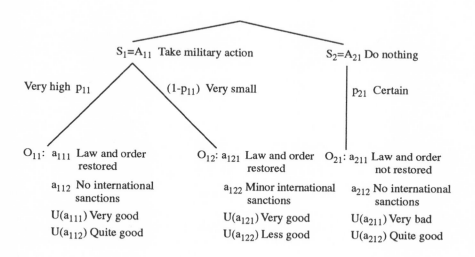

Symbols:	S_i	strategy i
	A_{ij}	alternative j under strategy i
	a_{ijm}	aspect m of outcome j under strategy i
	O_{ij}	outcome j under strategy i
	$U(a_{ijm})$	subjective utility of aspect m of outcome j under strategy i
	P_{ij}	subjective probability of the O_{ij}'s

From our discussion, it is clear that these models are quite complicated, since most of the time they require computations and estimates of probabilities and utilities. One can therefore assume that these arguments are very seldom used in political argumentation. This assumption is supported by evidence from psychological experiments (e.g., Tversky and Kahnemann 1986), which have shown that even in simple choice situations, individuals violate the implications of these models. Only in the case studies carried out by Saris and Gallhofer (1975), Gross-Stein and Tanter (1980) and Maoz (1981, 1986) did the MAUT-SEU model mostly fit the strategy choice. In our opinion, however, this result may have been due to the method used, which allowed inferences across documents when decision trees were being constructed.

In the next sections we will give ample evidence of argumentation in favor of strategies that are much simpler in the sense that they do not require any calculations on the part of the decision-maker or his audience. It should, however, also be said that such simplifications are only possible by reducing the complexity of the description of the decision problem, ignoring variations in the probabilities and/or utilities. We will come back to this problem later, after discussing the different types of argumentation.

Argumentation Rules in Class II

The rules of Class II (Table 2.4) are called "Risk-Avoidance rules." They require only probabilities with intensities, which means that the probability statements must at least indicate a rank order. The utility statements are supposed to be without intensities. The latter need only be indicated by positive or negative connotations in terms of "good" or "bad." These rules have been developed previously by the authors (Gallhofer and Saris 1979b). There are two versions of this model, the Positive Risk-Avoidance model and the Negative Risk-Avoidance model.

The decision rule for the Positive Risk-Avoidance model suggests selecting the strategy with the highest probability of positive outcomes, or

$$\text{If } P(O_{i+}) > P(O_{j+}) \text{ then } S_i \text{ must be chosen}$$

where $P(O_{i+})$ indicates the probability of a positive outcome under strategy i.

The Negative Risk-Avoidance model suggests selecting the strategy with the lowest probability of negative outcomes, or

$$\text{If } P(O_{i-}) < P(O_{j-}) \text{ then } S_i \text{ must be chosen}$$

where $P(O_{j-})$ indicates the probability of a negative outcome under strategy j.

Arguments using the Positive Risk-Avoidance Rule should be formulated as follows:

1. Description : Description of the outcomes with intensities for probabilities but not for utilities
2. Rule : If $P(O_{i+}) > P(O_{j+})$ then S_i must be chosen
3. Condition : $P(O_{i+}) > P(O_{j+})$
4. Conclusion : S_i must be chosen

Arguments using the Negative Risk-Avoidance Rule should be formulated as follows:

1. Description : Description of the outcomes with intensities for probabilities but not for utilities
2. Rule : If $P(O_{i-}) < P(O_{j-})$ then S_i must be chosen
3. Condition : $P(O_{i-}) < P(O_{j-})$
4. Conclusion : S_i must be chosen

The following text fragment illustrates one version of these rules :

If we take military action the chance is very high that we will restore law and order. But there is also a very small chance that we would lose our colony. If we do nothing, it is almost certain that we will lose our colony. I suggest that we select the strategy with the highest probability of a positive outcome, which is to take military action. Therefore I am in favor of military action.

Figure 2.6 presents the decision tree for the description of the decision problem. The description indicates that the probabilities are indicated with intensities but not the utilities. Therefore a Class II rule should apply. In the text, the Positive Risk-Avoidance Rule is mentioned, and indeed application of this rule leads to the choice of strategy 1.

It is, however, interesting to note that the writer could just as well have cited the negative version of the Risk-Avoidance Rule. Given the description of the decision problem, this would have led to exactly the same conclusion, which shows that sometimes different decision rules can lead to the same conclusion. Perhaps a more important point to note from this example is that conclusions can be drawn without any computations.

Argumentation Rules in Class III

Class III in Table 2.1 contains descriptions of arguments that use utilities with intensities and probabilities without intensities. The Class III models in Table 2.4 require utilities with intensities but no intensities for the probabilities. These models could therefore be good candidates for the argumentation rules in Class III. As we have seen in Table 2.4 this class contains several rules. We will illustrate the argumentation using each of these rules.

Figure 2.6:
Decision Tree for an Argument Using a Risk-Avoidance Rule

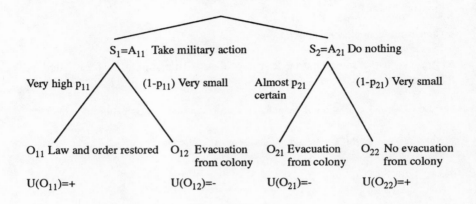

Symbols: S_i strategy i
              A_{ij} alternative j under strategy i
              O_{ij} outcome j under strategy i
              $U(O_{ij})$ subjective utility of outcome j under strategy i
              P_{ij} subjective probability of the O_{ij}'s

One of the rules in Class III is called the "Minimax Rule" (Thorngate 1980), according to which one should choose the strategy with the highest utility for the minimum outcome, or

> If Minimum $U(O_{ij})$ > Minimum $U(O_{kl})$ for all k, l then S_i must be chosen.

Arguments that use the Minimax Rule can be summarized formally in the following way:

1. Description : Description of outcomes with probabilities without and utilities with intensities
2. Rule   : If Minimum $U(O_{ij})$ > Minimum $U(O_{kl})$ for all k, l then S_i must be chosen
3. Condition   : Minimum $U(O_{ij})$ > Minimum $U(O_{kl})$ for all k, l
4. Conclusion : S_i must be chosen

This argumentation can be illustrated by the following example:

If we take military action we may possibly restore law and order, which would be the most desirable outcome for us. But it is also possible that we would only partly restore law and order in some regions. This would of course be less desirable. If we do nothing, it is possible that we can hold on to the colony despite the chaos. This outcome would be even worse than only partly restoring law and order. But it is also possible that we would lose the colony because of the chaos. This is the worst outcome I can imagine. We should take into account the bad outcomes, but choose the strategy where the worst outcome is still better than that of other strategies. I recommend taking military action because in that case the worst outcome is still better than that of the other strategy.

Figure 2.7 shows that the probabilities are indicated as "possible;" thus they appear without rank order. Since they are the same for both strategies, they play no role when the conclusion is drawn. The utilities are formulated in terms of a rank order, and the best minimum outcome is indeed O_{12} of the first strategy, since O_{22}, the minimum outcome of the second strategy, is evaluated as "worst ."

The verbal formulation of the Minimax rule in this case was, "We should take into account the bad outcomes, but choose the strategy where the worst outcome is still better than that of other strategies." Applying the Minimax Rule to this description, we arrive at the same conclusion as is drawn in the text. The choice for S_1 from this argumentation is therefore clear.

What the remaining rules mentioned in Class III have in common is that several aspects or dimensions of outcomes must be systematically used across strategies. The utilities of the aspects must be indicated at least by a rank order.

Figure 2.7:
Decision Tree for an Argument Using the Minimax Heuristics

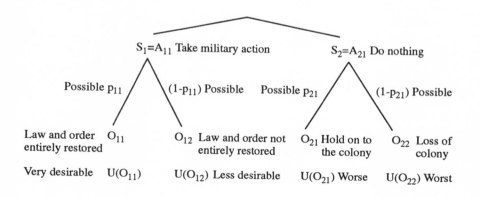

Symbols: S_i strategy i
           A_{ij} alternative j under strategy i
           O_{ij} outcome j under strategy i
           $U(O_{ij})$ subjective utility of outcome j under strategy i
           P_{ij} subjective probability of the O_{ij}'s

The fact that probabilities may be considered certain or uncertain is the same for all strategies and therefore does not play a role. These rules are called Multi-Attribute Utility (MAUT) models.

The first MAUT model mentioned in Table 2.4 is the Dominance Rule, which posits that the strategy selected must be better than the other(s) on at least one dimension of outcomes and not worse than any other strategy with regard to the remaining aspects, or formally:

$$\text{If } U(a_{ijm}) \geq U(a_{kjlm}) \text{ for all k, l, m then } S_i \text{ must be chosen}$$

Arguments referring to the use of the Dominance Rule can be summarized formally in the following way :

1. Description : Utilities with and probabilities without intensity
2. Rule   : If $U(a_{ijm}) \geq U(a_{kjlm})$ for all k, l, m then S_i must be chosen
3. Condition   : $U(a_{ijm}) \geq U(a_{kjlm})$ for all k, l, m
4. Conclusion : S_i must be chosen

The following example illustrates this rule:

If we take military action, I am convinced that we will restore law and order and there will be no national unrest. If we do nothing, I am certain that law and order will not be restored, and there will be no national unrest either. I recommend that we take military action, since we should choose a strategy which is better on at least one aspect and equally good on others, the situation in our colony will be much better if we take military action than if we do nothing, and nationally the outcome, which is quite good, is the same for both strategies.

Figure 2.8 presents the decision tree based on this text. This presentation makes clear that the probabilities are without intensities and the utilities with intensities. The rule specified in this case is a very clear one, and the choice can again be made without any computations and without any numerical information because one strategy, military action, is clearly better with regard to the colonial aspect and equally good with regard to the other aspect.

However, one can imagine situations where one aspect of an outcome is better while another is worse under a specific strategy, and in such a situation the Dominance Rule cannot be used.

One possible solution is suggested by the Lexicographic Rule mentioned in Table 2.4, Class III. This rule posits that the decision-maker must first rank-order the aspects according to their importance. Let us assume that there are three aspects, for example, a national, an international, and a legal one. According to the Lexicographic Rule, the decision-maker has first to establish which of the aspects is the most important to him, and then which is second and which is third in importance. He could, for instance, establish the following rank order: the international aspect is first in importance, the national dimension second, and the legal aspect third.

Figure 2.8:
Decision Tree for an Argument Using the Dominance Rule

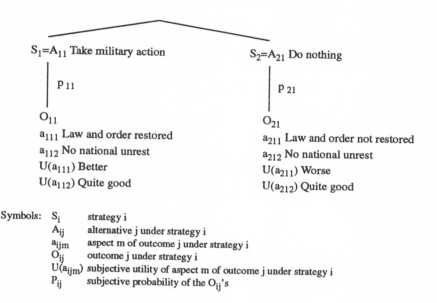

Symbols:
S_i strategy i
A_{ij} alternative j under strategy i
a_{ijm} aspect m of outcome j under strategy i
O_{ij} outcome j under strategy i
$U(a_{ijm})$ subjective utility of aspect m of outcome j under strategy i
P_{ij} subjective probability of the O_{ij}'s

The Lexicographic Rule, then suggests selecting the strategy that is most attractive with respect to the most important aspect, and eventually, if there is a tie, to continue to search for a strategy with highest utility regarding the second most important aspect, and so on. Formally this can be stated as follows:

> If $a_{..n}$ is the most important aspect and $U(a_{ijn}) > U(a_{kjn})$ for all k, j then S_i must be chosen

or

> If $U(a_{ijn}) = U(a_{kjn})$ and $a_{..o}$ is the second important aspect and $U(a_{ijo}) > U(a_{kjo})$ for all k, j then S_i must be chosen,

and so on.

Arguments referring to the use of the Lexicographic Rule can be summarized formally in the following way :

1. Description : The outcomes are described with systematic aspects, the order of importance of these aspects is indicated, and the utilities are given with intensities and probabilities without intensities.

2. Rule   : If $a_{..n}$ is the most important aspect and $U(a_{ijn}) > U(a_{kjn})$ for all k, j or if $U(a_{ijn}) = U(a_{kjn})$ and $a_{..o}$ is the second important aspect and $U(a_{ijo}) > U(a_{kjo})$ for all k, j then S_i must be chosen

3. Condition   : $U(a_{ijn}) > U(a_{kjn})$ for all k, j or $U(a_{ijn}) = U(a_{kjn})$ and $U(a_{ijo}) > U(a_{kjo})$
                  for all k, j

4. Conclusion : S_i must be chosen

An illustration of the use of this rule might look like this:

If we take military action, I am convinced that we will restore law and order, which is very good, but there will be national unrest, which is quite bad. If we do nothing, I am certain that law and order will not be restored, which is very bad, but it is quite attractive that there will be no national unrest. Since I consider the colonial aspect as the most important one, I select the strategy where this aspect has the highest value. I therefore recommend that we take military action.

Figure 2.9 presents the decision tree based on this argumentation. The decision tree indicates that the outcomes are specified in systematic aspects and that the utilities are expressed with intensities and the probabilities not. This suggests that a Class III model should be applied. In this case systematic aspects are specified but the Dominance Rule cannot be used because each of the two strategies is superior with regard to one aspect. Since the text clearly indicates that the author thinks the colonial aspect is the most important, it is clear that the Lexicographic Rule should be applied. This is corroborated by the fact that the author explicitly mentions this rule and indicates that military action scores best with regard to this aspect. Consequently, according to this argument, the choice of military action is correct.

If there is no dominant strategy available and there is no reason to say that one aspect is more important than another one, another solution still exists using the Addition-of-Utilities Rule. This rule suggests summing up the utilities of each aspect per strategy and then selecting the strategy with the highest total value. Formally this means:

$$\text{If } \sum_{j,m} U(a_{ijm}) > \sum_{l,m} U(a_{klm}) \text{ for all k then } S_i \text{ must be chosen}$$

Arguments that use the Addition-of-Utilities Rule can be summarized formally in the following way:

1. Description : The outcomes are described in aspects and at least the sum of the
                   utilities for each strategy should be specified with intensities while the
                   probabilities are specified without intensities.

2. Premise   : If $\sum_{j,m} U(a_{ijm}) > \sum_{l,m} U(a_{klm})$ for all k then S_i must be chosen

3. Premise   : $\sum_{j,m} U(a_{ijm}) > \sum_{l,m} U(a_{klm})$

4. Conclusion : S_i must be chosen

The following example illustrates the application of this rule:

If we take military action I am convinced that we will restore law and order, but there will be national unrest. If we do nothing, I am certain that law and order will not be restored, but there will be no national unrest. I think that we should select the alternative with the highest total value. Summing up the utilities for each strategy, the highest total value is achieved by taking military action. I therefore recommend that we take military action.

Figure 2.10 presents the decision tree based on this argument. The decision tree indicates that the aspects for the outcomes are systematically described and that each strategy is better with regard to one aspect. As a consequence, the choice is unclear unless one knows which aspect is the most important one or how the sums of the utilities of the different strategies compare.

In this argument a statement is made about the sum of the utilities suggesting that the sum for strategy S_1 is higher than that for S_2. Having specified this order, the choice for strategy S_1 also becomes clear.

A problem with this argument is of course that the sum is a subjective estimate; other people might think that the sum for strategy S_2 is much higher. The subjective aspect renders this argument an unconvincing one. A similar problem exists with the Lexicographic Rule, where the conclusion is immediately different if one suggests that another aspect is the most important one. In that sense the Dominance Rule is the most convincing one for MAUT-type decision problems, although not all decision problems have such a simple structure that Dominance argumentation can solve the problem.

Figure 2.9:
Decision Tree for an Argument Using the Lexicographic Rule

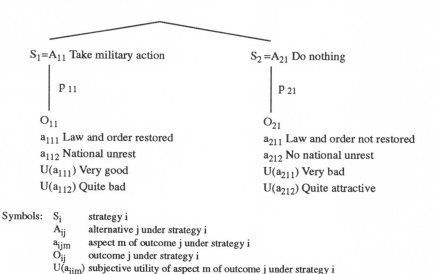

$S_1=A_{11}$ Take military action $S_2=A_{21}$ Do nothing

P_{11} P_{21}

O_{11} O_{21}
a_{111} Law and order restored a_{211} Law and order not restored
a_{112} National unrest a_{212} No national unrest
$U(a_{111})$ Very good $U(a_{211})$ Very bad
$U(a_{112})$ Quite bad $U(a_{212})$ Quite attractive

Symbols: S_i strategy i
            A_{ij} alternative j under strategy i
            a_{ijm} aspect m of outcome j under strategy i
            O_{ij} outcome j under strategy i
            $U(a_{ijm})$ subjective utility of aspect m of outcome j under strategy i
            P_{ij} subjective probability of the O_{ij}'s

Figure 2.10:
Decision Tree for an Argument Using the Addition-of-Utilities Rule

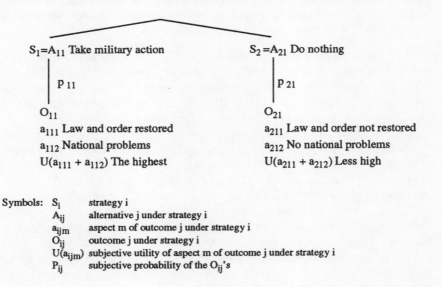

$S_1 = A_{11}$ Take military action	$S_2 = A_{21}$ Do nothing
P_{11}	P_{21}
O_{11}	O_{21}
a_{111} Law and order restored	a_{211} Law and order not restored
a_{112} National problems	a_{212} No national problems
$U(a_{111} + a_{112})$ The highest	$U(a_{211} + a_{212})$ Less high

Symbols: S_i strategy i
A_{ij} alternative j under strategy i
a_{ijm} aspect m of outcome j under strategy i
O_{ij} outcome j under strategy i
$U(a_{ijm})$ subjective utility of aspect m of outcome j under strategy i
P_{ij} subjective probability of the O_{ij}'s

Argumentation Rules in Class IV

The last class of decision problems is characterized by the fact that no intensities at all are specified (Table 2.1, Cell IV). The decision rules of Class IV of Table 2.4 do not require intensities for probabilites nor for utilities. These rules seem therefore the natural candidates for the argument of this class.

The first rule mentioned in this class is Simon's Rule, named for Herbert Simon's pioneering work on decision-making (Simon 1957b). The rule suggests selecting a strategy that leads only to satisfactory outcomes, while other strategies can also lead to negative outcomes. This rule should not be confounded with Simon's Satisficing Principle (1957), where a decision-maker forms some level of aspiration that the alternative he seeks must satisfy. As soon as he discovers an alternative which meets his aspiration level, he terminates the search and chooses this alternative. The Satisficing Principle assumes that the criterion values of the aspiration level are at least rank-ordered, while Simon's Rule only requires utilities without intensities and no acceptability threshold is postulated. Formally, Simon's Rule can be formulated as follows:

If $U(O_{ij}) > 0$ for all j and $U(O_{kl}) < 0$ at least for one l then S_i must be chosen

Arguments referring to the use of Simon's Rule can be summarized formally in the following way :

1. Description : The utilities and probabilities can be specified without intensities
2. Rule : If $U(O_{ij}) > 0$ for all j and $U(O_{kl}) < 0$ at least for one l then S_i must be chosen
3. Condition : $U(O_{ij}) > 0$ for all j and $U(O_{kl}) < 0$ at least for one l
4. Conclusion : S_i must be chosen

The following example provides an argument using Simon's Rule:

If we do nothing, we will not restore law and order in our colony. If we take military action, it is not only possible that we will restore law and order but it is even possible that the self-proclaimed rebel government will cease to exist. We should choose the strategy which leads only to positive outcomes if other strategies can not guarantee this. Therefore I recommend that we take military action.

Figure 2.11 summarizes the argumentation based on this text in a decision tree. It is clear that the probabilities and utilities are not expressed with intensities, which indicates that a Class IV rule should be used. The author clearly formulates the use of Simon's Rule, which of course also leads to the conclusion drawn by the author of the text.

The second rule mentioned in Class IV (Table 2.4) we call the Reversed Simon Rule. It was developed by the authors (Gallhofer and Saris 1979b) to cover political situations for which no satisfactory strategy was available. It consists of excluding all strategies that lead with certainty to negative outcomes only as long as there is another strategy that might lead to a positive outcome. Formally this rule can be formulated as:

If $U(O_{ij}) > 0$ for at least one j and $U(O_{kl}) < 0$ for all k, l then S_i must be chosen

Arguments referring to the Reversed Simon Rule can be summarized formally in the following way:

1. Description : the utilities and probabilities can be specified without intensities
2. Rule : if $U(O_{ij}) > 0$ for at least one j and $U(O_{kl}) < 0$ for all k, l then S_i must be chosen
3. Condition : $U(O_{ij}) > 0$ for at least one j and $U(O_{kl}) < 0$ for all k, l
4. Conclusion : S_i must be chosen

The following example illustrates the rule:

If we do nothing, we will not restore law and order in our colony. If we take military action, it is possible that we will restore law and order but it is also possible that we will lose our colony. I think we should choose the strategy where not only negative outcomes occur but where a positive outcome is also possible. Therefore I recommend that we take military action.

Figure 2.11:
Decision Tree for an Argument Using Simon's Rule

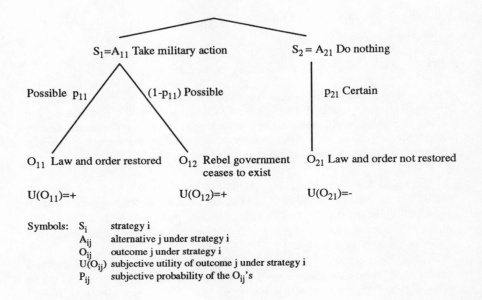

$S_1=A_{11}$ Take military action $S_2 = A_{21}$ Do nothing

Possible p_{11} $(1-p_{11})$ Possible p_{21} Certain

O_{11} Law and order restored O_{12} Rebel government O_{21} Law and order not restored
                                            ceases to exist

$U(O_{11})=+$ $U(O_{12})=+$ $U(O_{21})=-$

Symbols: S_i strategy i
          A_{ij} alternative j under strategy i
          O_{ij} outcome j under strategy i
          $U(O_{ij})$ subjective utility of outcome j under strategy i
          P_{ij} subjective probability of the O_{ij}'s

Figure 2.12 presents the argumentation in a decision tree. Again the probabilities and utilities are specified without intensities, but this time there is no single strategy that can guarantee a positive result. Therefore the Reversed Simon Rule is suggested; it can informally be described as a rule that recommends choosing the best of two evils. The Reversed Simon Rule suggests the choice of military action, and that is indeed the action that was chosen.

As the reader will no doubt have noticed, the heuristics in Class IV are very simple, making its use in arguments very plausible. On the other hand, the arguments may seem oversimplified, suggesting that much information has been ignored. The aims of a very evident argument and a complete presentation of the problem are often in conflict with each other. How the decision-makers solve this problem in practice will be the topic of the next chapters.

CONCLUSIONS

In this chapter we have seen that the descriptions of the decision problems can be classified under four different classes according to the amount of information provided about utilities and probabilities of the different outcomes. It was also shown that in decision theory, decision rules can be found that vary with respect to the amount of information they require with regard to utilities and probabil-

Figure 2.12:
Decision Tree for an Argumentation Using the Reversed Simon Rule

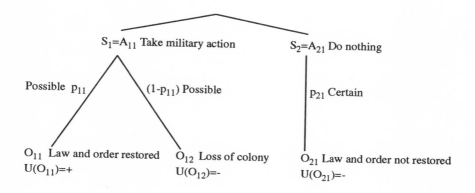

Symbols: S_i — strategy i
A_{ij} — alternative j under strategy i
O_{ij} — outcome j under strategy i
$U(O_{ij})$ subjective utility of outcome j under strategy i
P_{ij} — subjective probability of the O_{ij}'s

ities. Next we described how the four different classes of decision rules can be used to formulate arguments according to the four classes of decision problems. This combination leads to the formulation of a series of argumentations that decision-makers can use in order to convince their colleagues of their particular choice of a strategy. These argumentations have been described formally and using an example. We have used these examples in order to make it clear to the reader that the formulated argumentations are not strange and unusual: they can be formulated in normal words and, apart from the SEU type of argumentation, do not require any numerical values for utilities or probabilities.

Given this result, we think that the SEU type of argumentation will occur very infrequently since it requires too much information and calculation for real life. The other types of argumentation do not suffer from this disadvantage and are therefore expected to occur more frequently. On the other hand, we have said that this means these rules can only be applied if the description of the decision problem is simplified, if utilities and/or probabilities are specified without intensities. This would seem to require sacrificing part of the complexity of the decision problem for the sake of simplicity and strength of argument. How far this leads arguments to become unrealistic because of unacceptable simplification will be discussed later.

From another point of view, one may also ask whether the non-SEU rules represent acceptable arguments, a question that has been much debated in the literature (e.g., Svenson 1979; Von Winterfeldt and Edwards 1986). This question will be raised in Chapter 9.

It should be mentioned here that all examples in this chapter were constructed in order to simplify the discussion. In the minutes of meetings of decision-making bodies, arguments are much less clear, as we will show in the next chapter. The reasons for these complications are the following. First, a wealth of observation is included in the descriptive part of the text in order to clarify statements or to bolster the argument. Second, human decision-makers assume that their audience is very well informed about the way arguments are made, and therefore they often omit parts that seem essential from a logician's point of view. A consequence of these two complications is that one normally cannot so simply reconstruct the arguments from the texts as we have done so far for illustrative purposes. Therefore, in the next chapter we will employ a typical example from a real-life argument, show what the practical difficulties are in the detection of these arguments, and then discuss tools needed to do so.

Chapter 3

Detection of Argumentation in Documents

Reproduced here is a translation of the speech of a Dutch minister of foreign affairs during a meeting of the Council of Ministers on October 1, 1914. The argumentation in this document centers upon whether the Dutch should ask the Germans about their intentions with regard to the occupation of Antwerp or whether they should do nothing that might jeopardize their neutrality.

Par. 1: The minister of foreign affairs agrees with the chairman and declines firmly to ask the question either in the way proposed by the ministers of navy and war or in the amended version of the minister of agriculture. Our own interests have not yet been threatened. We can only guess, but do not know, how the war will end. This is therefore not the right moment to take sides, although our interests are closer to the British, especially with respect to our colonies.

Par. 2: If we ask the question, it will look like an appeal to stop the war or like taking sides. It is inconceivable that Germany will answer categorically at this stage of the war that it will not keep Antwerp or that it will only occupy it temporarily. Although it is unlikely that Germany will wish to incorporate Belgium, it will either answer evasively, or politely give us to understand that Germany's intentions are no concern of ours.

Par. 3: Shall we put this question aside or shall we insist on a clear answer? The latter could cause trouble, perhaps even war, and would certainly shake German confidence in our neutrality, which is of paramount importance.

Par. 4: To change our official position of neutrality now would not be in our interests, especially since we have declared it so forcefully and since Germany explicitly said that it would respect our position.

Par. 5: The minister of war's plan to grant the guarantors of Belgium's neutrality [France, Britain] access to our neutral territory in order to force back the German army is even less justifiable. Although it is unlikely that the British would even consider entering the Western Scheldt to relieve Antwerp, any British warship that tried would be sent to the bottom by the German artillery.

Par. 6: Actually it is unclear what we would gain at the final peace settlement by pressing
the Germans now. If we have to enter the war and Germany wins the war, we
have to pay the piper. If the British are victorious then we cannot expect much
reward, at most an equivalent piece of land from Germany in exchange for Dutch
Flanders and the Scheldt, which will be given as compensation to Belgium. If the
war ends with no clear winner, then we are left with a partially destroyed country
and the confidence of our Eastern neighbour, on whom we depend so much economically, much shaken.

Par. 7: The occupation of Antwerp is in no case worth any of these things.

Par. 8: It is not anticipated, that we would get into trouble with the British [i.e., that they
might take over the Dutch colony of Indonesia] if we remain silent.

(Source: Council of Ministers, Oct. 1, 1914, Minutes, *Bescheiden betreffende de Buitenlandse politiek van Nederland*, vol. 4, no. 171, 145–160.)

In the previous chapter we introduced different types of argumentation and
illustrated them with hypothetical arguments that were constructed by the authors. The text presented here shows that the analysis of real arguments provided
by decision-makers in a meeting is much more complex.

Reading this text over several times, one can distinguish the following points:

• It is assumed that the audience has ample knowledge of the situation and of previous
remarks.

• The different options are sometimes not clearly specified.

• Some arguments are repeated, even in a short text such as this one.

• The description is very unbalanced; one strategy has attracted far more attention than
the other.

• The description of the problem and the preferred option of the speaker are explicit.

• The argumentation rule, however, is not mentioned.

• Whether or not the condition leading to the conclusion is satisfied is also not
mentioned.

This text is a good example of the type of document we have encountered in
our study, which means that the remarks made about this text are valid in
general. Given this situation, we had to solve the following methodological
problems:

1. Since a description of the decision problems is often difficult to extract from a text, it
was necessary to develop a coding procedure in order to reconstruct such arguments.
In addition, since we wanted a procedure of high reliability and validity, we tested this
approach extensively before beginning to use it for the analysis of the texts. This
coding procedure will be the first topic of this chapter.

2. Since the argumentation rules were never mentioned in the text, there were two possibilities: either our approach was completely wrong and therefore there are no rules
to be mentioned, or the argumentation rules are so evident to the speakers and
audience that the rules do not need to be mentioned at all.

Obviously we would prefer the latter option, but we would not have accepted it without a test. The test of this hypothesis will be the second topic of this chapter. Readers who are not interested in these methodological issues can continue reading the subsequent chapters without problems.

PROCEDURES TO DETECT DESCRIPTIONS OF DECISION PROBLEMS

In the next sections, those coding procedures will be discussed that have been developed for the detection of the problem descriptions in the text. After the description of the coding procedure, the approach will be evaluated by presenting the results of the reliability studies.

The Coding Instrument

The purpose of text analysis is to derive a decision tree from the decision-maker's argument. In the following, all the steps of content analysis will be illustrated by examples drawn from the text just presented. The argument in this document centers upon whether the Dutch should ask the Germans about their intentions with regard to Antwerp or whether they should do nothing in order not to jeopardize their neutrality.

After reading the document carefully to gain insight into the structure of the discourse, a coder first has to register what the available strategies are and in which paragraphs they appear. A possible coding might be the following:

1. The strategies the decision-maker considers available:
   S_1: To question the Germans about their intentions with regard to Antwerp (Pars. 1, 2, 4).
   S_2: The minister of war's plan to grant the guarantors of Belgium's neutrality access to our territory (Par. 5).
   S_3: To remain silent (Par. 8).

Thereafter, the preferred course of action has to be registered and a subsequent brief summary is given of the content of each paragraph with respect to the presence or absence of an argument relating to available strategies and their possible consequences. This could be done as follows:

2. The course of action preferred by the decision-maker:
   S_3: Not to speak at all.

3. Brief summary of the content of each paragraph:
   Par. 1: The minister rejects S_1 to ask Germany the question about its intentions because Dutch interests are not yet threatened and the outcome of the war is uncertain. The consequences are very vaguely formulated.
   He supports S_3, not to speak at all, that is, not to take sides. But no consequences of this strategy are indicated here.

Par. 2: Consequences of S_1 are elaborated.

Par. 3: Further consequences of S_1 elaborated.

Par. 4: The decision-maker again rejects S_1, arguing that in the past they had announced their neutrality very loudly and Germany had promised to respect it.

Par. 5: He rejects S_2, to grant the guarantors of Belgium's neutrality access to Dutch territory, on the basis of the moral argument that it is "even less justifiable," and on the basis of the negative consequences for the British if they tried to exploit such access. The minister does not elaborate on the consequences for the Dutch of this strategy.

Par. 6: He continues to elaborate on the consequences of S_1.

Par. 7: He again rejects S_1 by referring vaguely to the consequences mentioned in Par. 7.

Par. 8: Consequences of S_3, not to speak at all.

On the basis of this summary, the relevant paragraphs for the construction of a decision tree are obtained. The consequences of strategy 1 are mainly mentioned in paragraphs 2, 3, and 6. No consequences are mentioned at all for strategy 2, which is rejected on moral grounds alone. For strategy 3, the consequences are set out in paragraph 8. The further coding activities consist of four steps.

The first and second step relate to the extraction of the decision theory concepts described in Chapter 2. Besides the actions of one's own nation (A), the possible actions of other nations (AO), possible new developments (ND), the possible outcomes for one's own nation (O), and their subjective probabilites (P) and utilities (U), the concept "undefined" (UNDF) is introduced for parts of the text that do not relate to decision theory concepts.

As already implied, a relevant paragraph is considered a context unit (Holsti 1969), that is, the largest body of text that has to be searched for decision theory concepts. The units we use to record these concepts (the specific segment of text into which the concept is classified; see also Holsti 1969) are grammatical units such as noun or verb phrases. This means that they can vary depending on the concept.

In the following analysis we illustrate this approach, beginning with the decomposition of sentences into semantic or recording units, the classification of concepts and the construction of partial argumentation trees.

Par. 2: ((A : If we ask the question)
            (O: it (P: will) look like an (U: appeal to stop or a taking of sides)))
         ((P: It is inconceivable)
            (O: that Germany will answer categorically at this stage of the war that it will
            (U: not keep Antwerp or that it will occupy it only temporarily)))
         ((UNDF: Although it is unlikely that Germany will wish to incorporate
            Belgium)
            (O: it (P: will) either answer (U: evasively) or politely give us to understand
            that Germany's intentions are (U: no concern of ours)))

This is one potential decomposition into semantic units and concept classification of paragraph 2. The first sentence consists of two main components: a noun and verb phrase classified as own action (A), "if we ask the question," and a noun and verb phrase classified as an outcome (O), "it will look like an appeal to stop or a taking of sides." Two other concepts are nested or embedded in the outcome concept, namely, a probability indication (P) "will," consisting of the modality of the verb signaling certainty, and a utility concept (U). The latter, "an appeal to stop or a taking of sides," contains mainly negative connotations for the decision-maker. The second sentence consists again of two main components, a rank-ordered probability statement (P), "it is inconceivable," indicating a probability of zero, and an outcome (O), "that Germany will answer categorically at this stage of the war that it will not keep Antwerp or that it will occupy it only temporarily." The outcome component contains value connotations (U) that are positive for the decision-maker, "not keep Antwerp" or that it will "occupy it only temporarily."

The last sentence is again decomposed into main components. The first part was considered by the coder as undefined (UNDF): "Although it is unlikely that Germany will wish to incorporate Belgium." The second part was classified as an outcome (O): "it will either answer evasively or politely give us to understand that Germany's intentions are no concern of ours." In the second main component, again, a probability (P) and a utility concept (U) are embedded.

Based on the coding of these concepts, the following partial decision tree can be constructed (Figure 3.1).

Figure 3.1:
Partial Decision Tree Based on Paragraph 2

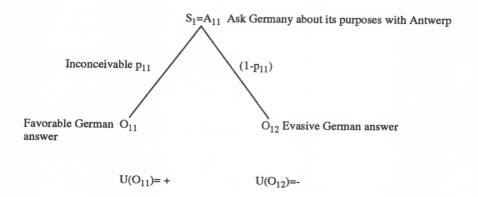

$S_1 = A_{11}$ Ask Germany about its purposes with Antwerp

Inconceivable p_{11} $\qquad$ $(1 - p_{11})$

Favorable German O_{11} answer $\qquad$ O_{12} Evasive German answer

$U(O_{11}) = +$ $\qquad$ $U(O_{12}) = -$

The construction of this partial decision tree is straightforward and needs no further comment. We now proceed to extract the concepts based on paragraph 3.

Par. 3:   ((A: Shall we put this question aside) or (A: shall we insist on a clear answer?))
        ((O: The latter (P: could cause (U: trouble)) (O: (P: perhaps) even (U: war))
            (O: and (P: certainly) would (U: shake German confidence) in our neutrality))

Since the decision-maker clearly indicates the further events that would follow from strategy 1, the decision tree in Figure 3.1 can be extended as in Figure 3.2.

Figure 3.2:
Partial Decision Tree Based on Paragraphs 2 and 3

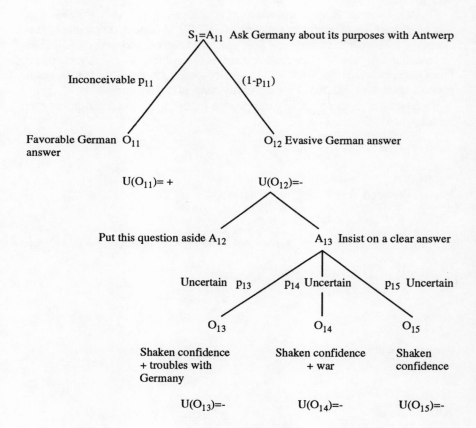

Figure 3.3:
Partial Decision Tree Based on Paragraphs 2, 3, and 6

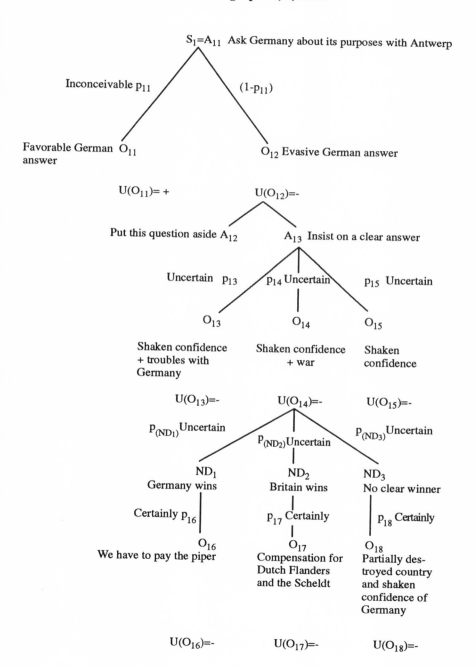

The last paragraph to deal with events foreseen under strategy 1 is paragraph 6. The concepts could be coded as follows:

Par. 6:

(UNDF: Actually it is unclear what we would gain at the final peace settlement (A: by pressing the Germans now.)))

((A: If we have to enter the war) (ND: and Germany wins the war) (O: we have (U: to pay the piper)))

((ND: If the British are victorious) (P: then (U: we cannot expect much reward,))) (O: at most an equivalent piece of land from Germany in exchange for Dutch Flanders and the Scheldt) (UNDF: which will be given as compensation to Belgium))

((ND: If the war ends with no clear winner) (O: then we are left with (U: a partially destroyed country and the confidence of our Eastern neighbour, on whom we depend so much economically, much shaken)))

Since the minister points out quite clearly in this paragraph what the consequences would be were the Netherlands to enter the war, the decision tree of Figure 3.2 can again be extended (Figure 3.3).

Having completed the scheme of events foreseen for strategy 1, the same can be repeated for strategy 3, the chosen alternative, for which only a few events were foreseen. As already pointed out, paragraph 8 relates to strategy 3. The decomposition into semantic units and the concept classification of this paragraph can be carried out in the following way:

((P: It is not anticipated) (O: that we would get into (U: trouble) with the British) (A: if we remain silent))

Based on this coding, the consequences for strategy 3 can be summarized in a tree structure (Figure 3.4).

The reader may have noticed that only O_{31}, "that we get into trouble with the British," was mentioned explicitly by the minister, but the probability statement "it is not to be anticipated" implies that the complementary outcome O_{32}, "that we do not get into trouble with the British," will actually occur. This implicit alternative outcome is also represented in the tree diagram. In the case of S_1, every outcome was mentioned explicitly by the decision-maker.

The argumentation text presented here was relatively clear. Frequently, however, decision-makers express themselves less clearly and texts contain many tacit implications, so that coders have to make more inferences when constructing decision trees. We have therefore developed coding instructions incorporating the findings of the reliability studies carried out at an early stage of this research project. Readers who are interested in more details of the coding approach are referred to Appendix A.

It is clear from the examples that coders may decompose sentences into semantic units in different ways. The same applies to the classification of concepts and the construction of decision trees. But in order to subject an argumentation tree to further analysis for detection of argumentation rules, a tree diagram is

Figure 3.4:
Partial Decision Tree for Strategy 3 Based on Paragraph 8

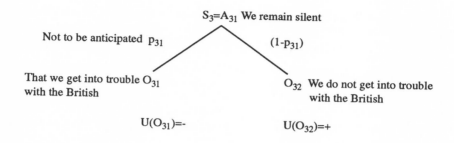

needed on which coders can agree. This led us to investigate the degree to which our coding approach reproduces similar results when carried out independently by different coders.

ASSESSING CODING RELIABILITY

Several reliability studies have been undertaken by the authors (Gallhofer and Saris 1978, 1979a, 1988) in order to assess the extent to which the coding instrument reproduces similar results when carried out independently by different coders. This is a necessary but not sufficient condition for the validity of the approach; it gives us some indication that we are measuring what we want to measure. The results obtained were satisfactory, although the studies also suggested several adjustments to the approach, which were subsequently implemented.

The reliability or the extent of agreement was studied for individual coders, replicating the same coding efforts across time (intracoder reliability), between pairs of individual coders (intercoder reliability) and also between pairs of groups of coders, as follows. First coders individually coded several documents. Then they were grouped in pairs, they compared their results, and where there were differences, they were asked to try to reach a common solution. The common solutions of a pair of coders were again subjected to a reliability test by comparing them with the common solutions of another pair of coders. A brief summary of the results of the various reliability studies follows.

Reliability of the Determination of Semantic Units and the Concept Assignment

Since, as mentioned earlier, the coding activities consisted of two steps, there was a possibility of disagreement among and between coders at each step.

Therefore, the reliability of the steps was studied separately.

First, we will concentrate on the reliability of the determination of semantic units. When coders decompose a sentence into semantic units, the results may differ in the number of main components and/or the number of levels with respect to embedded units. The measure we used was constructed for us by colleagues of the Mathematical Centre (Does and Overweel 1978) and is sensitive to these differences. The measure becomes 1 if the agreement is perfect and 0 if the agreement is zero.

After receiving basic instructions, four coders individually decomposed documents relating to two decision issues. They were then grouped into two pairs to compare their results; if there were differences, they tried to find a common solution. Two months later they repeated these efforts.

Here, for the sake of brevity, we will report only the most important scores of intercoder reliability.

The median coder reliability between an individual coder and the group result was already quite high for the first coding: .92, .83, .73, and .78 (n=81). When the second decision issue was coded, the scores were even better, probably because the coders had had more practice: 1.0, 1.0, .92, and .88 (n=48). The intercoder reliability between the two group codings for the first decision issue was .88 (n=81) and this also improved for the second decision issue because of more experience: .91 (n=48). Given these scores, individual coding results could have been used for the analysis, but we always used the results produced by groups of coders in order to correct for errors.

The second coding step consists of assigning concepts to the semantic units. To assess the reliability of the concept assignment, an association measure for nominal data was needed. We selected Scotts π, defined as the ratio of the above-chance agreement (Krippendorff 1970, 144).

When the level of agreement equals chance expectancy, the value of π is zero; if perfect, it is one, and if less than expected by chance, its value becomes negative.

The coder reliability between an individual coder and the group result for the classification of concepts was quite high even for the coding of the first decision issue: .81 (n=419), .78 (n=375), .82 (n=315), and .77 (n=299). The n's show that the total number of classified semantic units varied from coder to coder, because we could use only semantic units that were identically split up with the group coding result. The agreement measure, however, is size invariant. When the coders assigned concepts to the second decision issue the scores, were even better, probably because they had had more practice: .91 (n=112), .87 (n=103), .89 (n=96), and .87 (n=97). The intercoder reliability between two group codings for the first decision issue was .84 (n=356), and this also improved slightly for the second decision issue: .86 (n=98). Again, individual coding results could have been used for the analysis, but it was decided to use the results produced by groups of coders in order to correct for errors.

Reliability of the Construction of Decision Trees

For the assessment of the coding reliability of the construction of decision trees, individual and group data for both partial and complete trees—the latter represent the entire argumentation—were available. An ad hoc measure constructed for this purpose was used as the measure of agreement. The denominator of the agreement coefficient consists of the sum of the maximum number of branches for each node in the tree structure made by either of the coders. The numerator represents the sum of the branches that are identical for both coders, that is, with respect to the number of branches and their concepts. The measure of agreement is thus the ratio between the sum of the identical branches and the sum of the maximum number of branches. M can take on values ranging from 0 to 1. The results of the first reliability study led to the satisfactory construction of partial trees. The median agreement at the individual level was 1.0. The agreement with respect to the construction of complete tree diagrams, however, proved to be unsatisfactory, at both the individual and the group level. The agreement scores ranged between 0.3 and 0.7. In order to improve the procedure, the following steps were undertaken.

First, it was decided to use pairs of coders, who first coded the texts independently and then produced a joint coding. In this way they could correct each other's mistakes. Second, the instructions were changed. In the earlier study, coders had concentrated too much on details at the beginning. The new instructions insisted that they first become familiar with the general structure of the document before studying the details. Third, a procedure for the selection of good coders was developed. A detailed new reliability study (Gallhofer and Saris 1988) showed that, thanks to these improvements, the construction of complete tree diagrams could be carried out almost perfectly, that is, the procedure was repeatable.

With respect to the selection of good coders, some further explanation would seem to be in order. We used as a standard coding a decision tree derived by the joint coding of a group of four coders. The coders first constructed the tree individually; then came together in groups of two, producing a joint coding; and finally came together in a group of four to obtain the final coding. Since the individual agreement scores of the four coders with the standard coding are known, one can assess the score for good individual codings. For the selection of new coders it was decided that M should be > 0.8.

The results obtained by the coders trained according to the new instructions can be summarized as follows. Of the six coders who took part in this research (Gallhofer and Saris 1988), four arrived at an agreement greater than 0.8 with the standard coding. The remaining two coders achieved an agreement of between 0.6 and 0.8, and were not selected to take part in the further codings. The four good coders then coded 71 documents individually and achieved the following intercoder reliability: for 36 texts, the individual reliability scores between two coders were between 0.95 and 1.0; for 20 texts, the agreement ranged between 0.8 and 0.95; for 8 texts, the agreement was between 0.7 and 0.8; and for only 7 texts it ranged between 0.6 and 0.7. Taking into account that group codings rather than individual codings are used for the analysis, to correct for errors, one may assume that the agreement is almost perfect.

DETERMINATION OF THE CLASS OF DECISION RULES AND THE RULE USED

Given a highly reliable instrument of text analysis, it is possible to subject the argumentation trees to further analysis. In Figure 3.5 the entire tree of the argumentation studied in this chapter is presented, consisting of the two elaborated strategies.

In order to determine the argumentation rule used, it is first useful to reduce the data of the tree to a matrix representation of the decision problem as discussed in the previous chapter. Table 3.1 presents this reduction. It shows that all the intermediate outcomes of the decision tree leading to a final branch are summarized together. In this way one obtains outcomes for S_1 and for S_2. The table also indicates the utilities of the various outcomes. Then the probabilities of occurrence of the outcomes are summarized.

In order to make a summary of this kind, one has to take the "products" of the verbal probability statements leading to a specific final outcome. Taking, for example, the combinations of branches that lead to O_{16}, "that we have to pay the piper," under S_1 (Figure 3.5), the following probability statements have to be summarized: p (O_{12}) is (1-inconceivable), which means "certain"; p (O_{14}) is "uncertain"; p (ND_1) is "uncertain"; and p (O_{16}) is "certain." When taking the products of these statements, one obtains:

$$\text{"certain" * "uncertain" * "uncertain" * "certain"}$$

Knowing that the product of the probabilities cannot be greater than the smallest probability, one has to search for this latter. However, "uncertain" does not indicate an intensity and therefore the probability of finally having "to pay the piper" can only be considered "uncertain."

Table 3.1 shows that the utility statements are indicated only in terms of "good" and "bad." They are thus statements without intensities. The same is true for the probabilities. Two probability statements are indicated as zero: $p(O_{11})$ = "inconceivable" and $p(O_{21})$ = "it is not anticipated," which means that they can be excluded from the further argumentation, while the remaining probabilites are indicated in terms of "certain" or "uncertain," also without intensities.

Given this information about probabilities and utilities without intensities, we may expect that one of the rules in Class IV (Table 2.2) can reproduce the choice of the decision-maker. Summarizing the state of affairs, we get the following result:

1. Description : The outcomes are specified without intensities for utilities and probabilities.
2. Rule : Argumentation rule is absent, we expect a class IV rule to apply.
3. Condition : Not mentioned.
4. Conclusion : S_2 must be chosen.

Table 3.1:
Summary of the Argumentation of the Minister

Strategies	Outcomes								
	O_{11}: favorable German answer	O_{12}: evasive German answer	O_{12}: evasive German answer	O_{12}: evasive German answer	O_{12}: evasive German answer	O_{12}: evasive German answer	O_{12}: evasive German answer	O_{21}: trouble with the British	O_{22}: no trouble with the British
		O_{13}: shaken confidence + troubles	O_{14}: shaken confidence + war	O_{14}: shaken confidence + war	O_{14}: shaken confidence + war	O_{15}: shaken confidence			
			O_{16}: we have to pay the piper	O_{17}: compensation for Dutch Flanders and the Scheldt	O_{18}: partially destroyed country and Germany's confidence shaken				
S_1: Ask Germany about its intentions with regard to Antwerp	$U(O_{11})=+$	$UO_{12}=-$	$O(O_{12})=-$	$U(O_{12})=-$	$U(O_{12})=-$	$U(O_{12})=-$	$U(O_{12})=-$		
		$U(O_{13})=-$	$U(O_{14})=-$	$U(O_{14})=-$	$U(O_{14})=-$	$U(O_{15})=-$			
			$U(O_{16})=-$	$U(O_{17})=-$	$U(O_{18})=-$				
	p= inconceivable	p= uncertain	p= uncertain	p= uncertain	p= uncertain	p= uncertain	p= uncertain		
S_2: Remain silent (chosen)								$U(O_{21})=-$	$U(O_{22})=+$
								p= it is not anticipated	p= certain

Figure 3.5:
Decision Tree Based on the Argumentation of the Minister

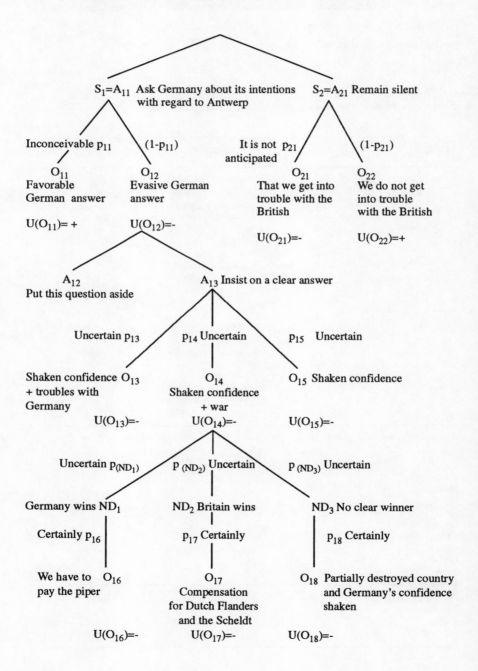

The next step to determine the complete argumentation is to apply the rule(s) of the class to the data and to determine which strategy should be chosen. Finally, the strategy obtained by a specific decision rule of the appropriate class must be compared with the strategy actually chosen by the decision-maker. If the strategies are identical, we say that the rule fits or explains the choice. If not, the model is not able to explain the choice.

Class IV (Table 2.2) contained two argumentation rules. One of these was Simon's Rule, which posits that one should select the first strategy one encounters that leads only to satisfactory outcomes. More formally, this rule can be summarized as follows:

1. Description : The outcomes are specified without intensities for utilities and probabilities.
2. Rule   : If $U(O_{ij}) > 0$ for all j and $U(O_{kj}) < 0$ at least for one j, then S_i must be chosen.
3. Condition   : $U(O_{ij}) > 0$ for all j and $U(O_{kj}) < 0$ at least for one j.
4. Conclusion   : S_2 must be chosen.

According to this argument, S_2 should be chosen, a choice that coincides with the actual choice and fits the data. The other rule in this class is the Reversed Simon Rule, according to which all strategies that lead only to negative outcomes are rejected as long as there is still a strategy that could lead to a positive outcome. This can formally be summarized as follows:

1. Description : The outcomes are specified without intensities for utilities and probabilities.
2. Rule   : If $U(O_{ij}) > 0$ for at least one j and $U(O_{kj}) < 0$ for all j, then S_i must be chosen.
3. Condition   : $U(O_{ij}) > 0$ for at least one j and $U(O_{kj}) < 0$ for all j.
4. Conclusion   : S_2 must be chosen.

The Reversed Simon Rule also fits the data, since S_2 must be chosen. We can therefore conclude that both rules are capable of explaining the choice of the decision-maker.

This example shows that the determination of the choice rule will always be carried out in two steps: First, given the value and probability statements, the appropriate class of rules is established. Second, this class is checked to see if one of its rules is able to predict the strategy chosen. In most cases only one rule applies, but in some cases several rules of the same class can explain the specified choice.

CONCLUSIONS

In this methodological chapter we have discussed how the arguments can be detected from written documents even though the texts contain a great deal of irrelevant information and some relevant parts are omitted. First we explained the procedure for the coding of the texts to identify the description of the decision problem. We have also shown that the coding of such texts to detect arguments can be conducted with very high reliability by pairs of coders. After that, we showed how this description gives indications of which class of argumentation one has to look to for a proper rule. If one of the rules of this class applies, we can say that the complete argument has been found because the description, the detected rule, the specified condition, and the choice are in agreement with each other.

In principle, this argument is not yet complete. It is not yet clear how frequently no appropriate argumentation rule could be found, and we have also not shown that the rules are self-evident to both the speakers and the audience. In Chapter 8 we will continue this discussion to show that for only very few texts could no fitting argumentation rule be found. In a separate study, we have shown that the audience, even with people less educated than politicians, has very little doubt about the decision rule used by a speaker in specific situations. But before we continue with these quantitative studies, we will use this approach to investigate the argumentations of politicians of different times, countries, and political regimes.

Chapter 4

War with Serbia or Not: The Initiation of World War I, July 1914

This chapter presents a case study of arguments of members of the Austro-Hungarian Common Council of Ministers on whether or not to declare war on Serbia following the assassination of the Austro-Hungarian heir to the throne and his wife at Sarajevo, the Bosnian capital, on June 28, 1914.

It is impossible to present here the full documents, since that would take too much space. For an example of such a text we refer to Chapter 3. In this chapter, the arguments of individual decision-makers will be presented in chronological order and analyzed, using the approach discussed in Chapter 3. After this analysis, each decision tree is transformed into a decision table, that is, that the descriptions of the decision problems will be presented in decision tables, as discussed in Chapter 3. In none of the arguments discussed in this chapter was the decision rule mentioned, nor the fact that the relevant condition was fullfilled in order to derive the conclusion. As we have mentioned before, this means either that our approach is completely wrong or that these rules are so obvious to both the speaker and the audience that they do not consider it important to mention them. If the latter is the case, we should be able to identify these obvious decision rules. In Chapters 2 and 3, it was suggested that the amount of information given in the problem description could be used as an indication of what class of rules should be applied. We will follow this procedure by first determining the class of the problem using the information on the utilities and probabilities, and then we will test the rules of this class to see if one or more of these rules can predict the choice of the decision-maker. If one rule of such a class of decision problems can predict the choice, we think that we have identified the complete argumentation of the decision-maker. This survey will show that in all individual arguments, at least one of the suggested decision rules could predict the choice mentioned by the decision-maker. This suggests that these simple decision rules probably are obvious to the speaker and the audience and that we probably have found the correct approach to the analysis of argumentation. More details on this issue follow in Chapter 8. First we present here the series of individual arguments of decision-makers.

POLITICAL BACKGROUND

From the second half of the nineteenth century, Austro-Hungarian foreign policy was aimed at minimizing the threat of Balkan nationalism and Russian-inspired Pan-Slavism in this region in order to protect the Habsburg territories of Croatia-Slavonia and Dalmatia. In 1878, the Great Powers had even agreed that Austria-Hungary should occupy the territories of Bosnia-Herzegovina, and this was changed into annexation of these territories in 1908. In the view of Austria-Hungary, this was necessary in order to protect its territories in this region from attack by Serbs or Pan-Slavs supported by Russians. After 1903, the Serbs changed their policy of good relations with Austria into an anti-Austrian policy with the aim of constructing a southern Slavian state under the leadership of Serbia with the consent of Russia, with whom, however, they had no agreement of military assistance in the event of a war with the Dual Monarchy.

When the Austro-Hungarian heir to the throne and his wife were assassinated in the Bosnian capital of Sarajevo on June 28, 1914, by Bosnian students who apparently had been supported by Serbia, the Dual Monarchy felt a threat to its Great Power status in the Balkans and its future prestige. Since neither the finances nor the army of the monarchy were in a condition to countenance a prolonged war with Serbia, the monarchy first discussed the matter with Germany, its ally. Germany readily offered its military support and encouraged Austria-Hungary to declare war on Serbia. Nevertheless, the responsible decision-makers were still hesitating, and a month elapsed between the assassination and the declaration of war. They anticipated difficulties in the event that the hostilities spread, since a war with Serbia could easily involve Russia, and Russia's ally France could also take sides. On the other hand, there were doubts over the monarchy's other allies, Italy and Romania, who were not considered very reliable.

In the following section we will study the arguments of members of the Common Austro-Hungarian Council of Ministers, whose ultimate decision provoked World War I.

DECISION PHASE 1, JULY 7, 1914

Although the decision process can be divided into several phases, the ministers mainly gave complete arguments in phase 1. Most of these arguments were made in the first meeting of the Common Council of Ministers, held on July 7, 1914. After having secured the German support, the common minister of foreign affairs convened a meeting of the Common Council of Ministers. Table 4.1 summarizes his argument.

Table 4.1:
Argument by the Common Minister of Foreign Affairs in the Common Council of Ministers on July 7, 1914, on the Declaration of War on Serbia

Strategies	Outcomes		
	O_{11}	O_{12}	O_{21}
	a_{111}: Unconditional support by Germany a_{112}: in war with Russia a_{113}: the negative development in the Balkans reversed	a_{121}: Unconditional support by Germany a_{122}: not in war with Russia a_{123}: the negative development in the Balkans reversed	The Balkan states consider it a sign of weakness and join with Russia against us
S_1*: Declare immediately war on Serbia	$U(a_{111})=+$ $U(a_{112})=-$ $U(a_{113})=+$ p=possible	$U(a_{121})=+$ $U(a_{122})=+$ $U(a_{113})=+$ p=possible	
S_2 Do nothing			$U(O_{21})=-$ p=certain

Source: Common Council of Ministers of the Austro-Hungarian Monarchy, July 7, 1914, Minutes, in M. Komjáthy, ed., *Protokolle des Gemeinsamen Ministerrates der Österreichisch-Ungarischen Monarchie (1914–1918)* (Budapest: Akadémiai Kiadó, 1966), no.1, 141–150.)

Symbols: S_i strategy i. S_i* chosen strategy. O_{ij} outcome j under strategy i. A_{ijk} aspect k of outcome j under strategy i. $U(O_{ij})$ utility of outcome j under strategy i. $U(a_{ijk})$ utility of aspect k of outcome j under strategy i. P probability of an outcome.
Cells that are empty for a specific strategy were not considered by the decision-maker.

The table shows that the minister of foreign affairs considered two strategies. If the monarchy did nothing in response of the heir to the throne's assassination (S_2), the Balkan states would certainly interpret this as a sign of weakness on the part of the monarchy and join with Russia against Austria-Hungary. He evaluated this outcome as negative and therefore rejected this strategy. If they declared immediate war on Serbia (S_1), they would at least have the unconditional support of Germany (O_{11}: a_{111} and O_{12}: a_{121}), and they would be able to reverse the negative development in the Balkans by restoring the mornarchy's prestige (O_{11}: a_{113} and O_{12}: a_{123}). But there was also the possibility that Russia would enter the war (O_{11}: a_{112}), which he evaluated as negative. On the basis of the utilities and probabilities, the minister of foreign affairs indicated his conclusion that S_1 should be adopted.

If one considers the evaluations of probabilities and utilities, it is clear that the minister used utilities and probabilities without intensities. Based on the probabilities and utilities he indicated, it would seem appropriate to test the heuristics of Class IV (Table 2.4) to see whether they produce his choice of S_1. Applictaion of Simon's Rule, which requires selection of a strategy leading only to satisfactory outcomes, does not reproduce his choice for S_1. Since he rejected S_2, where only a negative outcome could occur, and chose the strategy (S_1), where a positive outcome was also possible, the Reversed Simon Rule correctly predicts his choice and therefore seems to fit his argument.

The argument of the Hungarian prime minister (Table 4.2) was quite different. He also considered the strategy of immediately declaring war on Serbia (S_1), but rejected it, because the chance was very high, in his view, of finding his country in a struggle for life and death with a Russia coming to the assistance of the other Balkan states, who had all, with the exception of Bulgaria, turned against the monarchy (O_{11}). He then introduced another strategy, namely to deliver an ultimatum to Serbia with heavy but feasible demands, and if it did not accept them to initiate war but without the aim of destroying Serbia (S_2). According his view, the chance was high that the demands would be accepted, which would lead to a diplomatic success for the monarchy, restore its prestige in the Balkans, and humiliate the Serbs (O_{21}). There was, however, a small chance that the Serbs would not accept the demands, which would lead to only a local war with Serbia (O_{22}). This outcome he evaluated as less negative. On the basis of the values and probabilities, the Hungarian prime minister indicated his choice as S_2.

If one considers the evaluations of probabilities and utilities it is clear that the minister used probabilities with intensities. The utilities, however, are without intensities and can only be understood in terms of "good" and "bad." Based on the probabilities and utilities he indicated, models of Class II (Table 2.4) should be tested to see whether they produce his choice for S_2. We can try both versions, the Positive and the Negative Risk-Avoidance Rules.

Applying the Positive Risk-Avoidance Rule leads to the selection of S_2, and the same is true for the Negative Risk-Avoidance Rule. Therefore, both rules can predict the choice and the Risk-Avoidance argumentation seems to fit the argument of the Hungarian prime minister.

The next argument was presented by the Austrian prime minister (Table 4.3). He considered three strategies. If his government were to do nothing (S_1), they would certainly lose their provinces in the Balkans (O_{11}). If they were to deliver an ultimatum to Serbia with heavy but feasible demands and if, in the event these were not accepted, they were to initiate the war without the aim of destroy-

Table 4.2:

Argument of the Hungarian Prime Minister in the Common Council of Ministers on July 7, 1914, on the Declaration of War on Serbia

Strategies	Outcomes			
	O_{11} The Balkan states become our enemies with the exception of Bulgaria, which cannot help us, and we enter a fight for life and death with Russia	O_{12} The Balkan states do not become our enemies and we do not enter a fight for life and death with Russia	O_{21} Our demands are accepted, which leads to a diplomatic success with the restoration of our prestige in the Balkans and the humiliation of Serbia, improving our position	O_{22} Our demands are not accepted, but no fight for life and death
S_1: Declare immediately war on Serbia	$U(O_{11})=-$ p=highly probable	$U(O_{12})=+$ p=very small		
S_2*: Deliver an ultimatum to Serbia, with heavy but feasible demands, and if it does not accept them, initiate the war but without the aim to destroy Serbia entirely			$U(O_{21})=+$ p=highly probable	$U(O_{22})=$ less negative p=very small

Source: Common Council of Ministers of the Austro-Hungarian Monarchy, July 7, 1914, Minutes, in M. Komjáthy, ed., *Protokolle des Gemeinsamen Ministerrates der Österreichisch-Ungarischen Monarchie (1914–1918)* (Budapest: Akadémiai Kiadó, 1966), no.1, 141–150.

Symbols: S_i strategy i. S_i* chosen strategy. O_{ij} outcome j under strategy i. $U(O_{ij})$ utility of outcome j under strategy i. P probability of an outcome.

Cells that are empty for a specific strategy were not considered by the decision-maker.

Table 4.3:
Argument of the Austrian Prime Minister in the Common Council of Ministers on July 7, 1914, on the Declaration of War on Serbia

Strategies	Outcomes			
	O_{11} Loss of our provinces in the Balkans	O_{21} Our demands are accepted, which leads to a diplomatic success, but no improvement of our position in the Balkans	O_{22} No loss of our provinces in the Balkans	O_{31} With the aid of Germany, the prestige of the monarchy restored and no loss of our provinces in the Balkans
S_1: Do nothing	$U(O_{11})=-$ p=certain			
S_2*: Deliver an ultimatum to Serbia, with heavy but feasible demands, and if it does not accept them, initiate the war without the aim to destroy Serbia entirely		$U(O_{21})=-$ p=possible	$U(O_{22})=+$ p=possible	
S_3*: Deliver an ultimatum to Serbia, with infeasible demands, and initiate the war				$U(O_{31})=+$ p=certain

Source: Common Council of Ministers of the Austro-Hungarian Monarchy, July 7, 1914, Minutes, in M. Komjáthy, ed., *Protokolle des Gemeinsamen Ministerrates der Österreichisch-Ungarischen Monarchie (1914–1918)* (Budapest: Akadémiai Kiadó, 1966), no.1, 141–150.

Symbols: S_i strategy i. S_i* chosen strategy. O_{ij} outcome j under strategy i. $U(O_{ij})$ utility of outcome j under strategy i. P probability of an outcome.
Cells that are empty for a specific strategy were not considered by the decision-maker.

ing Serbia entirely (S_2), it was possible that Austria-Hungary would not lose its provinces in the Balkans (O_{22}). But in his view, it was also possible that the demands would be accepted, leading to a diplomatic success for the monarchy but not the improvement of its position in the Balkans (O_{21}). However, if they were to deliver an ultimatum to Serbia with demands that were not feasible and then were to initiate war (S_3), he was certain that with the assistance of Germany, the prestige of the monarchy in the Balkans would be restored and its provinces would not be lost (O_{31}).

Based on the probabilities and utilities the Austrian prime minister indicated (both without intensities), models of Class IV (Table 2.4) should be tested to see whether they produce his choice for S_3. Simon's Rule and the Reversed Simon Rule are mentioned in this class. Applying the Reversed Simon Rule, which demands the rejection of all strategies that lead only to negative outcomes and the selection of the strategy where a positive outcome is also possible, does not reproduce the choice for S_3. Since the prime minister chose the strategy leading only to satisfactory outcomes, Simon's Rule correctly predicts his choice for S_3 and therefore seems to fit his argument.

With the exception of the Hungarian prime minister, all the participants in the meeting opted for the ultimatum with infeasible demands in order to initiate war on Serbia. The group decision process will be studied in detail in another volume. Based on the outcome of this meeting, the common foreign minister went to the emperor to convey the advice of the Cabinet. Since the Hungarian prime minister was dissatisfied with this conclusion, it was decided that he would separately bring his point of view to the attention of the emperor in the form of a letter.

DECISION PHASE 2, JULY 8–13, 1914

In this phase only the Hungarian prime minister repeated a complete argument in the form of a letter to the emperor. Table 4.4 summarizes his argument. He now considered three strategies. If his government declared immediately war on Serbia (S_1) the chance was high that it would lead to a world war, involving Russia and other Great Powers, bringing about an unfavorable outcome for the monarchy (O_{11}). He also foresaw, although with a little probability, a less unfavorable outcome of the world war for the monarchy (O_{12}). If they did nothing (S_2), he reasoned that assassinations in the Balkans would continue, with the spread of hatred against the monarchy that would finally lead to a loss of its prestige (O_{21}). Neither strategies were viable in his opinion. However, if they were to deliver an ultimatum to Serbia with heavy but feasible demands (S_3), he foresaw the possibility that the Serbs would comply, resulting in a diplomatic success for the monarchy and humiliation of the Serbs (O_{33}). He also foresaw the possibility that the Serbian answer to the ultimatum (S_3) might be unsatisfactory or delayed, in which case war would be justified and might not lead to the involvement of the Great Powers. This would finally lead to a diminished Serbia

Table 4.4:
Advice of the Hungarian Prime Minister to the Emperor on July 8, 1914, on the Declaration of War with Serbia

Strategies	Outcomes					
	O_{11}	O_{12}	O_{21}	O_{31}	O_{32}	O_{33}
	Leads to a world war with an unfavorable outcome for our monarchy	Leads to a world war with a less unfavorable outcome for our monarchy	Continuation of assassinations and dissemination of hatred against us, loss of prestige by our monarchy	Serbian answer unsatisfactory or delayed, war is justified, no world war, Serbia diminished, right of monarchy to war reparations	Serbian answer unsatisfactory or delayed, war is justified, world war	Serbian answer satisfactory, diplomatic success of our monarchy, humiliation of Serbia
S_1: Declare immediately war on Serbia	$U(O_{11})=-$ p=high	$U(O_{12})=$ less negative p=small				
S_2: Do nothing			$U(O_{21})=$ -p=certain			
S_3*: Deliver an ultimatum to Serbia, with heavy but feasible demands, and if it does not accept them, initiate the war without the aim of destroying Serbia entirely				$U(O_{31})=+$ p=possible	$U(O_{32})=-$ p=possible	$U(O_{33})=+$ p=possible

Source: Hungarian prime minister to the emperor, July 8, 1914, Letter, in I. Geiss ed., *Julikrise und Kriegsausbruch 1914* (Hannover: Verlag für Literatur und Zeitgeschichte, 1963), no. 51, 128–131.

Symbols: S_i strategy i. S_i* chosen strategy. O_{ij} outcome j under strategy i. $U(O_{ij})$ utility of outcome j under strategy i. P probability of an outcome. Cells that are empty for a specific strategy were not considered by the decision-maker.

with the right of the monarchy to extract war reparations (O_{31}). In the event of a war, however, he also took into account the possibility of involvement of the Great Powers (O_{32}). On the basis of the utilities and probabilities he had indicated, the Hungarian prime minister advised the emperor to choose S_3, the same strategy he had in vain advocated during the Cabinet meeting.

If one considers the utilities, it is clear that the minister used utilities without intensities. The probabilities, however, are for the first strategy with intensities, while for the other strategies they are without intensities, so that they have to be considered without intensities. On the basis of the utilities and probabilities Simon's Rule and the Reversed Simon Rule (models of Class IV, Table 2.4) are appropriate to test. Simon's Rule does not reproduce the choice of S_3 since it demands the selection of the strategy that leads only to positive outcomes. But, the Reversed Simon Rule fits the data because it rejects the strategies that lead only to negative outcomes (S_1, S_2) and selects the alternative where positive outcomes are also possible (S_3).

The efforts of the Hungarian prime minister to convince the emperor to avoid war, however, proved to be in vain. The emperor accepted on July 9 the majority advice of the Common Council of Ministers to deliver to Serbia an ultimatum with demands that were not feasible, and to initiate war. Even the Hungarian prime minister was finally convinced by his colleagues of the necessity for war.

The events subsequently followed each other very quickly (see Bihl 1989). On July 23, the ultimatum was handed to the Serbian government. It contained such harsh demands as the renouncing by the Serbian government of the Pan-Slavic movement, the purge of the army, the civil service and the press from elements hostile to the Austro-Hungarian monarchy, and the dissolution of anti-Austrian secret organizations. It also demanded that officials of the Austro-Hungarian monarchy should take part in the investigations of the assassination. The Austro-Hungarian ambassador in Belgrade had received the instruction to demand "pure and simple" acceptance in order to secure war (Geiss 1963, no. 156, 237). On July 24, Britain had proposed a European mediation effort between Austria-Hungary and Russia; this was rejected by the Germans on July 28. On July 27, after receiving the Serbian answer, diplomatic relations between Austria-Hungary and Serbia were broken and the declaration of war followed on July 28. Britain vainly tried once again to mediate on July 29, proposing that Austria-Hungary would stop its hostile activities once the occupation of Belgrade and its differences with Russia were solved at the negotiation table. Thereafter, mobilizations and declarations of war followed each other.

CONCLUSIONS

In this chapter we have studied four arguments that were put forward by individual decision-makers in the crisis situation that finally initiated World War I. When arguing, the decision-makers described the available strategies and their consequences and evaluated the consequences and their likelihood of occurrence. Thereupon, they drew conclusions as to which strategy should be adopted. However, they never mentioned the choice rule they used in order to draw their conclusions, let alone indicated whether the conditions were satisfied under which the preferred strategy should be chosen. Based on the quality of the utilities and probabilities they indicated, it has been possible to establish for each argument an appropriate class of argumentation rules, which has been applied to the data to find a fitting choice rule. In one case the Risk-Avoidance Rules correctly predicted the choice, and in three cases rules of Class IV (Simon's and the Reversed Simon Rules) fitted the choice. These results show that the decision-makers generally avoided combining utilities and probabilities with intensities, which can lead to an overly complex computational operation, as we have already indicated. When studying these arguments one gets the impression that they are based on a number of simplifications or reductions of information.

One way of simplifying decision problems in order to reduce complexity is to reduce complex value problems to simple value problems. For example, decision-makers did not consider all relevant aspects of outcomes simultaneously across strategies. The common minister of foreign affairs, for instance, used in his argument for the first strategy (Table 4.1) three aspects systematically, namely, one aspect concerning the position of their ally, one regarding the occurrence of the kind of war (local or spread), and another referring to the position of the monarchy in the Balkans, in terms of its prestige and territorial integrity. For the second strategy, he considered only the position of the monarchy in the Balkans and omitted the other two aspects. These three dimensions also seemed to be relevant for the other decision-makers, as they sometimes considered them for one strategy, but they did not consider them systematically across all strategies. Table 4.5 summarizes for each strategy the dimensions of outcomes indicated by the decision-maker. The table shows that the decision-makers considered all three dimensions relevant but did not use them systematically across strategies. Sometimes they only referred to a single dimension when examining a strategy, for example, for S_2 they only considered the monarchy's position. It seems that they restricted themselves to considering only those aspects of outcomes they judged most important for each strategy.

Another way of reducing information is to omit uncertainty or reduce uncertainty to quasi certainty. In three cases (Tables 4.1, 4.3 and 4.4) the decision-makers formulated the problem in such a way that the outcomes for at least one strategy were considered certain, and in one case (Table 4.2) the outcomes had a very high or very low chance of occurring.

Another mode of simplification was to restrict the range of strategies considered. In total, four distinct strategies were mentioned in the course of the argumentations, but in two arguments the decision-makers only considered two alternatives simultaneously, and in the remaining two, they examined three. These data accord with Lindblom's assumption (Lindblom 1959, 1982) that decision-makers limit their analysis to a small range of alternatives that are familiar in order to make the decision problem manageable. Next to the alternative of maintaining the status quo ("do nothing"), they examined strategies that

Table 4.5:

Summary of the Aspects of Outcomes Considered for Each Strategy by the Decision-Makers

Strategies	Aspects of Outcomes		
	Ally's position	Kind of war	The monarchy's position
S_1:			
Declare immediately war on Serbia	Minister of foreign affairs	Minister of foreign affairs Hungarian prime minister	Minister of foreign affairs
S_2:			
Do nothing			Minister of foreign affairs Austrian prime minister Hungarian prime minister
S_3:			
Deliver an ultimatum to Serbia, with heavy but feasible demands, and if it does not accept them, initiate the war without the aim of destroying Serbia entirely		Hungarian prime minister	Hungarian prime minister Austrian prime minister
S_4:			
Deliver an ultimatum to Serbia, with infeasible demands, and initiate the war	Austrian prime minister		Austrian prime minister

quite drastically deviated from it, such as the "immediate declaration of war" and the ultimatum variants.

Having studied the arguments of ministers of a medium power that was confronted with a serious crisis situation at the beginning of this century and whose final decision provoked World War I, we will turn in the next chapter to the arguments of members of a dictatorial regime, who by the implementation of these decisions, provoked World War II.

Chapter 5

The Initiation of World War II

In this chapter we will study Hitler's arguments for the initiation of World War II, which was preceded by the annexations of Austria and Czechoslovakia and finally by the invasion of Poland. As usual, we will briefly introduce the political background and then describe the arguments presented. Since Hitler was a dictator who did not tolerate any criticism, his audience refrained from discussion and restricted itself mainly to applause. There are therefore only very few arguments from other individuals available on these topics.

POLITICAL BACKGROUND

When Hitler wrote *Mein Kampf* in the 1920s, he laid down his program for foreign policy. It consisted, among other things, of revising the Treaty of Versailles concluded after World War I, incorporating Austria, and transforming Czechoslovakia and Poland into satellite states for achieving more German Lebensraum (territory for raw materials and food). When Hitler came into power in the 1930s, he began by pursuing the rearmament of Germany against the provisions of the Treaty of Versailles, notwithstanding the protests of France, Britain, Italy, and the League of Nations, from which he withdrew Germany in 1933.

In 1936 Hitler launched a four-year plan to prepare Germany for war. In the same year he concluded a pact with Mussolini, whom he admired as his equal. The pact was the so-called Rome-Berlin axis, of which Japan became the third member in 1938. In November 1937, when Hitler disclosed to the leaders of the armed forces some of his plans for achieving German Lebensraum, he failed to convince his audience and consequently replaced the leaders of the army, abolished the position of minister of war and made himself commander-in-chief of the armed forces. By these means he avoided any further objections to the implementation of his decisions. In the spring of 1938, he annexed Austria with no protest from other European powers. This obviously encouraged him to take over Czechoslovakia also, a feat he accomplished in the spring of 1939. In this case, too, the German Army met little opposition. The next country from which he tried to acquire territory was Poland. When the Poles refused his request to give way on Danzig, the British felt obliged in March 1939 to guarantee Poland its independence. In regard to this British move, Hitler had by then formed the opinion that the British were too weak to stand by their guarantee. He also felt strengthened by his pact with Stalin, which was about to be concluded at the end of August 1939. Stalin also had an interest in carving up Poland, while for Hitler this treaty assured him of the time needed to concentrate on the West rather than open two fronts in the event that war did break out. Within this political context, he decided that the time had come to invade Poland. In the following sections, Hitler's argument for gaining more Lebensraum will be studied, arguments with respect to the annexation of Czechoslovakia will be analyzed, and finally the argument for invading Poland will be presented.

HITLER'S ARGUMENT FOR GAINING MORE LEBENSRAUM, NOVEMBER 10, 1937

On November 10, 1937, in the chancellery of the Reich, Hitler outlined to some ministers and his supreme commanders his foreign policy aims for the near future. Pointing out in advance that what they needed was more territory for raw materials and food, he considered several strategies (Table 5.1). If they were to continue with a strictly National Socialist governance (S_1), they would be able to achieve a conditional self-suffiency for raw materials, but not for food (O_{11}), and he considered this unacceptable. If they did participate in the world economy (S_2), they would certainly not achieve a safe economic basis in the long run, since there was no guarantee that trade agreements would be maintained in the long run. In the event of war, the food situation would become precarious because their foreign trade would lead through areas dominated by the British (O_{21}). Another strategy would be to ask for the restitution of former German colonies (S_3). But since he was certain that the British and the French would not meet this demand and at best would assign them some territories possessed by other countries—which would mean more people but not more agriculturally useful land (O_{31})—he rejected this alternative, too. However, if they were to annex Austria and Czechoslovakia at a favorable moment (S_4), there was a high probability that neither the French, the British, the Italians or the Polish would object, and provided they could force 3 million inhabitants of these countries to emigrate, they would gain territory to feed 5 or 6 million people. Militarily and politically, this would constitute a great relief because of the acquisition of better frontiers and the availability of the army for other purposes (O_{41}). However, there was also a very low chance that the French and the Russians would object, in which case the consequence would be war (O_{42}).

Table 5.1:
Hitler's Address to His Ministers and the Supreme Commanders,
November 10, 1937

Strategies	Outcomes				
	O_{11}	O_{21}	O_{31}	O_{41}	O_{42}
	Leads to conditional self-sufficiency with regard to raw materials but not with respect to food	No safe basis for an economic settlement in the long run	Denied by the British and French, at best, acquisition of colonies from other countries	No French, British, Italian or Polish objections, gain of territory to feed 5 or 6 million, military and political relief because of better frontiers, and use of army for other purposes	French and Russian objections and war
S_1: Strictly National Socialist governance	$U(O_{11})=-$ p=certain				
S_2: Participation in the world economy		$U(O_{21})=-$ p=certain			
S_3: Discussion about restitution of colonies			$U(O_{31})=-$ p=certain		
S_4*: Annexation of Austria and Czechoslovakia at a favorable moment				$U(O_{41})=+$ p=very high	$U(O_{42})=-$ p=very low

Source: Hitler, Adolf, Nov. 10, 1938, Address, *Akten zur Deutschen Auswärtigen Politik 1918–1945*, Series D (1937–1945), vol. 1 (Baden-Baden: Imprimerie Nationale, 1956), no. 19, 25–32.

Symbols: S_i strategy i. S_i* chosen strategy. O_{ij} outcome j under strategy i. $U(O_{ij})$ utility of outcome j under strategy i. P probability of an outcome.

The military warned Hitler that they were not yet prepared to take these measures, especially against Czechoslovakia, which had strong fortifications, and Hitler acknowledged that he did not intend to implement this plan in the immediate future. On the basis of the values and probabilities, the Führer indicated his choice of S_4.

If one considers the evaluations of probabilities and utilities, it is clear that Hitler used probabilities with intensities. The utilities, however, are without intensities and can only be understood in terms of "good" and "bad." Based on the probabilities and utilities that he indicated, models of Class II (Table 2.4) should be tested to see whether they produce his choice for S_4. We can try both versions, the Positive and the Negative Risk-Avoidance Rules. Applying the Positive Risk-Avoidance Rule leads to the selection of S_4, and the same is true for the Negative Risk-Avoidance Rule. Therefore, both rules are capable of predicting the actual choice, and the Risk-Avoidance argumentation seems to fit Hitler's argument.

However, during the early spring of 1938 extremely repressive measures against Austria were implemented in the hope that the annexation would evolve of itself (see also Botz 1976). When the Austrian chancellor announced a plebiscite with the intention of asking the population whether or not they preferred a free and autonomous Austria, Hitler invaded the country under the pretext of responding to a request for help by the Austrian National Socialists. The invasion began on March 11. The Western powers did not react, and Hitler's expectations in this respect seemed to be fulfilled. The next adventure concerned Czechoslovakia.

ARGUMENTS LEADING TO THE ANNEXATION OF CZECHO-SLOVAKIA, 1938

On April 22, 1938, Hitler gave the army his reasons for favoring a lightning action in order to annex Czechoslovakia. The military had to prepare the operation plan, which was code-named Operation Green. Hitler considered three strategies (Table 5.2). One was a strategic attack out of the blue (S_1) which he thought might provoke hostile world opinion and lead to a serious crisis, since the Western powers might not accept it (O_{11}). But it was also possible that only hostile world opinion would occur (O_{21}). Another alternative was to act after a period of diplomatic discussion (S_2). But the Führer was certain that this course also would lead only to negative outcomes, such as a crisis and war with the Western powers (O_{21}). However, lightning action after an incident such as the murder of a German minister in the course of an anti-German demonstration in Czechoslovakia (S_3) might lead to a positive result achieved by quick military success (O_{31}). If there was no quick military success, a European crisis and war would ensue (O_{32}).

Based on the probabilities and utilities indicated by the Führer (both without intensities), models of Class IV (Table 2.4) should be tested to see whether they

Table 5.2:
Memorandum on Operation Green, April 22, 1938

Strategies	Outcomes				
	O_{11}	O_{12}	O_{21}	O_{31}	O_{32}
	Hostile world opinion, which leads to a serious situation	Hostile world opinion	Crisis and war	Military success	No military success and a European crisis
S_1: A strategic attack out of the blue	$U(O_{11})=-$ p=possible	$U(O_{12})=-$ p=possible			
S_2: An action after a period of diplomatic discussion			$U(O_{21})=-$ p=certain		
$S_3{}^*$: A lightning action on the basis of an incident				$U(O_{31})=+$ p=possible	$U(O_{32})=-$ p=possible

Source: Hitler, Adolf, April 22, 1938, Memorandum on Operation Green, *Akten zur Deutschen Auswärtigen Politik 1918–1945*, Series D (1937–1945), vol. 2 (Baden-Baden: Imprimerie Nationale, 1956), no. 133, 239–240.

Symbols: S_i strategy i. $S_i{}^*$ chosen strategy. O_{ij} outcome j under strategy i. $U(O_{ij})$ utility of outcome j under strategy i. P probability of an outcome.

produce his choice for S_3. Simon's Rule and the Reversed Simon Rule are mentioned in this class. Applying Simon's Rule, which demands the rejection of all strategies that lead only to negative outcomes and the selection of the strategy leading only to satisfactory outcomes, does not reproduce his choice for S_3. But the Reversed Simon Rule, which demands the rejection of all strategies that lead only to negative outcomes and the selection of the strategy where a positive outcome is also possible, correctly predicts his choice for S_3 and therefore seems to fit his argument.

However, the annexation of Czechoslovakia did not progress so easily. Although unrest was fomented with the help of the Sudeten German minority in Czechslovakia, in the course of the summer of 1938, Czech mobilization ensued and a crisis developed. In the light of these events, the following two pieces of advice by a state secretary to the minister of foreign affairs were formulated. The minister in turn had to discuss the matter with Hitler.

The state secretary considered two strategies on June 2 (Table 5.3). If they were to immediately attack Czechoslovakia (S_1), they would possibly invite a conflict with the British and the French that the German army could not withstand (O_{11}), although it was also possible, of course, that the Western powers would not interfere (O_{12}). If they were to start a gradual annexation process by demanding self-determination for the Sudeten Germans (S_2), he was certain that they would prepare the ground for the disruption of Czechoslovakia (O_{21}).

Based on the probabilities and utilities indicated by the state secretary (both without intensities), models of Class IV (Table 2.4) should be tested to see whether they produce his choice for S_2. Simon's Rule and the Reversed Simon Rule are mentioned in this class. Applying the Reversed Simon Rule, which demands the rejection of all strategies that lead only to negative outcomes and the selection of the strategy where a positive outcome is also possible, does not

Table 5.3:
Memorandum by a State Secretary for the Foreign Minister, June 20, 1938

Strategies	Outcomes		
	O_{11}	O_{12}	O_{21}
	Conflict with British and French, which our strength could not bear	No conflict with British and French	Prepares the ground for the disruption of Czechoslovakia
S_1: An immediate attack	$U(O_{11})=-$ p=possible	$U(O_{12})=+$ p=possible	
S_2*: Start a gradual process with the aim of self-determination for the Sudeten Germans and amputation of districts			$U(O_{21})=+$ p=certain

Source: State Secretary, June 20, 1938, Memorandum, *Akten zur Deutschen Auswärtigen Politik 1918–1945*, Series D (1937–1945), vol. 2 (Baden-Baden: Imprimerie Nationale, 1956), no. 259, 420–422.

Symbols: S_i strategy i. S_i* chosen strategy. O_{ij} outcome j under strategy i. $U(O_{ij})$ utility of outcome j under strategy i. P probability of an outcome.

reproduce his choice for S_2. But Simon's Rule, which demands the rejection of all strategies that lead only to negative outcomes and the selection of the strategy leading only to satisfactory outcomes, does correctly predict his choice for S_2 and therefore seems to fit his argument.

It seemed that Hitler was hesitating himself about the course of action to follow, because on August 30 the same state secretary produced similar advice for the foreign minister (Table 5.4). He again stated that an invasion of Czechoslovakia (S_1) would make the Western powers their enemies and would consequently lead to a European war, which would sooner or later lead to German capitulation (O_{11}). If his government were to negotiate with the British,

Table 5.4:

Memorandum by a State Secretary for the Foreign Minister, August 30, 1938

Strategies	Outcomes		
	O_{11}	O_{21}	O_{22}
	Western powers are our enemies, war develops in a European war and ends sooner or later with German defeat	Autonomy of Sudeten Germans achieved	Autonomy of Sudeten Germans not achieved, Czechs forfeit French and British help, and the country is incorporated into the Reich
S_1: An immediate attack	$U(O_{11})=-$ p=certain		
S_2*: Negotiate, reduce military preparations, tighten economic screws and start a military action if the Sudeten Germans continue to be oppressed		$U(O_{21})=+$ p=possible	$U(O_{22})=+$ p=possible

Source: State Secretary, August 30, 1938, Memorandum, *Akten zur Deutschen Auswärtigen Politik 1918–1945*, Series D (1937–1945), vol. 2 (Baden-Baden: Imprimerie Nationale, 1956), no. 409, 662–663.

Symbols: S_i strategy i. S_i* chosen strategy. O_{ij} outcome j under strategy i. $U(O_{ij})$ utility of outcome j under strategy i. P probability of an outcome.

scale down military preparations and tighten economic screws on Czecho-slovakia (S_2), it was possible that the Sudeten Germans would achieve their autonomy (O_{21}). If that did not occur (O_{22}), they could resort to military action (S_2) because the Czechs would have forfeited British and French help. They could then incorporate Czechoslovakia (O_{22}).

Based on the probabilities and utilities indicated by the state secretary (both without intensities), models of Class IV (Table 2.4) should be tested to see whether they produce his choice for S_2. Simon's Rule and the Reversed Simon Rule are mentioned in this class. Applying the Reversed Simon Rule, which demands the rejection of all strategies that lead only to negative outcomes and the selection of the strategy where a positive outcome is also possible, does not reproduce his choice for S_2. But Simon's Rule, which demands the rejection of all strategies that lead only to negative outcomes and the selection of the strategy leading only to satisfactory outcomes, does correctly predict his choice for S_2 and therefore seems to fit his argument.

Hitler indeed negotiated with the British, and at the end of the Munich Conference of September 1938, at which Czechoslovakia was not represented, the Sudeten German territories were ceded to Germany. In this cession, Czechoslovakia lost its important defense lines, and in March 1939 Hitler invaded the rest of Czechoslovakia, meeting hardly any opposition and turning Bohemia and Moravia into a protectorate and Slovakia into a satellite of the Reich. Encouraged by this success, he concentrated thereafter on Poland.

HITLER'S ARGUMENT FOR INVADING POLAND, AUGUST 22, 1939

On August 22, 1939, Hitler made two speeches to the heads of the armed forces in which he gave his reasons for invading Poland and demanded from his audience implementation of the move. Table 5.5 shows that the Führer discussed two strategies: doing nothing (S_2) and invading Poland (S_1). If his forces did nothing (S_2), he reasoned that it would certainly lead sooner or later to the destruction of Germany, because the four-year plan had failed and economically the country was close to bankruptcy (O_{21}). If they were to invade Poland (S_1), in his opinion, the chance was high that the Western nations would not meet their commitments to Poland because they were not prepared for a war. Germany could thus destroy Poland and secure its own material future by occupying Poland and making use of its resources (O_{11}). But there was also a chance, however slight, that the Western nations would enforce an embargo against Germany, break off diplomatic relations, and initiate war (O_{12}). Another possibility, although with very low probability, was that the Western nations would enforce an embargo and break off diplomatic relations, but no war would ensue and Germany could then secure its economic resources (O_{13}). The chance of a Western blockade without war and the securing of economic resources (O_{14}), Hitler qualified as zero. On the basis of the values and probabilities, the Führer indicated his choice of S_1.

Table 5.5:
Address of Hitler to the Supreme Commanders, August 22, 1939

Strategies	Outcomes				
	O_{11} The Western countries do not meet their commitments to Poland; Poland destroyed and our future secured	O_{12} Economic embargo from the Western countries; break off of diplomatic relations and war with the Western countries	O_{13} Economic embargo from the Western countries; break off of diplomatic relations; no war and our economic resources secured	O_{14} Blockade from the Western countries; no war and our economic resources secured	O_{21} Leads sooner or later to the destruction of Germany
S_1: Invade Poland	$U(O_{11})$=+ p=high	$U(O_{12})$=- p=slight	$U(O_{13})$=+ p=very low	$U(O_{14})$=+ p=zero	
S_2: Do nothing					$U(O_{21})$=- p=certain

Source: Hitler, Adolph, August 22, 1939, Address, *Akten zur Deutschen Auswärtigen Politik 1918–1945*, Series D (1937–1945), vol. 7 (Baden-Baden: Imprimerie Nationale, 1956), nos. 192, 193; 167–172.

Symbols: S_i strategy i. S_i* chosen strategy. O_{ij} outcome j under strategy i. $U(O_{ij})$ utility of outcome j under strategy i. P probability of an outcome.

If one considers the evaluations of probabilities and utilities, it is clear that Hitler used probabilities with intensities. The utilities, however, are without intensities and can only be understood in terms of "good" and "bad." Based on the probabilities and utilities he indicated, models of Class II (Table 2.4) should be tested to see whether they produce his choice for S_1. We can try both versions, the Positive and the Negative Risk-Avoidance Rules. Applying the Positive Risk-Avoidance Rule leads to the selection of S_1, and the same is true for the Negative Risk-Avoidance Rule. Therefore both rules are capable of predicting the choice, and the Risk-Avoidance argumentation seems to fit Hitler's argument.

After the Führer's speech, only Minister Goering seemed to have applauded this decision enthusiastically. The other members of the meeting preferred to keep silent. On August 31 Hitler gave the order to invade Poland, which was carried out on September 1. On September 3 Britain and France declared war on Germany, a possibility that Hitler had severely underestimated (see Table 5.5), and by these acts World War II was initiated.

CONCLUSIONS

The argumentations discussed show that members of a totalitarian regime argue in the same fashion as other decision-makers, since their conclusions can be derived from argumentation rules that also fit the arguments of decision-makers belonging to a constitutional monarchy (Chapter 4), a democratic presidential regime of a superpower (Chapter 6), and a small power democracy (Chapter 7). The Führer twice used the Risk-Avoidance Rules (Tables 5.1 and 5.5), and in the remaining three cases the simplest rules (Class IV, Table 2) produced the choices of Hitler and the state secretary. The results also show that these decision-makers generally avoided combining utilities with intensities and probabilities with intensities, a move that can lead to an overly complex computational operation, as we have already indicated. Other simplifications concerned the reduction of uncertainty to quasi certainty or certainty. In the argumentations presented in Tables 5.1 and 5.5, the chosen strategy had a very high chance of ensuring a positive outcome while the rejected alternatives were considered certain to be negative. In Table 5.3 the chosen strategy was formulated as certain to be positive.

Yet another way of simplifying decision problems in order to reduce complexity is to reduce complex value problems to simple value problems. When studying the arguments just presented, two aspects of outcomes could be seen as relevant, one aspect relating to the position of the Western powers in terms of their reactions, and the other relating to the condition of Germany's economy. Both decision-makers used them selectively but never systematically across strategies.

Having studied arguments of members of the totalitarian regime that initiated World War II, we will turn in the next chapter to arguments of the decision-makers of a superpower, whose decision almost initiated a nuclear war at about middle of this century.

Chapter 6

The World at the Brink
of a Nuclear War: October 1962

This chapter presents a case study of the arguments of President Kennedy's advisers during the Cuban missile crisis in October 1962. In the following sections we will briefly introduce the political background and then describe the individual arguments, which took place in two phases. The case study will show that members of the advisory board of a superpower reasoned in a similar way as advisers of smaller powers or dictators.

POLITICAL BACKGROUND

On October 16, 1962, President Kennedy called together a group of his closest advisers to discuss the Central Intelligence Agency's discovery of Soviet missile site installations under construction on the island of Cuba. The relations between the United States and the Soviet Union with respect to Cuba had already been strained for some time. The attempt to install nuclear weapons in Cuba can therefore be considered as the culmination of deteriorating relations between these nations. (For an extended political analysis, see Chang and Kornbluh 1992.)

The motive for the Soviets to deploy nuclear weapons 90 miles away from the United States seemed to be at least twofold. One of the reasons was the presence of U.S. nuclear installations and military bases close to and even along Soviet borders. In 1959 the United States had deployed nuclear missiles, the so-called Jupiter missiles, in the NATO countries of Italy and Turkey. These rockets became operational in April 1962. Another reason was the constant threat from the United States to overthrow Castro's regime in Cuba. Before the advent of Castro, the pro-American military government of Cuba had enjoyed largely American support. When Castro, a Marxist, came to power in 1959 by a national revolution, Washington withdrew its military assistance to Cuba and the planning of operations initiated by the CIA to overthrow this regime had begun by 1960. Notwithstanding the disaster of the U.S.-sponsored invasion attempt of Cuban exiles in April 1962 at the Bay of Pigs, the U.S. government continued to authorize another covert program to oust Castro. The latter had meanwhile become a major ally of the Soviet Union in the Western hemisphere and had thus intensified the challenge to U.S. security.

On the other hand, the covert operations and military maneuvers, combined with a full economic embargo on Cuba and a diplomatic initiative instigated by the United States to expel Cuba from the Organization of American States, increased the fear of Soviets and Cubans of an impending American invasion of the island. In order to take precautions against an invasion, Soviet and Cuban officials secretly negotiated the deployment of nuclear missiles as well as other military equipment and a large contingent of conventionally armed Soviet troops. During the summer of 1962, the Soviets had begun to transfer the troops and equipment, and this was monitored with great concern by the CIA. But only on October 15 could the CIA identify with certainty the construction of Soviet missile installations.

There were a number of meetings of presidential advisory groups held from October 16 till October 28, when chairman Khrushchev finally announced his withdrawal of the missiles. In the following sections, we will present individual arguments of decision-makers about how to resolve the problem. The arguments took place in two phases. Group decision-making processes will be studied in detail in another volume.

DECISION PHASE 1, OCTOBER 16 THROUGH OCTOBER 22, 1962

In this phase, most of the advice to the president was given by individuals. Following a meeting in the State Department on October 16, U.N. Ambassador Stevenson advised the president strongly against a surprise air attack on Cuba. Table 6.1 summarizes his argument. The table shows that the ambassador considered two strategies. If the United States made a surprise air attack against Cuba in order to remove the missiles (S_1), in his opinion it was very unlikely that the Soviets would not make reprisals elsewhere (O_{11}). According to his view, Soviet reprisals would very likely occur (O_{12}, O_{13}). More specifically, he considered the possibility of an attack on the Jupiters in Turkey or countermeasures in Berlin, the Western enclave in communist East Germany, where the Soviets could, for instance, deny access to the Western powers. But in his opinion it was also possible that the Soviets could provoke a nuclear war, and furthermore they would encounter sharp differences with the Latin American republics and the NATO allies (O_{12}). There was, of course, also the possibility that only Soviet reprisals would occur (O_{13}). If the United States was to send emissaries to Castro and to the Soviets with the message that they had to restore the status quo ante or otherwise the United States would restore it, and thereafter negotiate about missile bases in the context of a disarmament treaty (S_2), the ambassador thought that there was a greater chance of a positive outcome, and in fact, that there might even be no Soviet reprisals (O_{21}). On the basis of the utilities and probabilities, the ambassador had indicated his conclusion that S_2 should be adopted.

If one considers the evaluations of probabilities and utilities, it is clear that the ambassador used utilities without intensities and probabilities with intensities. Based on the probabilities and utilities indicated, it would seem appropriate to test heuristics of Class II (Table 2.4) to see whether they produce his choice of S_2. We can try both versions, the Positive and Negative Risk-Avoidance Rules.

Table 6.1:

Argument of U.N. Ambassador Adlai Stevenson in Support of Negotiations, October 17, 1962

Strategies	Outcomes		
	$O_{11}=O_{21}$	$O_{12}=O_{22}$	$O_{13}=O_{23}$
	No Soviet reprisals anywhere else	Soviet reprisals in other areas, a nuclear war, Latin American republics divided, sharp differences with NATO allies	Soviet reprisals in other areas, but no nuclear war
S_1: Surprise air attack on Cuba	$U(O_{11})=+$ $p_{11}=$very unlikely	$U(O_{12})=-$ $p_{12}=$ possible	$U(O_{13})=$less negative $p_{13}=$possible
S_2*: Let personal emissaries deliver messages to Castro and Khrushchev to restore the status quo ante and negotiate thereafter about missile bases	$U(O_{21})=+$ $p_{21}=$ higher	$U(O_{22})=-$ p_{22} and p_{23} together=lower	$U(O_{23})=$less negative

Source: Stevenson, Adlai, Oct. 17, 1962, Letter, in L. Chang and P. Kornbluh, eds., *The Cuban Missile Crisis, 1962* (New York: Free Press, 1992), doc. 19, 199–120.

Symbols: S_i strategy i. S_i* chosen strategy. O_{ij} outcome j under strategy i. U (O_{ij}) utility of outcome j under strategy i. P probability of an outcome.

Cells that are empty for a specific strategy were not considered by the decision-maker.

Applying the Positive Risk-Avoidance Rule leads to the selection of S_2, and the same is true for the negative version of the Risk-Avoidance Rule. Therefore, both rules can predict the choice and the Risk-Avoidance argument seems to fit the argument of the ambassador.

The same day, the secretary of the treasury, having participated in several advisory meetings the previous day, also produced his written advice to the president. Contrary to the U.N. ambassador, he advocated a stronger action (Table 6.2). The secretary of the treasury reviewed four strategies. If his government did nothing (S_1), he was certain that, at least in the long run, they would lose all Latin America to communism, and elsewhere in Third World countries there would be similar reactions because the United States had lost its prestige in not resisting communism (O_{11}). If they merely implemented a naval blockade on Cuba (S_2) in order to intercept ships bringing weapons to Cuba, he was certain that it would lead to endless negotiations, with similar results in Latin America and Third World countries (O_{21}). If they carried out without prior warning an air attack on Cuba (S_3), he was certain that the weapons could be eliminated but there would be difficulties with public opinion (O_{31}). But if they initiated action with a blockade and intensive low-level surveillance over Cuba, coupled with a demand to remove the weapons immediately and to accept international inspection, and in the event of a refusal made an air strike, in his opinion it was certain that they could eliminate the weapons (O_{41}, O_{42}).

Based on the probabilities and utilities indicated by the secretary of the treasury (both without intensities), models of Class IV (Table 2.4) should be tested to see whether they produce his choice for S_4. Simon's Rule and the Reversed Simon Rule are cited in this class. Applying the Reversed Simon Rule, which demands the rejection of all strategies that lead only to negative outcomes and the selection of the strategy where a positive outcome is also possible, produces two possible options $(S_4$ or $S_3)$ and not one. Simon's Rule suggests the choice of a strategy leading only to satisfactory outcomes, which actually coincides with the proposed strategy and therefore correctly predicts the decision-maker's choice for S_4.

The next piece of advice containing a complete argumentation was produced around October 18 by the undersecretary of state (Table 6.3). The undersecretary of state considered two strategies. One was a surprise attack (S_1), which he rejected because it would destroy the U.S. moral position and alienate friends and allies (O_{11}). The second alternative he reviewed was a blockade (S_2), which he was certain would not prevent the missiles from becoming operational. It would, however, be generally accepted by friends and allies (O_{21}, O_{22}), and it also was possible that the Soviets would accept it, which would isolate the Cubans and topple the Castro regime (O_{21}). It was also possible, though, that the Soviets would not accept it and would take reprisals elsewhere (O_{22}).

Based on the probabilities and utilities indicated by the undersecretary of state (both without intensities), models of Class IV (Table 2.4) should be tested to see whether they produce his choice for S_2. Simon's Rule and the Reversed Simon

Table 6.2:
Argument of Secretary of the Treasury Douglas Dillon, for Initiating a Blockade Combined with Other Military Measures, ca. October 17, 1962

Strategies	Outcomes				
	O_{11} We will lose all Latin America to communism and elsewhere we will have similar reactions	O_{21} Leads to negotiations either in the UN or directly with Khrushchev, we will lose all Latin America to communism, and elsewhere we will have similar reactions	O_{31} a_{311}: Elimination of weapons from Cuba a_{312}: Difficulties with public opinion	O_{41} Cuban refusal and weapons eliminated from Cuba	O_{42} No Cuban refusal and weapons from Cuba eliminated
S_1: Do nothing	$U(O_{11})=-$ $p=$certain				
S_2: Blockade of Cuba		$U(O_{21})=-$ $p=$certain			
S_3: Surprise air attack against Cuba			$U(a_{311})=+$ $U(a_{312})=-$ $p=$certain		
S_4^*: Initiate action with a blockade and intensive low-level surveillance, coupled with a demand to Cuba to immediately remove the weapons and to accept international inspection. If they refuse, make an air strike.				$U(O_{41})=+$ $p=$possible	$U(O_{42})=+$ $p=$possible

Source: Dillon, Douglas, Oct. 17, 1962, Memorandum, in L. Chang and P. Kornbluh, eds., *The Cuban Missile Crisis, 1962* (New York: Free Press, 1992), doc. 18, 116–118.

Symbols: S_i strategy i. S_i^* chosen strategy. O_{ij} outcome j under strategy i. A_{ijk} aspect k of outcome j under strategy i. $U(O_{ij})$ utility of outcome j under strategy i. $U(a_{ijk})$ utility of aspect k of outcome j under strategy i. P probability of an outcome.

Table 6.3:
Argument of Undersecretary of State George W. Ball in Support of a Blockade against Cuba, ca. October 18, 1962

Strategies	Outcomes		
	O_{11}	O_{21}	O_{22}
	We destroy our moral position and alienate our friends and allies	Missiles not prevented from becoming operational, but generally accepted as legal, accepted by Soviets; Cubans feel isolated, days of Castro regime numbered	Missiles not prevented from becoming operational, but generally accepted as legal, not accepted by Soviets, who create a counter-thrust elsewhere
S_1: Surprise air attack on Cuba	$U(O_{11})=-$ p=certain		
S_2*: Blockade of Cuba		$U(O_{21})=+$ p=possible	$U(O_{22})=-$ p=possible

Source: Ball, George W., Oct. 18, 1962, Note, in L. Chang and P. Kornbluh, eds., *The Cuban Missile Crisis, 1962* (New York: Free Press, 1992), doc. 20, 121–122.

Symbols: S_i strategy i. S_i* chosen strategy. O_{ij} outcome j under strategy i. U (O_{ij}) utility of outcome j under strategy i. P probability of an outcome.

Rule are cited in this class. Simon's Rule does not reproduce the choice of S_2, since it demands the selection of the strategy that leads only to positive outcomes, which was not available to the decision-maker. But the Reversed Simon Rule fits the data because it rejects the strategies that only lead to negative outcomes (S_1) and selects the alternative where positive outcomes are also possible (S_2).

Meanwhile, the deliberations of the presidential advisory groups continued, and in the morning meeting of the Executive Committee on October 19, two speakers set out complete argumentations about the course of action to follow. Table 6.4 summarizes the argument of the national security assistant, who reviewed two strategies. If the United States introduced a naval blockade (S_1), this would not, in his opinion, remove the missiles and would only very slowly be felt by the Cubans. Furthermore, the United Nations would exert pressure for a negotiatied settlement (O_{11}). However, if they made a surprise attack, the missiles would be taken out in a clean, surgical way and the world would be confronted with a fait accompli. He advised the implementation of S_2.

Based on the probabilities and utilities indicated by the national security assistant (both without intensities), models of Class IV (Table 2.4) should be tested to see whether they produce his choice for S_2. Simon's Rule and the Reversed Simon Rule are cited in this class. Applying the Reversed Simon Rule, which demands the rejection of all strategies that lead only to negative outcomes and the selection of the strategy where a positive outcome is possible, thus predicts S_2. But in this simple case, Simon's Rule also predicts the choice for S_2, since the adviser chose the strategy leading only to satisfactory outcomes. Therefore, both rules fit his argument.

The other speaker who rejected the air strike strategy with a complete argument was the attorney general (Table 6.5). If the United States made a surprise attack (S_2), thousands of Cubans and many Russians would be killed without

Table 6.4:

Argument of Assistant to the President for National Security Affairs McGeorge Bundy, in Support of a Surprise Attack against Cuba, October 19, 1962

Strategies	Outcomes	
	O_{11}	O_{21}
	Does not remove the missiles, would be slow to take effect, leads to pressures from the UN for a negotiated settlement	Takes out the bases in a clean, surgical way, world confronted with a fait accompli
S_1: Blockade of Cuba	$U(O_{11})=-$ p=certain	
S_2*: Surprise air attack on Cuba		$U(O_{21})=+$ $p(O_{21})$=certain

Source: Bundy, McGeorge, Executive Committee Meeting, Oct. 19, 1962, Minutes, in L. Chang and P. Kornbluh, eds., *The Cuban Missile Crisis, 1962* (New York: Free Press, 1992), doc. 21, 123–127.

Symbols: S_i strategy i. S_i* chosen strategy. Oij outcome j under strategy i. $U(O_{ij})$ utility of outcome j under strategy i. P probability of an outcome.

Table 6.5:
Argument of Attorney General Robert F. Kennedy, in Support of a
Blockade against Cuba, October 19, 1962

Strategies	Outcomes		
	O_{11}	O_{12}	O_{21}
	Soviets pull back from their over-extended position	Soviets do not pull back from their over-extended position	Thousands of Cubans and many Russians are killed without warning, a U.S.-initiated Pearl Harbor
S_1*: Blockade of Cuba	$U(O_{11})=+$ p=possible	$U(O_{12})=-$ p=possible	
S_2: Surprise attack against Cuba			$U(O_{21})=-$ p=certain

Source: Kennedy, Robert, Executive Committee Meeting, Oct. 19, 1962, Minutes, in L. Chang and P. Kornbluh, eds., *The Cuban Missile Crisis, 1962* (New York: Free Press, 1992), doc. 21, 123–127.

Symbols: S_i strategy i. S_i* chosen strategy. O_{ij} outcome j under strategy i. $U(O_{ij})$ utility of outcome j under strategy i. P probability of an outcome.

warning, which would amount to a U.S.-initiated Pearl Harbor (O_{21}). He rejected this alternative on moral grounds. But if they blockaded Cuba, he saw a possibility of the Russians removing the missiles (O_{11}).

Based on the probabilities and utilities outlined by the attorney general (both without intensities), models of Class IV (Table 2.4) should be tested to see whether they produce his choice for S_1. Simon's Rule and the Reversed Simon Rule are cited in this class. Simon's rule does not reproduce the choice of S_1 since it demands selection of the strategy that leads only to positive outcomes. But the Reversed Simon Rule fits the data because it rejects the strategies that lead only to negative outcomes (S_2) and selects the alternative where positive outcomes are also possible (S_1).

During this meeting, a tentative consensus was already reached to advise the president to set up a blockade, although the military advisers were not yet convinced. In the course of further meetings on this day, however, proponents of the air strike also began to shift their support to the blockade option (Chang and

Kornbluh 1992, 362).

The next complete argument in favor of the blockade alternative was given by the president's special counsel on October 20 (Table 6.6). He reasoned as follows. If the United States made a surprise attack (S_2), this would lead to an invasion of Cuba because air strikes alone would prove to be insufficient. There would then be many casualities and the stigma of a U.S.-initiated Pearl Harbor. If the United States started with a blockade (S_1), which in his opinion did not preclude further steps, there would be no Pearl Harbor posture (O_{11}, O_{12}). Probably no general war would ensue, and the Soviets would back down and abandon Castro.

If one considers the evaluations of probabilities and utilities, it is clear that the president's special counsel used utilities without intensities and probabilities with intensities. Based on the probabilities and utilities indicated, it would seem appropriate to test heuristics of Class II (Table 2.4) to see whether they produce his choice of S_1. We can try both versions, the Positive and Negative Risk-

Table 6.6:

Argument of Special Counsel to the President, Theodore Sorensen, in Support of a Blockade against Cuba, October 20, 1962

Strategies	Outcomes		
	O_{11}	O_{12}	O_{21}
	Does not preclude other steps, no Pearl Harbor posture, general war	Does not preclude other steps, no Pearl Harbor posture, no general war, and Soviets back down and abandon Castro	Leads to an invasion with all the consequences and means U.S.-initiated Pearl Harbor
S_1*: Blockade of Cuba	$U(O_{11})$=- p=least likely	$U(O_{12})$=+ p=most likely	
S_2: Surprise attack against Cuba			$U(O_{21})$=- p=certain

Source: Sorensen, Theodore, Oct. 20, 1962, Note, in L. Chang and P. Kornbluh, eds., *The Cuban Missile Crisis, 1962* (New York: Free Press, 1992), doc. 22, 133.

Symbols: S_i strategy i. S_i* chosen strategy. O_{ij} outcome j under strategy i. $U(O_{ij})$ utility of outcome j under strategy i. P probability of an outcome.

Table 6.7:
Argument of the Central Intelligence Agency in Support of a Major Air Attack against Cuba Followed by an Invasion, October 20, 1962

Strategies	Outcomes			
	O_{11} Buildup continues, other confrontations such as Berlin, loss of confidence in U.S., decline of U.S. influence in Latin America, strong encouragement to communists	O_{12} Buildup continues, other confrontations such as Berlin, loss of confidence in U.S., decline of U.S. influence in Latin America, strong encouragement to communists	$O_{21}=O_{31}$ Cuba linked with Berlin in negotiations, removes element of surprise in a subsequent attack	$O_{22}=O_{32}$ Deployment halted
S_1: Do nothing	$U(O_{11})=-$ p=probable	$U(O_{12})=-$ p=improbable		
S_2: Confront Khrushchev with knowledge			$U(O_{21})=-$ p=probable	$U(O_{22})=+$ p=improbable
S_3: Confront Castro with knowledge			$U(O_{31})=-$ p=higher	$U(O_{32})=+$ p=slightly more chance
S_4: A Blockade against Cuba				
$S_5{}^*$: A major attack against Cuba followed by an invasion				
S_6: A selective attack against Cuba				

Source: Central Intelligence Agency, Oct. 20, 1962, Note, in L. Chang and P. Kornbluh, eds., *The Cuban Missile Crisis, 1962* (New York: Free Press, 1992), doc. 24, 134–143.

			Outcomes		
O_{41} Buildup continues, Soviets use force	O_{42} Buildup continues, Soviets compel U.S. to desist, adverse reactions of allies, Cuban regime not brought down, threats of retaliation in Berlin	O_{43} Buildup continues, Soviets compel U.S. to desist, adverse reactions of allies, Cuban regime not brought down, no threats of retaliation in Berlin	$O_{51}=O_{61}$ Weapons eliminated, no nuclear war, retaliations in Berlin or elsewhere	$O_{52}=O_{62}$ Weapons eliminated, no nuclear war, no retaliations elsewhere	$O_{53}=O_{63}$ A nuclear war
$U(O_{41})=-$ p=very unlikely	$U(O_{42})=-$ p=very likely	$U(O_{43})=-$ p=less likely			
			$U(O_{51})=-$ p=less likely	$U(O_{52})=+$ p=more likely	$U(O_{53})=-$ p=almost excluded
			$U(O_{61})=-$ p=more likely	$U(O_{62})=+$ p=less likely	$U(O_{63})=-$ p=almost excluded

Symbols: S_i strategy i. S_i^* chosen strategy. O_{ij} outcome j under strategy i. $U(O_{ij})$ utility of outcome j under strategy i. P probability of an outcome.

Avoidance Rules. Applying the Positive Risk-Avoidance Rule leads to the selection of S_1, and the same is true for the negative version of the Risk-Avoidance Rule. Therefore, both rules can predict the choice and the Risk-Avoidance argument seems to fit the argument of this adviser.

The last complete complete piece of advice produced during this first phase came from the Central Intelligence Agency (CIA). The argumentation of this agency is summarized in Table 6.7. The CIA considered six strategies. If the United States was to do nothing (S_1), the Soviet military buildup would certainly continue (O_{11}, O_{12}) and this would probably lead to a confrontation in Berlin (O_{11}). This course would lead, in any case, to the decline of U.S. influence in Latin America and to strong encouragement for the spread of communism in this area (O_{11}, O_{12}). If the Unites States government confronted Khrushchev with their knowledge of the missiles (S_2), the CIA held that it was unlikely that he would stop the deployment (O_{22}) but probable that he would link Cuba with Berlin in negotiations. This would remove the element of surprise in any subsequent U.S. air attack on Cuba (O_{21}). If the United States government confronted Castro with their knowledge of the missiles (S_3), the chance was slightly higher than under S_2 that the deployment could be stopped (O_{32}), although the agency thought that here also it was more probable that Cuba woud be linked with Berlin in negotiations (O_{31}). If the United States initiated a blockade against Cuba (S_4), in the CIA's opinion it was very likely that the buildup would continue, that the Soviets would compel them to desist, that allies would disagree with them, that the Cuban regime would not be brought down, and that the Soviets would threaten with retaliations in Berlin (O_{42}). If they initiated a major air attack against Cuba followed by an invasion (S_5), the agency estimated the chances of a nuclear war as almost zero, because the Soviets would not dare to take these risks (O_{53}). In the CIA's opinion it was more likely that the missiles would be eliminated and that, no nuclear war nor retaliations such as in Berlin would ensue (O_{52}). However, if they made a selective air attack on Cuba (S_6), the chance of success, that is, the removal of the missiles, was less likely, and also the chance that no retaliations in Berlin or elsewhere would ensue was less likely (O_{62}). Based on the values and probabilites they had indicated, the CIA recommended S_5.

If one considers the evaluations of probabilities and utilities, it is clear that the Central Intelligence Agency used utilities without intensities and probabilities with intensities. Based on the probabilities and utilities indicated, it would seem appropriate to test heuristics of Class II (Table 2.4) to see whether they produce their choice of S_5. We can try both versions, the Positive and Negative Risk-Avoidance Rules. Applying the Positive Risk-Avoidance Rule leads to the selection of S_5, and the same is true for the negative version of the Risk-Avoidance Rule. Therefore both rules can predict the choice, and the Risk-Avoidance argument seems to fit the argument of the CIA.

As stated, on about October 20 the majority of the president's advisers recommended initiation of a blockade based on the consequences considered in the arguments. The CIA advocated a different option. But the president was informed on October 21 by General Sweeney (Chang and Kornbluh 1992, 145) that even with a major air attack against Cuba followed by an invasion, the military could only guarantee the elimination of 90% or less of the known missiles.

Given these prospects, the president approved initiation of the blockade. Parallel to the preparations for implementing the blockade option, also called quarantine measures, which consisted of briefing foreign nations about the crisis and addressing the nation at home at 7 P.M. on October 22, the military was readied for an eventual air strike. Alert levels were raised and the naval base in Cuba, Guantánamo, was reinforced. On October 22, the secretary of state also handed an advance of the president's speech to the Soviet ambassador.

DECISION PHASE 2, OCTOBER 23 THROUGH OCTOBER 28, 1962

On October 23, Chairman Khrushchev wrote a letter to President Kennedy in which he stated in reaction to Kennedy's's radio broadcast that Soviet armaments were intended solely for defensive purposes in order to secure Cuba against an aggressor, and in a Security Council meeting the Russians called for negotiations to end the crisis. The same day, the Cuban and the Warsaw Pact forces were put on alert. The United States in turn started low-level reconnaissance flights over Cuba, and on October 24 the quarantine of Cuba officially went into effect.

In addition to a Turkey-for-Cuba missile trade-off, the presidential advisers explored other options should the quarantine measures prove ineffective in removing the missiles. Within this context, on October 25 a group including the secretary of the treasury agreed on advice in support of an air strike to be followed by an invasion (Table 6.8). The group argued that if they started with air strikes followed by an invasion (S_1), this would certainly eliminate the missiles, and also avoid any erosion of U.S. prestige. The attack would relate solely to the Soviet presence in Cuba, avoid the growth of a hands-off-Cuba movement in Latin America, signal that the United States was not prepared to trade off Cuba for other positions such as Berlin or within NATO, and deny Khrushchev a cheap victory (O_{11}: a_{111}-a_{116}; O_{12}: a_{121}-a_{126}; O_{13}: a_{131}-a_{136}). Although escalation to a major war seemed unlikely (O_{11}: a_{117}), and although the chance of a missile being fired from Cuba by a local commander was estimated as very small (O_{13}: a_{137}), the chances of a Soviet reaction in kind (O_{12}: a_{127}) were considered to be high, but with the positive effect of undermining Castro and the Cuban reliance on the Soviets (O_{12}: a_{128}). If the United States was to continue with the blockade (S_2), the advisory group estimated that further escalation and a Soviet riposte in kind would be most likely (O_{22}).

If one considers the evaluations of probabilities and utilities, it is clear that the secretary of the treasury's advisory group used utilities without intensities and probabilities with intensities. Based on the probabilities and utilities indicated, it would seem appropriate to test heuristics of Class II (Table 2.4) to see whether

Table 6.8:
Argument of the Secretary of the Treasury's Group in Support of an Air Strike against Cuba, October 25, 1962

Strategies	Outcomes	
	O_{11}	O_{12}
	a_{111}: Eliminates offensive threat to United States and hemisphere from Cuba	a_{121}: Eliminates offensive threat to United States and hemisphere from Cuba
	a_{112}: Avoids any erosion of U.S. momentum and position	a_{122}: Avoids any erosion of U.S. momentum and position
	a_{113}: Keeps issue focused on Soviet presence in Cuba	a_{123}: Keeps issue focused on Soviet presence in Cuba
	a_{114}: Avoids dangers of growth of hands-off-Cuba movement throughout Latin America	a_{124}: Avoids dangers of growth of hands-off-Cuba movement throughout Latin America
	a_{115}: Signals United States is not prepared to bargain Cuba for positions in Berlin, NATO, etc.	a_{125}: Signals United States is not prepared to bargain Cuba for positions in Berlin, NATO, etc.
	a_{116}: Denies Khrushchev cheap victory	a_{126}: Denies Khrushchev cheap victory
	a_{117}: Escalation to major war	a_{127}: Soviet riposte in kind
		a_{128}: Undermines Castro and Cuban reliance on the Soviets
S_1*: An air-strike against Cuba followed by an invasion	$U(a_{111})=+$ $U(a_{112})=+$ $U(a_{113})=+$ $U(a_{114})=+$ $U(a_{115})=+$ $U(a_{116})=+$ $U(a_{117})=-$ p=unlikely	$U(a_{121})=+$ $U(a_{122})=+$ $U(a_{123})=+$ $U(a_{124})=+$ $U(a_{125})=+$ $U(a_{126})=+$ $U(a_{127})=$less negative $U(a_{128})=+$ p=more likely
S_2: Blockade against Cuba		

Source: Secretary of the Treasury's Group, Oct. 25, 1962, Discussion paper, in L. Chang and P. Kornbluh, eds., *The Cuban Missile Crisis, 1962* (New York: Free Press, 1992), doc. 37, 168–171.

Outcomes			
O_{13}	O_{21}	O_{22}	O_{23}
a_{131}: Eliminates offensive threat to United States and hemisphere from Cuba	Further escalation and major war	Further escalation and riposte in kind	No further escalation
a_{132}: Avoids any erosion of U.S. momentum and position			
a_{133}: Keeps issue focused on Soviet presence in Cuba			
a_{134}: Avoids dangers of growth of hands-off-Cuba movement throughout Latin America			
a_{135}: Signals United States is not prepared to bargain Cuba for positions in Berlin, NATO, etc.			
a_{136}: Denies Khrushchev cheap victory			
a_{137}: Firing of a missile from Cuba by local commander			

$U(a_{131})=+$
$U(a_{132})=+$
$U(a_{133})=+$
$U(a_{134})=+$
$U(a_{135})=+$
$U(a_{136})=+$
$U(a_{137})=-$

p=very small chance

	$U(O_{21})=-$ p=unlikely	$U(O_{22})=-$ p=more likely	$U(O_{23})=-$ p=small

Symbols: S_i strategy i. S_i^* chosen strategy. O_{ij} outcome j under strategy i. A_{ijk} aspect k of outcome j under strategy i. $U(O_{ij})$ utility of outcome j under strategy i. $U(a_{ijk})$ utility of aspect k of outcome j under strategy i. P probability of an outcome.

they produce the choice of S_1. We can try both versions, the Positive and Negative Risk-Avoidance Rule. Applying the Positive Risk-Avoidance Rule leads to the selection of S_1 and the same is true for the negative version of the Risk-Avoidance Rule. Therefore, both rules can predict the choice, and the Risk-Avoidance argument seems to fit the argument of these advisers.

On October 26, Chairman Khrushchev proposed removal of the missiles under U.N. inspection in return for a U.S. noninvasion pledge in regard to Cuba. While the president and his advisers were considering this proposal, a new offer came from the Soviets demanding instead of the noninvasion pledge a missile trade-off. The same day, two incidents with airplanes increased the tension: an American U-2 violated Soviet air space, and a U-2 reconnaissance plane was shot down in Cuba. After long deliberation, the president and his advisers ignored Khrushchev's second letter (they expected problems within NATO if they openly removed the missiles from Turkey) and proposed to give a non-invasion pledge after the removal of the missiles. The Soviets also received the oral message that without the prompt removal of the missiles, U.S. military action would be initiated.

On October 28, while the advisory committee was reviewing various military measures for the next day, a new broadcast from Chairman Khrushchev reached them, indicating that he would withdraw the missiles. With this message, the missile crisis was effectively terminated and the world was saved from the threat of an impending nuclear war.

CONCLUSIONS

In this chapter, eight arguments have been studied that were put forward by the decision-makers of a superpower in a crisis situation at the brink of a nuclear war. When arguing, the decision-makers described the available strategies and their consequences and evaluated the consequences and their likelihood of occurrence. Thereafter, they drew conclusions as to which strategy should be adopted. However, they never mentioned the choice rule they used in order to draw their conclusions, let alone indicated whether the conditions were satisfied for choosing their preferred strategy. Based on the quality of the utilities and probabilities they indicated, it has been possible to establish for each argument an appropriate class of argumentation rules, which was applied to the data to find a fitting choice rule. In four cases the Risk-Avoidance Rules correctly predicted the choice, and in the remaining four cases rules of Class IV (Simon's Rule and the Reversed Simon Rule) fitted the choice. Thus with respect to their argumentation, these decision-makers did not differ from the dictator or the decision-makers of a medium power at the beginning of this century, studied in earlier chapters.

This case study also demonstrates that the decision-makers generally avoided combining utilities with intensities and probabilities with intensities, a move that can lead to an overly complex computational operation, as we have already indicated.

Table 6.9:

Summary of the Aspects of Outcomes for Each Strategy Considered by the Decision-Makers

Strategies	Aspects of Outcomes			
	Allies' position	Kind of war	The United States' position	Enemies' position
S_1: Do nothing	Secretary of the treasury CIA	CIA	CIA	CIA
S_2: Surprise attack on Cuba	Ambassador to U.N. Undersecretary of state	Ambassador to U.N. National security assistant Special counsel to the president CIA	Secretary of the treasury Undersecretary of state National security assistant Attorney general Special counsel to the president	Ambassador to U.N. Secretary of the treasury Attorney general CIA
S_3: Surprise attack and invasion	Secretary of the treasury's group	Secretary of the treasury's group CIA	Secretary of the treasury's group	Secretary of the treasury's group CIA
S_4: Blockade of Cuba	Secretary of the treasury Undersecretary of state CIA	Special counsel to the president CIA Secretary of the treasury's group	National security assistant Special counsel to the president	Secretary of the treasury Undersecretary of state National security assistant Attorney general Special counsel to the president CIA Secretary of the treasury's group
S_5: Message to Khrushchev	Ambassador to U.N.	Ambassador to U.N.	CIA	Ambassador to U.N. CIA
S_6: Message to Castro			CIA	CIA
S_7: Blockade of Cuba and if missiles are not removed, make an air attack			Secretary of the treasury	Secretary of the treasury

In addition, these arguments were based on a number of simplifications or on a reduction of information. One way of simplifying the decision problems in order to reduce complexity is to reduce complex value problems to simple value problems. For example, decision-makers did not consider all relevant aspects of outcomes simultaneously across strategies.

The Central Intelligence Agency, for instance, used in its argument for the first strategy (Table 6.7) four aspects systematically, namely, one aspect concerning the position of their allies and friends, one regarding the occurrence of the kind of war (local or general), another referring to the position of the United States in terms of its prestige, and yet another concerning the position of its enemies in terms of their reactions other than declaring war and their prestige. For the other strategies, the CIA for the most part considered only two of these aspects (see also Table 6.9). For the other decision-makers, these four dimensions also seemed to be relevant, since they sometimes employed them in considering one strategy, but they did not consider them systematically across all strategies. Table 6.9 summarizes for each strategy the dimensions of outcomes indicated by the decision-makers. The table shows that the decision-makers considered all four dimensions as relevant but did not use them systematically across strategies. It seems that they restricted themselves to considering only those aspects of outcomes that they judged most important for each strategy.

Another way of reducing information is to omit uncertainty or reduce uncertainty to quasi certainty. In two cases (Tables 6.2 and 6.4), the decision-makers formulated the problem in such a way that the outcomes for at least one strategy were considered certain, and in one other case (Table 6.6), the outcomes had a very high or very low chance of occurring.

Still another mode of simplification is to restrict the range of strategies considered. In total, seven distinct strategies were mentioned in the course of the argumentations, but in six argumentations the decision-makers only considered simultaneously two alternatives when giving their arguments. These data also accord with Lindblom's assumption (Lindblom 1959, 1982) that decision-makers limit their analyses to a small range of alternatives that are familiar in order to make the decision problem manageable. Next to the alternative of the status quo (i.e., "do nothing"), they examined strategies that quite drastically deviated from this, to the extent of a surprise attack on Cuba and its variants.

Having studied the arguments of advisers of a superpower in a crisis situation at the brink of a nuclear war, we will turn in the next chapter to the arguments of ministers of a small power that tried to avert the loss of a colony after World War II.

Chapter 7

The Decision whether to Take Measures against Indonesia or Not, the Netherlands in the Autumn of 1948

This chapter presents a case study of argumentations presented to the Dutch government by the Dutch authorities in Indonesia and by participants of meetings of the Dutch goverment, which led in the end to the second military action in Indonesia, in December 1948.

POLITICAL BACKGROUND

During World War II, the Dutch East Indies (later to become Indonesia) were occupied by Japan. On August 17, 1945, after Japan's capitulation to the Allies, the Indonesian nationalist leaders Sukarno and Hatta proclaimed the independence of the republic of Indonesia. Their government exercised its authority mainly over the most densely populated and economically most developed islands, Java and Sumatra.

When the Dutch returned under leadership of Lieutenant Governor General H. J. Van Mook, they regained control mainly on islands that did not include Java and Sumatra. Van Mook very soon developed the idea that the archipelago should be reorganized on a federal basis, comprising four equally autonomous components—Java, Sumatra, Borneo, and the Great East. After an interim period in which the Dutch would still exercise power, these should become sovereign, forming the United States of Indonesia (USI). They would be linked with the kingdom of the Netherlands by a union headed by the Queen, in order to administer joint interests such as foreign relations and defense. This program of principles constituted the main body of the agreement between the Netherlands and the republic, the Linggadajti agreement, which was signed in March 1947. However, subsequent talks on the implementation of the program made no progress, and between May and July 1947, the negotiations reached a deadlock. Each side had attempted to put its primary objective forward: the Dutch wanted to create a federal state, which would diminish the position and role of the republic, while the republic was aiming at the hegemony of the Indonesian archipelago.

On July 20, 1947, the Dutch took military measures against the republic, the so-called first police action, in order to create conditions of law and order that would permit the implementation of the Linggadjati program. Since military action did not lead, as expected, to quick cooperation between the Indonesians and the Dutch, the Dutch authorities seriously considered occupying the republican capital, Jocyakarta, in order to destroy the republic as a political entity and obtain the desired cooperation.

The intervention of the Security Council in August 1947, however, prevented the destruction of the republic. Subsequently a Good Offices Committee (GOC) was brought into being by the Security Council to assist both parties in working out a peaceful settlement of the dispute. The committee consisted of American, Australian, and Belgian delegates. The period from September 1947 to mid-December 1948 was characterized by various efforts at negotiation between the republic and the Dutch, mainly under the auspices of the GOC. However, Dutch-republican relations deteriorated to a point where not even the truce agreement was observed.

By August 1948 a change of cabinet had taken place in the Netherlands. Although the Labor Party supplied the prime minister, who was seen as a dove on the Indonesian question, the Confessional Parties, especially the Roman Catholics, represented in the cabinet were determined to pursue a hard line in the matter. They also supplied the minister of overseas territories and the High Representative of the Crown, the former governor.

DECISION PHASE 1, OCTOBER 1948

While awaiting the republic's answer to the new Dutch proposals for continuing negotiations, the Dutch authorities in Indonesia seriously considered taking military action against the republic if it continued to ignore the truce.

The Dutch commander of the troops in Indonesia sent a memorandum giving his advice to the Dutch government in the Hague. Table 7.1 shows that he considered two strategies: sending an ultimatum to the U.S. delegation of the GOC and quickly starting military action if the republic failed to agree (S_1), or doing nothing (S_2). The second strategy amounted to the continuation of the status quo, the unsuccessful negotiation efforts under the auspices of the GOC. He rejected this strategy on the grounds that it would certainly lead to the loss of Indonesia (O_{21}). If his government sent an ultimatum to the U.S. delegation (S_1), the chance of an agreement with the republic was almost excluded (O_{11}), but then they could turn to military action, which had, in his opinion, a fairly high chance of bringing about positive and acceptable consequences.

He foresaw quick military success (O_{12}: a_{121}), only limited international sanctions (O_{12}: a_{122})—the closing of some harbors and airfields to Dutch transport—

Table 7.1:

Argument Given by the Dutch Commander of the Troops in Indonesia to the Government Regarding Military Action, October 20, 1948

Strategies	Outcomes			
	O_{11}	O_{12}	O_{13}	O_{21}
	Agreement reached	a_{121}: Quick military success	a_{131}: No quick military success	Loss of Indonesia
		a_{122}: Limited international sanctions	a_{132}: No limited international sanctions	
		a_{123}: Morale of republic quickly broken	a_{133}: Morale of republic not broken	
		a_{124}: Limited material and personal losses	a_{134}: Material and personal losses not limited	
		a_{125}: No loss of Indonesia	a_{135}: Loss of Indonesia	
S_1*: Send an ultimatum to the U. S. delegation of the GOC and take quickly military action if the republic does not agree	$U(O_{11})=+$	$U(a_{121})=+$ $U(a_{122})=$acceptable $U(a_{123})=+$ $U(a_{124})=$acceptable $U(a_{125})=+$	$U(a_{131})=-$ $U(a_{132})=-$ $U(a_{133})=-$ $U(a_{134})=-$ $U(a_{135})=-$	
	p=almost excluded	p=fairly high	p=small	
S_2: Do nothing				$U(O_{21})=-$ p=certain

Source: Dutch Commander of the Troops in Indonesia, Oct. 20, 1948, Archive of Van Mook, record no. 238.

Symbols: S_i strategy i. S_i* chosen strategy. O_{ij} outcome j under strategy i. A_{ijk} aspect k of outcome j under strategy i. $U(O_{ij})$ utility of outcome j under strategy i. $U(a_{ijk})$ utility of aspect k of outcome j under strategy i. P probability of an outcome. Cells that are empty for a specific strategy were not considered by the decision-maker.

the breakdown of the morale of the republic (O_{12}: a_{123}), limited personal and material losses (O_{12}: a_{124}), and the possibility of holding on to Indonesia (O_{12}: a_{125}). However, there was also a small chance that things would not work out so well. There might be no quick military success (O_{13}: a_{131}), severe international sanctions might be imposed (O_{13}: a_{132}), such as the closing of a large number of harbors and airfields to Dutch transport and suspension of Marshall aid to Indonesia or the Netherlands itself, the morale of the republic might not be so easily crushed (O_{13}: a_{133}); personal and material losses might be high (O_{13}: a_{134}); and, finally, Indonesia might be lost after all (O_{13}: a_{135}). On the basis of the utilities and probabilities he indicated, the commander of the troops concluded that S_1 should be adopted.

If one considers the evaluations of probabilites and utilities, it is clear that the commander of the troops used probabilities with intensities. The utilities, however, are without intensities and can only be understood in terms of "good" and "bad." Based on the utilities and probabilities he indicated, it would seem appropriate to test heuristics of Class II (Table 2.4) to see whether they produce his choice of S_1. We can try both versions, the Positive and the Negative Risk-Avoidance Rules. Applying the Positive Risk-Avoidance Rule leads to the selection of S_1, and the same is true for the negative version of the Risk-Avoidance Rule. Therefore, both rules can predict the choice, and the Risk-Avoidance argument seems to fit the argument of the Dutch commander of the troops in Indonesia.

Meanwhile, the republic's answer to the demand to reduce the truce violations was received. As expected, the Dutch received very vague promises from some members of the republican government, while others made statements to the contrary in public. In separate telegrams, the Dutch authorities in Batavia (later to be called Jakarta) urged the minister of overseas territories to come quickly to a decision. At the Department of Foreign Affairs, an official prepared some advice for the prime minister (see Table 7.2).

The official from foreign affairs also considered only two strategies. The first strategy consisted of the commander of the troops' advice to send an ultimatum to the U.S. delegation of the GOC and take military measures if the republic did not agree (S_1). In the official's opinion, the chance of reaching an agreement with the republic under this condition could be excluded (O_{11})—the commander of the troops also gave it only a very small chance—but in contrast to the commander of the troops, the official foresaw with certainty severe international sanctions (O_{12}). Fearing the consequences, he rejected this strategy. The option he proposed consisted of negotiating directly with the republic without the intervention of the GOC on the most controversial issues and taking military action only if these efforts failed (S_2). In his opinion, there was a very small chance that his government could reach an agreement with the republic (O_{21}). If they did not reach an agreement and had to resort to military measures, the risk of attracting severe international sanctions (O_{22}) was small, though there was a greater risk of attracting limited international measures (O_{23}). Based on the values and probabilities he indicated, the official advised choosing S_2.

If one considers the evaluations of probabilites and utilities, it is clear that this official used probabilities with intensities. The utilities, however, are without intensities and can only be understood in terms of "good" and "bad." Based on

Table 7.2:
Argument of an Official from Foreign Affairs to the Government on the Continuation of Negotiations in Indonesia, October 24, 1948

Strategies	Outcomes		
	$O_{11}=O_{21}$ Agreement reached	$O_{12}=O_{22}$ No limited international sanctions	O_{23} Limited international sanctions
S_1: Send an ultimatum to the U. S. delegation of the GOC and take quickly military action if the republic does not agree	$U(O_{11})=+$ p=excluded	$U(O_{12})=-$ p=certain	
S_2*: Negotiate with the republic about the most controversial issues and take military action if no agreement is reached	$U(O_{21})= +$ p=very small	$U(O_{22})= -$ p=less likely	$U(O_{23})=+$ p=more likely

Source: Foreign Affairs Official, Oct. 24, 1948, Note, Archive of the Ministry of Foreign Affairs, record Indonesia in the transition period, no. 147.

Symbols: S_i strategy i. S_i* chosen strategy. O_{ij} outcome j under strategy i. $U(O_{ij})$ utility of outcome j under strategy i. P probability of an outcome.

the utilities and probabilities he indicated, it is appropriate to test heuristics of Class II (Table 2.4) to see whether they produce his choice of S_2. We can try both versions, the Positive and the Negative Risk-Avoidance Rules. Applying the Positive Risk-Avoidance Rule leads to the selection of S_2, and the same is true for the negative version of the Risk-Avoidance Rule. Therefore, both rules can predict the choice, and the Risk-Avoidance argumentation seems to fit the argument of this official.

On October 26, the Council of Ministers made its decision. The minister of foreign affairs gave a complete argument, which was quite similar to his official's; Table 7.3 summarizes this argument.

The minister considered the same strategies as his official. If his government informed the GOC of the failure of negotiations and started military action (S_1), he was convinced that there would be serious international and national repercussions (O_{11}). If they negotiated informally with the republic on the most controversial issues and took military action only if no agreement could be reached (S_2), there was at least some possibility of reaching an agreement (O_{21}), though if they had to start military action there would probably still be serious international and national repercussions (O_{22}), in his opinion.

Based on the probabilities and utilities the minister indicated (both without intensities), models of Class IV (Table 2.4) should be tested to see whether they produce his choice for S_2. Simon's Rule and the Reversed Simon Rule are mentioned in this class. Applying Simon's Rule, which demands selection of a strategy leading only to satisfactory outcomes, does not reproduce his choice for S_2.

Table 7.3:
Argument of the Minister of Foreign Affairs in the Council of Ministers on the Continuation of Negotiations in Indonesia, October 26, 1948

Strategies	Outcomes		
	O_{11} Serious international repercussions, serious national repercussions	O_{21} Agreement reached	O_{22} Serious international repercussions, serious national repercussions
S_1: Send an ultimatum to the U. S. delegation of the GOC and take quick military action if the republic does not agree	$U(O_{11})= -$ p=certain		
S_2*: Negotiate with the republic about the most controversial issues and take military action if no agreement is reached		$U(O_{21})= +$ p=possible	$U(O_{22})= -$ p=possible

Source: Council of Ministers, Oct. 26, 1948, Minutes, *Officiële Bescheiden betreffende de Nederlands Indonesische betrekkingen, 1945–1950*, vol. 15, no. 259, 517–525.

Symbols: S_i strategy i. S_i* chosen strategy. O_{ij} outcome j under strategy i. $U(O_{ij})$ utility of outcome j under strategy i. P probability of an outcome.

Since he rejected the strategy (S_1) where only a negative outcome could occur and chose the one (S_2) where a positive outcome was also possible, the Reversed Simon Rule correctly predicts his choice and therefore seems to fit his argument.

The minister's proposal was accepted by the cabinet. In a telegram of October 27, 1948, to the Dutch authorities in Indonesia, the minister of overseas territories announced that the cabinet agreed with the advice of the minister of foreign affairs and that the latter should go immediately to Indonesia to start preliminary negotiations with the republic. Another adviser who was already in Indonesia would assist him in this task. By mid-November it was expected that they would be able to decide whether an agreement with the republic seemed possible or the Netherlands would have to resort to military measures.

DECISION PHASE 2, EARLY NOVEMBER 1948

Between November 3 and November 9, 1948, the minister of foreign affairs and his adviser held meetings with members of the republican government. On November 10 they received a memorandum from the Indonesians in which the republicans put forward their views, making some concessions with respect to the observation of the truce but mentioning that it was impossible to dismantle the republican army. It seemed that they had no control over several guerilla factions. The Dutch authorities in Indonesia and the negotiators now had to decide whether there were sufficient grounds for continuing the negotiations.

Table 7.4 summarizes the advice of the High Representative of the Crown sent to The Hague. He considered three strategies. If they continued with informal negotiations (S_1), in his opinion, only negative outcomes could occur: the situation might get even worse (O_{11}) or perhaps no favorable results would be achieved from the negotiations (O_{12}). On these grounds he rejected S_1. Another option would be to demand from the republic and the GOC unconditional agreement on the main points (S_2). But if this was done, he was certain that international pressure would force the Dutch to abandon their point of view (O_{21}). Thus this strategy was not viable either. However, to inform the GOC of the failure of negotiations and start military action (S_3) could, he considered, offer a genuine, satisfactory solution in Indonesia (O_{31}), though it was also possible that it might not lead to a genuine, satisfactory solution (O_{32}).

Based on the probabilities and utilities he indicated (both without intensities), models of Class IV (Table 2.4) should be tested to see whether they produce his choice for S_3. Simon's Rule and the Reversed Simon Rule are mentioned in this class. Applying Simon's Rule, which requires selection of a strategy leading only to satisfactory outcomes, does not reproduce his choice for S_3. Since he rejected all strategies where only negative outcomes could occur (S_1 and S_2) and chose the one where a positive outcome was also possible (S_3), the Reversed Simon Rule correctly predicts his choice and therefore seems to fit his argument.

The Minister of foreign affairs also sent his advice to The Hague (Table 7.5). He considered two strategies. S_1 coincided with the High Representative of the

Table 7.4:
Argument of the High Representative of the Crown in Indonesia to the Minister of Overseas Territories in The Hague, November 13, 1948

Strategies	Outcomes				
	O_{11}	O_{12}	O_{21}	O_{31}	O_{32}
	Worsening of the situation in Indonesia	No favorable result	We are forced by international pressure to give up our point of view	A genuine, satisfactory solution	No genuine, satisfactory solution
S_1: Continue with the informal negotiations	$U(O_{11})=-$ p=possible	$U(O_{12})=-$ p=possible			
S_2: Demand from the republic and the GOC unconditional agreement with the main points			$U(O_{21})=-$ p=certain		
S_3*: Inform the GOC about the failure of the negotiations and take military action				$U(O_{31})=+$ p=possbile	$U(O_{32})=-$ p=possible

Source: High Representative of the Crown to the Minister of Overseas Territories, Nov. 13, 1948, Telegrams, *Officiële Bescheiden betreffende de Nederlands Indonesische betrekkingen, 1945–1950*, vol. 15, no. 321, 322, 650–657.

Symbols: S_i strategy i. S_i* chosen strategy. O_{ij} outcome j under strategy i. $U(O_{ij})$ utility of outcome j under strategy i. P probability of an outcome.

Crown's choice. If his government informed the GOC of the failure of the negotiations and started military action, according to the minister, the chance was very high of a highly negative outcome (O_{11}): heavy material damage, an increased breeding ground for subversion, international sanctions, and a diminished willingness on the part of nonrepublican Indonesians (federalists) to cooperate. There was, however, a lesser chance that material damage would not be

Table 7.5:

Argument of the Minister of Foreign Affairs to the Government in The Hague for the Continuation of the Negotiations with the Republic, November 10, 1948

Strategies	Outcomes		
	$O_{11}=O_{21}$	$O_{12}=O_{22}$	O_{23}
	Heavy material damage, increased breeding ground for subversion, international repercussions, willingness of federalists to cooperate diminished	Less heavy material damage, breeding ground for subversion not increased, fewer international repercussions, willingness of federalists to cooperate not diminished	Compromise reached, guaranteeing a strong position of the republic in the interim federal government, not all details settled, and a quicker transfer of sovereignity
S_1: Inform the GOC about the failure of the negotiations and take military action	$U(O_{11})$=very negative p=very high	$U(O_{12})$=less negative p=very low	
S_2*: Continue with the negotiations, try to reach an agreement before December 1, and if this fails, take military action	$U(O_{21})$=very negative p=less likely	$U(O_{22})$=less negative p=less likely	$U(O_{23})$=less negative p=more likely

Source: Minister of Foreign Affairs, Nov. 10, 1948, Note, *Officiële Bescheiden betreffende de Nederlands Indonesische betrekkingen, 1945–1950,* vol. 15, no. 313, 639–643.

Symbols: S_i strategy i. S_i* chosen strategy. O_{ij} outcome j under strategy i. $U(O_{ij})$ utility of outcome j under strategy i. P probability of an outcome.

too heavy, that the breeding ground for subversion would not be increased, that the international sanctions would not be too severe, and that the remaining Indonesians would still be willing to cooperate with the Dutch (O_{12}).

The second strategy he considered was to continue with the negotiations and to try to reach a less demanding agreement before December 1, and only if this ended in failure to initiate military action (S_2). Here, too, he anticipated that the same highly negative outcome (O_{21}) could occur, though he considered it less likely. The less negative outcome (O_{22}) was also less likely to occur, and still another less negative outcome (O_{23}) was, in his opinion, most likely to result from the negotiations, entailing a strong position for the republic in the interim federal government, a delay in settling all details, and a more rapid transfer of the sovereignty. The minister saw the situation in very gloom terms. He mentioned that a really good solution was beyond their reach and that he had to choose "the lesser of two evils," that is, S_2. He could perceive only negative outcomes.

At first sight, these outcomes seem to be evaluated with intensitity statements. But since this minister did not indicate a rank order between O_{23} and O_{22} (they are both evaluated as less negative but contain very different elements), we consider them to be without intensities. The probabilities are intensity statements. Based on the information about values and probabilities, it is appropriate to test rules of Class II (Table 2.4), that is, the Risk-Avoidance Rules. Since the minister chose the strategy with the highest chance of a less negative outcome, the negative version of the Risk-Avoidance Rule predicts his choice of S_2. The positive version is not applicable, since there are no positive outcomes.

Now the cabinet in The Hague had to decide what to do. Despite the two divergent trends, the policy advocated by the prime minister gained ground (Table 7.6). The prime minister generated no new strategies. He considered only the two strategies suggested by the High Representative of the Crown and the minister of foreign affairs. He rejected the representative's choice (S_1) by stating that there was a high chance that it would lead both in Indonesia and in the international arena to serious repercussions, such as the closing of harbors and airports to the Dutch; great human and material losses; and endless guerrilla warfare in Indonesia (O_{11}). The chance that there would be no serious repercussions either in Indonesia or in the international arena was low (O_{12}). With respect to the minister of foreign affairs negotiation proposal (S_2), he was more optimistic, as he anticipated a high chance of some positive result, which meant that the republic would agree in some way with the essential demands (O_{21}). If negotiations did not succeed, then they would have to resort to military measures, with a low chance of serious repercussions both in Indonesia and in the international arena (O_{22}).

Based on the utilities without intensities and the probabilities with intensities indicated by the prime minister, it is appropriate to test heuristics of Class II (Table 2.4) to see whether they produce his choice of S_2. We can try both versions, the Positive and the Negative Risk-Avoidance Rules. Applying the Positive Risk-Avoidance Rule leads to the selection of S_2, and the same is true for the negative version of the Risk-Avoidance Rule. Therefore, both rules can predict the choice, and the Risk-Avoidance argumentation seems to fit the argument of the prime minister.

Table 7.6:

Argument of the Prime Minister for the Continuation of Negotiations in Indonesia, November 15, 1948

Strategies	Outcomes			
	O_{11}	O_{12}	O_{21}	O_{22}
	Serious repercussions, both in Indonesia and in the international arena	No serious repercussions either in the international arena or in Indonesia	Negotiations lead to a result	Serious repercussions, both in Indonesia and in the international arena
S_1: Inform the GOC about the failure of the negotiations and take military action	$U(O_{11})=-$ p=high	$U(O_{12})=+$ p=low		
S_2*: Continue with negotiations, and if they fail, inform the GOC and take military action			$U(O_{21})=+$ p=high	$U(O_{22})=-$ p=low

Source: Council of Ministers, Nov. 5, 1948, Minutes, *Officiële Bescheiden betreffende de Nederlands Indonesische betrekkingen, 1945–1950,* vol. 15, no. 328, 662–670.

Symbols: S_i strategy i. S_i* chosen strategy. O_{ij} outcome j under strategy i. $U(O_{ij})$ utility of outcome j under strategy i. P probability of an outcome.

The minister of foreign affairs thus had to continue with the negotiations. In the eyes of most of the Dutch authorities in Indonesia, this was not a viable solution, and therefore the minister of overseas territories, himself a hawk, went to Indonesia to explain the decision. Table 7.7 contains the arguments of the minister of overseas territories for his choice of continuing first with the negotiations (S_2). The minister of overseas territories argued that if the government had adopted the advice of the High Representative of the Crown to inform the GOC of the failure of the negotiations and turn to military action (S_1), an irreparable division would have occurred within the cabinet (O_{11}: a_{111} and O_{12}: a_{121}), possibly followed by international sanctions (O_{12}: a_{122}), though not necessarily so (O_{11}: a_{112}). These consequences are fairly negative, and for the first time an in-

Table 7.7:
Argument of the Minister of Overseas Territories for the Continuation of Negotiations, November 24, 1948

Strategies	Outcomes						
	O_{11}		O_{12}		O_{21}	O_{22}	O_{23}	O_{24}
	a_{111}: Irreparable division within the cabinet	a_{112}: No international sanctions	a_{121}: Irreparable division within the cabinet	a_{122}: International sanctions	Agreement reached but not carried out by the republic; the Security Council considers the conflict an internal affair	Agreement reached but not carried out by the republic; the conflict is more acceptable to the international arena	Agreement reached and carried out by the republic; the Security Council removes the case from its agenda, and the GOC is dissolved	No agreement reached but we can cope with the international sanctions
S_1: Inform the GOC about the failure of the negotiations and start with military action	$U(a_{111})=-$ $U(a_{112})=+$ p=possible		$U(a_{121})=-$ $U(a_{122})=-$ p=possible					
S_2^*: Continue with the negotiations and if they fail, or the agreement is not carried out, start with military action					$U(O_{21})=+$ p=possible	$U(O_{22})=+$ p=possible	$U(O_{23})=+$ p=possible	$U(O_{24})=+$ p=possible

Source: Dutch negotiators in Indonesia, Nov. 24, 1948, Minutes of meeting, Archive of Stikker, record no. 7D, Batavia II.

Symbols: S_i strategy i. S_i^* chosen strategy. O_{ij} outcome j under strategy i. $U(O_{ij})$ utility of outcome j under strategy i. P probability of an outcome. Outcomes O_{11} and O_{12} are split up in aspects since the decision-maker evaluated each aspect separately.

ternal aspect (the division of the government) is mentioned as playing a role in the decision.

With regard to S_2, the minister anticipated only positive outcomes. Outcomes O_{21}, O_{22}, and O_{23} depend on reaching an agreement with the republic. If an agreement was reached but the republic did not abide by it, there was a possibility that the Security Council would finally consider the conflict an internal affair, which would mean that the Dutch were free to do what they deemed necessary without fear of sanctions (O_{21}). But it was also possible in this case that the conflict, even if it were not considered an internal affair, would be more acceptable to the international arena (O_{22}). There was even the possibility that the republic would abide by the agreement, which would lead to the Security Council removing the case from its agenda and dissolving the GOC (O_{23}). If no agreement was reached, the minister of overseas territories argued, the Netherlands could cope with any international sanctions (O_{24}).

Given value and probability statements without intensities, it is appropriate to test heuristics of Class IV (Table 2.4) to see whether they produce the minister's choice of S_2. The Reversed Simon Rule, which requires rejection of all strategies that lead with certainty to negative outcomes and selection of the one where a positive outcome is also possible, does not fit the choice of S_2 since S_2 leads with certainty only to positive outcomes. But Simon's Rule, which requires the choice of the alternative that leads only to positive outcomes, correctly predicts the choice of S_2 .

DECISION PHASE 3, END OF NOVEMBER TO DECEMBER 13, 1948

Negotiations with the Indonesians continued between November 27 and December 1. The minister of overseas territories was now the leader of the Dutch delegation and the minister of foreign affairs, and his adviser merely participated. A delegation of five members of parliament had also joined them to offer advice. The crucial points for an agreement concerned the observation of the truce, the position of the High Representative of the Crown as supreme commander of the troops during the transition period, and the gradual dismantling of the republican army. The minister of foreign affairs was convinced that without American support, the republic would not comply, and he therefore sought it desperately, though in vain. The Indonesians did not make any serious concessions and even retracted some earlier concessions because of internal pressure.

On November 30, the ministers therefore had to decide whether to continue with the negotiations or to stop.

Table 7.8 summarizes the advice of the Minister of Foreign Affairs. He considered two strategies. His government could either take military action (S_1) or conclude an unsatisfactory agreement (S_2). If they concluded an unsatisfactory agreement, the minister was certain that there would be no law and order in Indonesia, since the republican leaders were unable to keep their own army under control, and so the position of the High Representative of the Crown would become untenable (O_{21}). If they resorted to military action, there was a high risk of serious international sanctions and a diminished willingness on the part of the remaining Indonesians to cooperate with the Dutch (O_{11}), but there was also a low chance of a less negative outcome (O_{12}), namely, that the international sanctions would be less serious and that the willingness of the remaining Indonesians to cooperate might even increase. The minister again mentioned that he was having to choose "the lesser of two evils," and opted for military action. At first sight, these outcomes seem to be evaluated with intensity statements, but since the Minister did not indicate a rank order between O_{11} and O_{21} and they are both evaluated as negative despite containing different elements, the utilities must be considered to be without intensities.

Given utilities without intensities and probabilities with intensities, it is appropriate to test models of Class II (Table 2.4) to see whether they produce the minister's choice of S_1. We can try both versions, the positive and the negative Risk-Avoidance Rules. Applying the Positive Risk-Avoidance Rule does not lead to the selection of S_1 since there is no higher chance of a positive outcome.

Table 7.8:
Argument of the Minister of Foreign Affairs for Taking Military Action, November 30, 1948

Strategies	Outcomes		
	O_{11} Serious international sanctions, willingness of remaining Indonesians to co-operate diminished	O_{12} Less serious international sanctions, willingness of remaining Indonesians to cooperate increased	O_{21} No law and order in Indonesia, position of the High Representative of the Crown untenable
S_1*: Take military action	$U(O_{11})$=negative p=high	$U(O_{12})$=less negative p=low	
S_2: Conclude an unsatisfactory agreement with the republic			$U(O_{21})$=negative p=certain

Source: Dutch negotiators in Indonesia, Nov. 30, 1948, Minutes of meeting, Archive of Stikker, record no. 7D, Batavia II.

Symbols: S_i strategy i. S_i* chosen strategy. O_{ij} outcome j under strategy i. $U(O_{ij})$ utility of outcome j under strategy i. P probability of an outcome.

But the negative version of the Risk-Avoidance Rule predicts the choice of S_1, and therefore this rule seems to fit the argument of the minister.

The adviser to the ministers also advocated resorting to military measures (Table 7.9). He considered the same strategies as the minister of foreign affairs but anticipated only such outcomes as might affect Indonesia. For both strategies he considered the same two outcomes, and only their chances of occurrence differed. If the government concluded an unsatisfactory agreement with the republic (S_2), the chance was less, in his opinion, that more cooperation would be achieved (O_{21}). In fact, he would have expected less cooperation, since the republican army would not have been dismantled and therefore the breeding ground for communism would increase (O_{22}). If they took military action (S_1), the chance was greater that more cooperation would be achieved, because they could dismantle the republican army and reduce the breeding ground for communism (O_{12}).

Based on the utilities without intensities and the probabilities with intensities indicated by the adviser, it is appropriate to test heuristics of Class II (Table 2.4) to see whether they produce the adviser's choice of S_1. We can try both versions,

Table 7.9:

Argument of the Minister's Adviser for Taking Military Action, November 30, 1948

Strategies	Outcomes	
	$O_{11}=O_{21}$ More cooperation achieved in Indonesia by the elimination of the republican army and the destruction of the breeding ground for communism	$O_{12}=O_{22}$ No cooperation achieved since the republican army is not eliminated and the breeding ground for communism increases
S_1*: Take military action	$U(O_{11})=+$ p=greater	$U(O_{12})=-$ p=smaller
S_2: Conclude an unsatisfactory agreement with the republic	$U(O_{21})=+$ p=smaller	$U(O_{22})=-$ p=greater

Source: Dutch negotiators in Indonesia, Nov. 30, 1948, Minutes of meeting, Archive of Stikker, record no. 7D, Batavia II.

Symbols: S_i strategy i. S_i* chosen strategy. O_{ij} outcome j under strategy i. $U(O_{ij})$ utility of outcome j under strategy i. P probability of an outcome.

the Positive and the Negative Risk-Avoidance Rules. Applying the Positive Risk-Avoidance Rule leads to the selection of S_1, and the same is true for the negative version of the Risk-Avoidance Rule. Therefore, both rules can predict the choice, and the Risk-Avoidance argumentation seems to fit the argument of this adviser.

Before leaving Indonesia, the ministers informed the GOC of the result of the negotiations, indicating that they would still welcome constructive moves from the republic. Having received the unanimous advice of the three negotiators, the cabinet deliberated on December 9 and 13 on the course of action to follow. Here again we will discuss only the individual arguments of ministers. The minister of the interior and the prime minister set out complete arguments. The arguments of the minister of the interior are summarized in Table 7.10. He considered three available strategies. The first strategy was to start military action (S_1), as recommended by the negotiators. Another option, a new one in this situation, was inaction (S_2), and the third strategy, consisting of two steps, was to let the GOC formally handle the matter and then take military action later (S_3). The first step is slightly different from those options that proposed informing the GOC (discussed after the second phase), and the second step is already very familiar. If his government were to first let the matter be formally handled by the GOC and thereafter turn to military action (S_3), the minister was certain that the Americans would force the Dutch to ease their demands (O_{31}), and obviously they would not be able to carry out the second step. If they were to undertake nothing (S_2), he was certain that the extremists in Indonesia would improve their position (O_{21}), meaning that the risk of chaos would be increased. If they were simply to go ahead with military action (S_1), he anticipated a high probability of gaining the cooperation of the population in the republican territory (O_{11}), while the probability of achieving no cooperation (O_{12}) was very small. Based on the probabilities and values of the consequences, the minister chose S_1.

Since the minister indicated utilities without intensities and probabilities with intensities, it is appropriate to test the rules of Class II (Table 2.4) to see whether they produce his choice of S_1. We can try both versions, the Positive and the Negative Risk-Avoidance Rules. Applying the Positive Risk-Avoidance Rule leads to the selection of S_1, and the same is true for the negative version of the Risk-Avoidance Rule. Therefore, both rules can predict the choice, and the Risk-Avoidance argumentation seems to fit the argument of this minister.

The prime minister also considered three strategies (Table 7.11): continuing negotiations with the aid of the GOC (S_1), which would have been slightly different from the status quo, where they were negotiating independently; doing nothing (S_2), the strategy the minister of the interior had also considered; or sending a message to the United States and the GOC with the theoretical possibility of pressuring the republic to accept the most important Dutch demands, and if this did not succeed turning to military action (S_3). The latter strategy differs only slightly from the minister of the interior's (S_3), which asks the GOC for a formal handling of the matter, while the prime minister would ask for an

Table 7.10:
Argument of the Minister of the Interior for Taking Military Action, December 9, 1948

Strategies	Outcomes			
	O_{11}	O_{12}	O_{21}	O_{31}
	Cooperation of the population in republican territory	No cooperation of the population in republican territory	The position of the extremists improves	We are forced by the Americans to ease our demands
S_1*: Take military action	$U(O_{11})=+$ p=very high	$U(O_{12})=-$ p=very small		
S_2: Do nothing			$U(O_{21})=-$ p=certain	
S_3: Let the matter be formally handled by the GOC and take military action				$U(O_{31})=-$ p=certain

Source: Council of Ministers, Dec. 9, 1948, Minutes, *Officiële Bescheiden betreffende de Nederlands Indonesische betrekkingen, 1945–1950*, vol. 16, no. 41, 73–82.

Symbols: S_i strategy i. S_i* chosen strategy. O_{ij} outcome j under strategy i. $U(O_{ij})$ utility of outcome j under strategy i. P probability of an outcome.

eventual last-resort intervention not only from the GOC but also directly from the United States.

If his government was to continue with the negotiations under the auspices of the GOC (S_1), the prime minister was certain that no solution would be achieved (O_{11}). If they were to do nothing at all (S_2), he was certain that Indonesia would be plagued by anarchy and dictatorship (O_{21}). However, if they were to send a message to the United States and the GOC with the theoretical possibility of pressuring the republic to accept the main Dutch demands (S_3), there was at least a very small chance that the republic would give in (O_{33}); otherwise they would initiate military action. In this case, the prime minister thought that the probability was high that only small-scale internal opposition would be encountered (O_3: a_{311}), the Dutch international position would not suffer so badly (O_{31}: a_{312}), and although many people and material resources would be destroyed (O_{31}: a_{313}), Indonesia would not be plagued by anarchy and dictatorship (O_{31}: a_{314}). The

Table 7.11:
Argument of the Prime Minister for Taking Military Action, December 9, 1948

Strategies	Outcomes				
	O_{11} No solution	O_{21} Anarchy and dictatorship in Indonesia	O_{31} a_{311}: Only small scale internal opposition a_{312}: Our international position is not badly affected a_{313}: Many people killed and a good deal of material destroyed a_{314}: No anarchy and dictatorship in Indonesia	O_{32} a_{321}: General strikes in the Netherlands a_{322}: Our international position is severely damaged a_{323}: Many people killed and a good deal of material destroyed a_{324}: Anarchy and dictatorship in Indonesia	O_{33} The republic agrees to our main demands
S_1: Continue the negotiations with the aid of the GOC	$U(O_{11})=-$ p=certain				
S_2: Do nothing		$U(O_{21})=-$ p=certain			
S_3*: Send a message to the United States and the GOC with the theoretical possibility of putting pressure on the republic to accept our main demands, and if this does not succeed, take military action			$U(a_{311})$=acceptable $U(a_{312})$=acceptable $U(a_{313})=-$ $U(a_{314})=+$ p=high	$U(a_{321})=-$ $U(a_{322})=-$ $U(a_{323})=-$ $U(a_{324})=-$ p=small	$U(O_{33})=+$ p=very small

Source: Council of Ministers, Dec. 9, 1948, Minutes, *Officiële Bescheiden betreffende de Nederlands Indonesische betrekkingen, 1945–1950*, vol. 16, no. 41, 73–82.

Symbols: S_i strategy i. S_i* chosen strategy. O_{ij} outcome j under strategy i. $U(O_{ij})$ utility of outcome j under strategy i. P probability of an outcome.

probability of a totally adverse outcome (O_{32}), although small, was not excluded, in the prime minister's opinion. In this case there would be general strikes in the Netherlands (O_{32}: a_{321}), the Dutch international position would be severely damaged (O_{32}: a_{322}), many people would be killed and a good portion of material resources would be destroyed (O_{32}: a_{323}), and despite all efforts to the contrary, Indonesia would be plagued by anarchy and dictatorship (O_{32}: a_{324}). Based on the utilities and probabilities he indicated, the prime minister chose the third strategy.

Since the prime minister indicated utilities without intensities and probabilities with intensities, it is appropriate to test the rules of Class II (Table 2.4) to see whether they produce his choice of S_3. We can try both versions, the Positive and the Negative Risk-Avoidance Rules. Applying the Positive Risk-Avoidance Rule leads to the selection of S_3, and the same is true for the negative version of the Risk-Avoidance Rule. Therefore, both rules can predict the choice, and the Risk-Avoidance argumentation seems to fit this argument.

On December 13, the cabinet agreed unanimously to carry out the course of action preferred by the prime minister. Aides-mémoires were sent to the United States and the GOC, and the High Representative of the Crown received instructions to get ready for military action, which was to start at midnight December 18.

DECISION PHASE 4, DECEMBER 14 AND 15, 1948

On December 13 at around midnight, the High Representative of the Crown cabled a letter from the Indonesian deputy president to The Hague, advising that this letter be ignored, since it contained only vague personal views dictated by the American delegate to the GOC in response to the Dutch aide-mémoire. That same night, the prime minister had contact with the ministers of foreign affairs and overseas territories. The next day, December 14, the cabinet convened and they had to decide whether to go ahead with the military action as planned or to once more insert an interim step where they would ask for clarification and/or negotiate. Three ministers gave complete arguments for their choice, as presented here.

The argument of the prime minister is summarized in Table 7.12. He considered three strategies, the first being the advice of the High Representative of the Crown—for which the latter had not indicated the consequences—to ignore the letter and go straight ahead with military action (S_1). The second one was to negotiate step-by-step (S_2), a familiar cooperative strategy. The third strategy consisted of two steps, namely to postpone action for several days and then to deliver an ultimatum to the republic reiterating the primary demands (S_3).

The prime minister argued that if the government ignored the letter and started military action (S_1), there would certainly be serious international trouble (O_{11}: a_{111}), and nationally it would also be unacceptable (O_{11}: a_{112}). He therefore rejected this strategy. If they postponed military action for several days and delivered an utlimatum to the republic (S_3), there was a high risk of serious

Table 7.12:
Argument of the Prime Minister for Continuing with Negotiations, December 14, 1948

Strategies	Outcomes			
	O_{11}	O_{21}	O_{31}	O_{32}
	a_{111}: Serious international trouble, not only with respect to Indonesia	a_{211}: No international troubles	A satisfactory answer	Serious international trouble, not only with respect to Indonesia
	a_{112}: Nationally unacceptable	a_{112}: Nationally acceptable		
S_1: Ignore the letter and take military action	$U(a_{111})=-$ $U(a_{112})=-$ p=certain			
S_2*: Negotiate step-by-step		$U(a_{211})=+$ $U(a_{212})=$acceptable p=certain		
S_3: Ask the republican government for clarification in an ultimatum; if the answer is unsatisfactory take military action			$U(O_{31})=+$ p=small	$U(O_{32})=-$ p=high

Source: Council of Ministers, Dec. 14, 1948, Minutes, *Officiële Bescheiden betreffende de Nederlands Indonesische betrekkingen, 1945–1950*, vol. 16, no. 88, 141–147.

Symbols: S_i strategy i. S_i* chosen strategy. O_{ij} outcome j under strategy i. $U(O_{ij})$ utility of outcome j under strategy i. P probability of an outcome.

international trouble (O_{32}), while the chance of a satisfactory answer from the republic (O_{31}) was small. If they negotiated step-by-step (S_2), he anticipated no international trouble (O_{21}: a_{211}) and nationally the choice would also be acceptable (O_{21}: a_{212}).

Based on the values and probabilities he indicated, the prime minister advocated S_2. Given utilities without intensities and probabilities with intensities, it is appropriate to test heuristics of Class II (Table 2.4) to see whether they produce the choice of S_2. We can try both versions, the Positive and the Negative Risk-Avoidance Rules. Applying the Positive Risk-Avoidance Rule leads to the selection of S_2 and the same is true for the negative version of the Risk-Avoidance Rule. Therefore, both rules can predict the choice, and the Risk-Avoidance argumentation seems to fit this argument.

The prime minister's colleague, the minister of social affairs, who was also a member of the Labor Party, considered only two strategies (Table 7.13). If his government ignored the letter and took military action (S_1), he argued, this would be certain to stir up serious trouble both at home and in the international arena, and in Indonesia the breeding ground for communism would be increased (O_{11}).

Table 7.13:
Argument of the Minister of Social Affairs for Continuing with Negotiations, December 14, 1948

Strategies	Outcomes	
	O_{11} Serious trouble at home and in the international arena, breeding ground for communism in Indonesia increased	O_{21} No serious trouble either at home or in the international arena, loss of Indonesia
S_1: Ignore the letter, take military action	$U(O_{11})$=more disastrous p=certain	
S_2*: Negotiate step-by-step		$U(O_{21})$=less disastrous p=certain

Source: Council of Ministers, Dec. 14, 1948, Minutes, *Officiële Bescheiden betreffende de Nederlands Indonesische betrekkingen, 1945–1950*, vol. 16, no. 88, 141–147.

Symbols: S_i strategy i. S_i* chosen strategy. O_{ij} outcome j under strategy i. $U(O_{ij})$ utility of outcome j under strategy i. P probability of an outcome
Since the decision-maker gave total evaluations for each outcome we did not decompose them into aspects.

If they negotiated step-by-step (S_2), he was certain that there would be no serious trouble either at home or in the international arena, but Indonesia would be lost (O_{21}). Since he evaluated the outcome of S_1 as more disastrous than the outcome of S_2, he chose the strategy with the least disastrous outcome (S_2).

It is clear from his argument that for each strategy this minister considered an outcome that systematically took into account international, national, and Indonesian aspects. The probabilities are the same for both strategies, and therefore his choice is based only on the utilites with intensities. MAUT models of Class III (Table 2.4) are thus the appropriate ones to test in order to find a fitting decision rule. Since the minister did not indicate utilities for each aspect, the Dominance Rule cannot predict this choice. The same is true for the Lexicographic Rule, which also requires an indication of the most important aspect. But the Addition-of-Utilities Rule* which requires a total value for each outcome, and selects the strategy with the highest value of the total outcome correctly predicts his choice of S_2 and thus fits the argument.

This minister was one of the few who dared to make a value trade-off, a move generally unpopular among politicians (e.g., Farnham 1990, 100; Maoz 1990, 230). The arguments of the minister of social affairs hint that within the Labor Party the ultimate loss of Indonesia, which can be considered a more long-term outcome, was evaluated as a less disastrous outcome than the more immediate internal and international uproar.

The argument of the minister of overseas territories, a member of the Roman Catholic Party, was very different (Table 7.14). He considered the same three strategies as the prime minister but focused only on outcomes with respect to Indonesia, and drew a different conclusion. If his government postponed military action for several days and delivered an ultimatum to the republic (S_3), he reasoned that they would certainly lose Indonesia (O_{31}). The same would would be true (O_{21}), in his opinion, were they to negotiate step-by-step (S_2). Only if they ignored the letter and initiated military action (S_1) would there be a possibility of holding on to Indonesia (O_{12}), but it was still possible that Indonesia would be lost (O_{11}). The minister thus advocated S_1.

Based on the values and probabilities he had indicated (both without intensities), it is appropriate to test models of Class IV (Table 2.4). Simon's Rule does not predict the choice of S_1, since this strategy does not lead only to positive outcomes. But the Reversed Simon Rule, which requires rejection of all alternatives that lead with certainty to negative outcomes and the selection of the one where a positive outcome is also possible, correctly predicts the minister's choice of S_1.

The cabinet was very divided on this day, December 14, 1948, and several sessions of deliberations took place one after the other in an effort to arrive at a collective choice (this process will be discussed in detail in the volume on political decision-making).

---

* "Addition" is a mental operation that we cannot verify.

Table 7.14:
Argument of the Minister of Overseas Territories for Ignoring the Letter and Taking Military Action, December 14, 1948

Strategies	Outcomes	
	$O_{11}=O_{21}=O_{31}$ Loss of Indonesia	O_{12} No loss of Indonesia
S_1*: Ignore the letter and take military action	$U(O_{11})=-$ p=possible	$U(O_{12})=+$ p=possible
S_2: Negotiate step-by-step	$U(O_{21})=-$ p=certain	
S_3: Ask the republican government for clarification in an ultimatum; if the answer is unsatisfactory, take military action	$U(O_{31})=-$ p=certain	

Source: Council of Ministers, Dec. 14, 1948, Minutes, *Officiële Bescheiden betreffende de Nederlands Indonesische betrekkingen, 1945–1950,* vol. 16, no. 88, 141–147.

Symbols: S_i strategy i. S_i* chosen strategy. O_{ij} outcome j under strategy i. $U(O_{ij})$ utility of outcome j under strategy i. P probability of an outcome.

CONCLUSIONS

In this chapter, fourteen arguments put forward by individual decision-makers of a small power in a worsening crisis situation have been studied. When arguing, these decision-makers described similarly to their colleagues from other types of nations the available strategies and their consequences, and they evaluated the consequences and their likelihood of occurrence. Thereafter, they drew conclusions as to which strategy should be adopted. However, they never mentioned the choice rule they used in order to draw their conclusions, let alone indicated whether the conditions were satisfied under which the preferred strategy should be chosen. Based on the quality of the utilities and probabilities they indicated, it has been possible to establish for each argument an appropriate class

Table 7.15:
Summary of the Aspects of Outcomes Considered for Each Strategy by the Decision-Makers

Strategies	Aspects of outcomes Indonesian
S_1: Do nothing	Commander of the troops, prime minister, minister of overseas territories, minister of the interior
S_2: Negotiate with the republic	High Representative of the Crown, minister of social affairs
S_3: Continue the negotiations with the aid of the GOC	Prime minister
S_4: Negotiate with the republic and if the negotiations fail, take military action	Official of foreign affairs, minister of foreign affairs, prime minister, minister of overseas territories
S_5: Demand from the republic and the GOC the unconditional agreement with the main points	—
S_6: Send an ultimatum to the U.S. delegation of the GOC and take quick military action, if the republic does not agree	Commander of the troops, official of foreign affairs, prime minister, ministers of foreign affairs, overseas territories
S_7: Inform the GOC about the failure of the negotiations and take military action	High Representative of the Crown, minister of foreign affairs, prime minister
S_8: Send a message to the United States and the GOC with the theoretical possibility of pressuring the republic into accepting our main demands; if this does not work, take military action	Prime minister
S_9: Conclude an unsatisfactory peace treaty with the republic	Minister of foreign affairs, adviser on foreign affairs
S_{10}: Take military action	Adviser on foreign affairs, minister of foreign affairs, minister of the interior, minister of social affairs, minister of overseas territories

Aspects of outcomes	
International	National
—	—
Prime minister, minister of social affairs	Prime minister, minister of social affairs
—	—
Official of foreign affairs, minister of foreign affairs, prime minister, minister of overseas territories	Minister of foreign affairs
High Representative of the Crown	—
Secretary of foreign affairs, prime minister, minister of foreign affairs	—
Minister of foreign affairs, prime minister, minister of overseas territories, minister of the interior	—
Prime minister	Prime minister
Minister of foreign affairs	—
Ministers of foreign affairs, minister of social affairs	Minister of social affairs

of argumentation rules, which was applied to the data to find a fitting choice rule.

In nine cases, the Risk-Avoidance Rules correctly predicted the choice, in three cases the Reversed Simon Rule fitted the choice, in another case it was Simon's Rule, and in yet another case it was the Addition-of-Utilities Rule. These results show that the Dutch decision-makers, like others, generally avoided combining utilities with intensities and probabilities with intensities, which can lead to an overly complex computational operation, as we have already indicated. In nine cases the Dutch decision-makers used probabilities with intensities, while the utilities were indicated without intensities (Risk-Avoidance Rules); in one case the utilities were indicated with intensities while the probabilities were without intensities (Addition-of-Utilities Rule); and in four cases both utilities and probabilities were indicated without intensities (Simon's and Reversed Simon Rules).

When studying these arguments, one gets the impression that they are based on a number of simplifications or a reduction of the information. One way of simplifying decision problems in order to reduce complexity is to reduce complex value problems to simple value problems. For example, decision-makers did not consider all relevant aspects of outcomes simultaneously across strategies. As was shown, only one argument required a MAUT Rule for its description, namely, the Addition-of-Utilities Rule. In this case the decision-maker systematically mentioned three relevant aspects of outcomes: an Indonesian dimension, an international one, and a national one. For the other decision-makers, these three dimensions also seemed to be of relevance, as they sometimes used them for one strategy, but they did not consider them systematically across all strategies. Table 7.15 summarizes for each strategy the dimensions of outcomes indicated by the decision-maker. The table shows that with the exception of the minister of social affairs, who used all three dimensions for S_2 and S_{10} simultaneously, the other decision-makers considered them relevant but did not use them systematically across strategies. Sometimes they only referred to a single dimension when examining a strategy. For example, the prime minister, when dealing with S_1, considered only the Indonesian aspect and evaluated the utility of this simple outcome. When he examined the consequences for S_2, he considered both the national and international dimensions, and when dealing with S_4, the consequences related to the Indonesian and international dimensions. For S_8, he even considered consequences containing all three dimensions. The evaluations were given either by indicating utilities for each dimension or by using a holistic utility for all dimensions together instead of evaluating them separately and comparing them across strategies. A further inspection of the table shows that other decision-makers argued in a similar way. Only the commander of the troops restricted himself to outcomes referring to the Indonesian dimension. In our view, these data suggest that although the decision-makers were generally aware that three aspects played a role in the decision problem, in order to keep things manageable, they restricted themselves to considering only those aspects of outcomes that they judged most important for each strategy.

Table 7.16:
Summary of the Total Number of Strategies Considered

Strategies	Decision-maker who generated the strategy	Decision-maker(s) who considered the strategy
S_1: Do nothing	Commander of the troops	Minister of the interior, prime minister
S_2: Negotiate with the republic	High Representative of the Crown	Prime minister, minister of social affairs, minister of overseas territories
S_3: Continue the negotiations with the aid of the GOC	Prime minister	—
S_4: Negotiate with the republic and if the negotiations fail, take military action	Official of foreign affairs	Minister of foreign affairs, prime minister, minister of overseas territories
S_5: Demand from the republic and the GOC unconditional agreement with the main points	High Representative of the Crown	—
S_6 Send an ultimatum to the U. S. delegation of the GOC and take quickly military action if the republic does not agree	Commander of the troops	Official of foreign affairs, minister of foreign affairs, prime minister, minister of overseas territories
S_7: Inform the GOC about the failure of the negotiations and take military action	High Representative of the Crown	Minister of foreign affairs, prime minister, minister of overseas territories, minister of the interior
S_8: Send a message to the United States and the GOC with the theoretical possibility of pressuring the republic into accepting our main demands, and if this does not work, take military action	Prime minister	—
S_9: Conclude an unsatisfactory peace treaty with the republic	Minister of foreign affairs	Adviser on foreign affairs
S_{10}: Take military action	Minister of foreign affairs	Adviser on foreign affairs, prime minister, minister of social affairs, minister of overseas territories

Another way of reducing information is to omit uncertainty or reduce uncertainty to quasi certainty. In nine cases (Tables 7.1, 7.2, 7.4, 7.8, and 7.10 through 7.14) the decision-makers formulated the problem in such a way that the outcomes for at least one strategy were considered certain, and in two cases (Tables 7.12 and 7.13) the outcomes of the other strategy had a very high or very low chance of occurring.

Another mode of simplification is to restrict the range of strategies considered. In total, ten distinct strategies were mentioned in the course of the argumentations, but in nine argumentations the decision-makers only considered two alternatives simultaneously, and in the remaining five they examined three.

Table 7.16 summarizes all the strategies mentioned in the course of the arguments and indicates who generated them first and which other decision-makers also considered them. The table shows that S_5 and S_8 were only considered by the persons who generated them. The other strategies were also examined occasionally by other decision-makers. As far as their contents are concerned, the strategies were not very original either. "Doing nothing" (S_1) relates to the status quo, and must have been quite familiar to decision-makers. The varying negotiation strategies S_2 through S_4 were also known from past experience. The same is true of the strategies that suggest preceding military action with an ultimatum (S_6), information (S_7), or a request to exercise pressure (S_8).

These data accord with Lindblom's assumption (Lindblom 1959, 1982) that decision-makers limit their analysis to a small range of alternatives that are familiar in order to make the decision problem manageable. Some, though not all, of the strategies are also only incrementally different from the status quo, which is also suggested by Lindblom. The alternatives that contain military action at least as a second step (S_6-S_8, S_{10}) clearly depart drastically both from the status quo and also from the eventual conclusion of an unsatisfactory peace treaty (S_9). Another simplification stratagem mentioned by Lindblom (1959, 1982) is to consider a restricted number of consequences. The data show that in three arguments no more than three outcomes were indicated, and in eleven argumentations no more than six outcomes were considered, as can be seen in the tables.

From Tables 7.15 and 7.16, which present all possible alternatives and aspects of outcomes, and the discussion of the probabilities, it follows that political decision problems are in essence complex value problems with a large degree of uncertainty. Since these problems are so complex, decision-makers intuitively apply a variety of simplifications.

The Practice of Political Argumentation

CHOICE OF A THEORETICAL FRAMEWORK

In Part 1 we discussed different approaches to the analysis of argumentation. It was shown that the more or less classical argumentation theory was very general and did not provide specific access to arguments that would allow the selection of alternatives from a set of possibilities, because there were no rules that indicated which of the alternatives would be the best in any sense. The cognitive mapping approach was also discussed, and it was concluded that it was less attractive where arguments pro or contra different alternatives were concerned because the choice rule in this approach was too crude to take into account probabilities. The means-and-ends approach came very close to the type of instrument we were looking for. But it seemed to be best suited for situations where a certain goal had to be realized than for situations where the decision-maker had to evaluate the consequences of options in order to select an alternative. Given that none of these approaches was satisfactory for our purposes, we developed within the framework of decision theory a text analysis instrument.

SIX TYPES OF ARGUMENTATIONS

Based on the concepts of decision theory, the argument of an individual politician could be described by a decision tree and further summarized in a decision table. We showed that the descriptions of the decision problems could be classified under four different classes according to the amount of information provided about utilities and probabilities of the different outcomes. It was also demonstrated that in decision theory, decision rules can be found that vary with respect to the amount of information they require with regard to utilities and probabilities. Next we described how the four different classes of decision rules could be used to formulate arguments according to the four classes of decision problems. This combination led to the formulation of a series of argumentations that decision-makers could use in order to convince their colleagues of their particular choice of a strategy. These argumentations were described formally and illustrated by examples. Following this, we showed how the description indicates which class of argumentations provides the appropriate rule. If one of the rules of this class applied, we could say that the complete argument had been found because the description, the detected rule, the specified condition, and the choice were in agreement with each other.

TEXT ANALYSIS OF REAL-LIFE ARGUMENTS

When presenting a real-life argument, neither the decision rule used nor the fact that the relevant condition was fulfilled were mentioned in deriving the conclusion. This either meant that our approach was completely wrong or that these rules were so obvious to both the speaker and his audience that they did not consider it important to mention them. We assumed that the latter was the case and used the amount of information given in the problem description as an indication of what class of rules should be applied. The procedure we used was as follows: first, the class of the problem using the information given about utilities and probabilities, was determined; then the rules of this class were tested, and if one or more rules of this class could predict the choice, we assumed that the complete argumentation of the decision-maker had been found.

CROSS-NATIONAL CASE STUDIES

Subsequently we studied individual argumentations of crucial decisions relating to decision-makers belonging to four different types of regimes and to different periods of time. From these studies, it emerged that these individuals used independently of each other similar argumentation rules and similar methods of simplifying complex decision problems in order to make them manageable. Although further cross-national research is required to strengthen the idea that the argumentation rules we presented in this book are more or less universally used, we adduced clear evidence in this direction. In Part 2 of this book, we will show in a quantitative study that these rules are very commonly used in the Netherlands.

REDUCTION OF INFORMATION AND SIMPLIFICATIONS

Before we proceed with Part 2, however, the simplification of decision problems or reduction of information that we observed at the cross-national level should be briefly summarized. It was shown that on the basis of the nature of the utilities and probabilities that the decision-makers indicated, an argumentation rule in the appropriate class could be found that described their choice. We studied in total thirty-one individual arguments and observed that the decision-makers indeed avoided combining utilities and probabilities with intensities, which would have led to overly complex computational operations, as had already been indicated. Only in one case were utilities with intensities indicated (Addition-of-Utilities Rule). In sixteen arguments probabilities with intensities were used, while the utilities were indicated without intensities (Risk-Avoidance Rules), and in the other fourteen cases both utilities and probabilities were indicated without intensities (Simon's and Reversed Simon Rules).

Another simplifying strategem was to reduce complex value problems to simple value problems. As mentioned, only one argument required a MAUT Rule for its description, namely, the Addition-of-Utilities Rule. In this case, the decision-maker systematically mentioned some relevant aspects of outcomes for each strategy. For the other decision-makers, several aspects of outcomes also seemed to be of some relevance, since they sometimes used them for one strategy, yet they did not consider them systematically across all strategies.

Still, another mode of simplification was to restrict the range of strategies considered. In twenty of the thirty-one individual arguments (65 percent) only two alternatives were considered simultaneously while in only eleven cases (35 percent) were three or more considered. Yet another way of reducing information was to omit or reduce uncertainty to quasi certainty. Decision-makers formulated the problem in twenty arguments (65 percent of the cases) in such a way that the outcomes for at least one strategy were considered certain or having a very high or very low probability of occurrence.

With these observations, we wish to conclude the qualitative part of our studies. We proceed with the quantitative studies, where questions such as whether or not the expected decision rules predict the chosen strategy and whether or not the decision-makers and their audiences actually applied the argumentation rules we expected will be investigated in a systematic way based on a sample of arguments of Dutch decision-makers.

Part 2

A Quantitative Study of Arguments

In this part we will demonstrate the universal character of this argumentation (Chapter 8) and discuss the quality of the arguments found (Chapter 9).

Subsequently, we will investigate whether or not there are specific external and internal characteristics that produce different types of argumentations. Chapter 10 will review the literature, specify our selection of explanatory variables, and discuss the methodology used. On the basis of our studies of the literature, Chapter 11 then introduces the propositions that can be tested with respect to the specification and selection of strategies and presents the results. Chapter 12 deals with the detection of conditions under which decision-makers consider different kinds of outcomes, and Chapter 13 investigates conditions that could lead to the use of specific argumentation rules.

Chapter 8

The Decision Rules Are Universal

It has been shown that decision-makers do not specify the argumentation rules that must lead to their choices. It seems (see, e.g., Chapter 6) that they assumed these rules were obvious to their audiences. We have suggested that this means it must be possible to discover this "obvious rule" that correctly predicts their choice. Second, we also have to show that this decision rule is indeed obvious to others. Both points require quantitative research. Studies on both points will be reported in this chapter.

First of all, the hypothesis that an obvious rule can be found will be studied, as already suggested, by first determining the class of decision problem on the basis of the problem description. After that, the decision rules of this class will be tested to investigate whether one can predict the suggested strategy. If our hypothesis is correct, the result of this test on a sample of arguments should be nearly perfect. As a side effect of this study, we will also see how frequently the different decision rules are used.

Given that we can predict the choices by applying a number of argumentation rules, the question remains whether the decision-makers and the general population actually applied the argumentation rules that we expect. If people in general are able to recognize the argumentation rule when presented with the information provided by the politicians, this would indicate that the expected rules are generally obvious for human decision-makers and do not have to be mentioned explicitly. The second part of the chapter deals with the test of this hypothesis.

DO THE EXPECTED DECISION RULES PREDICT THE CHOSEN STRATEGY?

In Chapter 2 it was shown that decision rules can be divided into four different classes according to the information concerning the probabilities and utilities they require. For convenience, Table 2.4 is reproduced here (Table 8.1). The table clearly shows that the classification is based on the dichotomy of utilities and probabilities.

Previously, it was shown that what the decision-makers did was to indicate the facts, which we summarized in decision trees and decision matrices. The specification of the facts can be further characterized by two mental steps. First, a decision-maker selects the components that are necessary to formulate the decision problem, that is, the strategies, outcomes, potential aspects of outcomes and the presence or absence of uncertainty. This activity is frequently called "structuring." The second step relates to the "evaluation" of the outcomes and the probabilities.

Having structured the situation and evaluated the probabilities and utilities, the decision-makers completed their arguments by drawing a conclusion. The fact that they do not mention the choice rule can only be explained, in our opinion, by assuming that the decision-makers considered it to be self-evident. Given the function of the evaluation in the formulation of the argument, we made the following hypothesis: The information on utilities and probabilities is a sufficient condition for the use of a specific decision rule to describe the choice.

This hypothesis suggests that we expect to find a practically perfect relationship between the formulation of the decision problem by the decision-maker and the decision rule used. In practice, this means that given the information on utilities and probabilities, where use is made of all the available information, a rule should exist that is sufficiently complex to require this information, and we should then be able to predict the choice of strategy. It is this hypothesis that will be tested next by a quantitative study based on a sample of arguments of Dutch decision-makers.

Table 8.1:
Relationship between Decision Rules and the Precision of the Information about Utilities and Probabilities

	Utilities with intensities	Utilities without intensities
Probabilities with intensities	SEU model MAUT-SEU model I	Risk-Avoidance Rules II
Probabilities without intensities	Minimax Rule MAUT Rules: Dominance Rule Lexicographic Rule Addition-of-Utilities Rule etc. III	Simon's Rule Reversed Simon Rule IV

Research Design

For this study we decided to try to draw a random sample of decisions made by the Dutch government concerning foreign policy during the twentieth century. Before the raw data of the decision cases could be collected, two problems were encountered that had to be resolved.

First, there was the problem that there was no way of knowing the total number of foreign policy decisions between 1900 and 1955—the period for which we were allowed access to documents—because the various state offices did not keep systematic inventories of all the decisions made in their departments. Second, when all available means are used to gather as complete as possible an inventory of decisions, it is still possible that some cases will be omitted, since the records may be incomplete or inappropriate, perhaps not containing arguments relevant to the selection of a strategy.

In order to eliminate these problems as far as possible, the study population of foreign policy decisions between 1900 and 1955 was defined as follows: only those decisions were selected that were described in historical or political studies in such a manner that one could assume documents existed containing the relevant choice arguments. We thus collected the most important decisions for which material was available. With respect to the choice of historico-political studies from which we drew our raw data, we first consulted handbooks for an overview of the existing literature (e.g., Stapel 1943; Smit 1950, 1962; Leurdijk 1978; Voorhoeve 1979; Hommes 1980; Klein and van der Plaat 1981). We then consulted the most recent studies of historical periods, and complementary material was gathered from the diaries and memoirs of officials (e.g., Hirschfeld 1959; Drees 1963; Stikker 1966; Beyen 1968; Smit 1972; Jonkman 1977; De Beus 1978; Manning 1978; Kersten 1981; Van Kleffens 1983; De Jong 1988). In this way we collected 136 decision situations. We defined "decision situation" as a situation in which one or more persons individually formulate advice about choices. Table 8.2 summarizes the number of decision situations in the study population for the time periods under investigation.

Table 8.2:
Description of the Population of Decision Situations in the Given Time Periods

Time period	Number of decision situations
World War I–World War II (1914–1945)	42
Indonesian War of Independence and postwar recovery in the Netherlands (1945–1955)	94
Total	136

The table shows that for the period between the beginning of World War I and the end of World War II, relatively few decision situations (42) were available. This was partly due to the fact that some archives were no longer intact and some documents relating to these decision situations had disappeared. But it was also partly caused by the practice of several government agencies, such as the Council of Ministers, not to make verbatim minutes of the arguments during this time. For this period we intended to study all the available material, but an inspection of the documents showed that for 33 situations the material was incomplete, leaving only 9 situations to study. The 94 decision situations after World War II consisted on average of 4.3 individual arguments, which means that the text of approximately 404 individual pieces of advice would have to be analyzed. Since this task would have been too time-consuming and too costly for the available research funds, a random sample without replacement of 50 decision situations was drawn from the population of 94.

Table 8.3 summarizes the number of decision situations studied for each time period, the number of individual pieces of advice for each situation, and the mode of selection. The table shows that for the period World War I–World War II, all available situations are included. For the later period, our random sample without replacement left us with 50 situations containing 178 individual argumentations. The selection of arguments in the period before the Second World War was not very good, but we decided to keep these cases in the study because the study of the arguments could indicate whether or not the same argumentation rules were used in that period as in the later period.

In the first period, two decision situations related to World War I. One situ-

Table 8.3:
Description of the Decision Situations Studied

Time period	Number of decision situations	Number of individual pieces of advice	Mode of selection
World War I– World War II (1914–1945)	9	53	All complete documents
Indonesian War of Independence and postwar recovery in the Netherlands (1945–1955)	50	178	Random sample without replacement
Total	59	231	

ation concerned the maintenance of Dutch neutrality during the impending invasion of neutral Belgium by the German Reich. The other situation related to maintenance of the Dutch armed forces in 1916. Although the Netherlands managed to stay neutral, it had a relatively large armed force at the ready for any belligerent transgressions of its borders. Other situations studied in this period concerned changes in trade treaties with Britain in Indonesia and the Netherlands' maintenance of the gold standard in the interwar period when other European countries were giving it up.

Another five decision situations related to World War II. They referred to quite diverse matters and were made by advisers to or members of the government in exile in London. These decisions concerned the negotiation of a peace treaty with the German Reich, transferring the seat of government to Indonesia, maintaining the status quo in the Far East, restoring diplomatic relations with the Soviet Union, and lending gold stocks to the British for their war effort. With respect to the War of Independence in Indonesia (1945–1949), the decision situations analyzed concerned the two military interventions by the Netherlands and the two interventions by the United Nations in response to Dutch military efforts.

The remaining 46 decision situations studied concerned postwar recovery in the Netherlands (1945–1955). They related to a variety of subjects, such as claiming war reparations from Germany, extending trade relations with the Soviet Union and Italy, taking part in the negotiations that created the Benelux and the European Economic Community (EEC), taking part in negotiations to set up defense organizations such as the Western European Union and NATO, granting development aid to Third World countries, participating in weapons embargoes of Third World countries, ratifying the peace treaty with Japan, recognizing governments in Third World countries, and so on. In matters concerning the EEC and NATO, it should be mentioned that only a few documents were available, because the majority of documents were still classified.

The data can also be described in terms of the kinds of documents. Of the 231 individual pieces of advice studied, 61 were individual arguments from meetings of the Council of Ministers. They pertained to 49 sets of minutes of the Council of Ministers. Another 55 pieces of advice consisted of notes to the Council of Ministers authored by ministers or high officials. We also analyzed 44 interdepartmental pieces of advice, where officials from different government agencies exchanged points of view. The 38 telegrams we studied came largely from governors of Indonesia and diplomats. Finally, 33 pieces of advice consisted of letters. Diplomats frequently used this form of communication with the minister of foreign affairs and vice versa.

In conclusion, it can be said that the sample of arguments for the time period after World War II is representative of the population of interest. The data collection for the earlier period is incomplete because of the lack of documents, and it can therefore be used only to test whether or not the argumentation of this earlier period differs from the later instances.

Results

Having described the variety of topics and sources used for this study, we will now look at the results. Table 8.4 indicates the frequency with which the different descriptions of the decision problems occurred.

The table shows that the decision-makers tried to avoid complicated descriptions that use intensity statements of utilities and probabilities at the same time (Class I models); this class occurred only three times. Descriptions using intensity statements of probabilities (Class II models) occurred more frequently than descriptions using intensities of utilities (Class III models). Descriptions that did not use intensities at all occurred most frequently (Class IV models).

We hypothesized that there would be a practically perfect relationship between the formulation of the decision problems by the decision-maker and the decision rule used. Table 8.5 shows that the decision rules that used all the information available could almost always predict the choice. Only in 12 of the 231 cases was no decision rule found in the appropriate class that could describe the choice. Our hypothesis is thus confirmed, and it seems that in general the expected decision rules could very well predict the decision-maker's suggested choice.

The cases where no fitting argumentation rule could be found in the appropriate class need some further explanation. Table 8.6 displays an example. The decision problem in Table 8.6 is formulated with utilities with intensities and probabilities without intensities, and two aspects are considered systematically across the strategies. The models of Class III (Table 8.1) are appropriate to test. But neither of these rules (Dominance, Lexicographic, or Addition-of-Utilities Rules) can produce the choice of S_1. It is clear that the decision-maker should have mentioned explicitly some additional information. For instance, if he had rank-ordered the aspects according to their importance and the second aspect had been the most important one, then the Lexicographic Rule could have produced his choice. Or if he had given a total evaluation of O_{11} by stating that it was better than O_{21} the Addition-of-Utilites Rule could have produced his choice.

Table 8.4:
The Frequency of the Different Descriptions of Decision Problems
Classified by Information on Probabilities and Utilities

	Utilities with intensities	Utilities without intensities
Probabilities with intensities	3	70
Probabilities without intensities	49	109

Table 8.5:

Prediction of Fitting Argumentation Rules on the Basis of the Measurement Level of the Information

Information about utilities and probabilities	Classes of argumentation rules	Correct prediction of the argumentation rule	No fitting argumentation rule available	Total
Probabilities with intensities and utilities with intensities	I SEU model	2	1	3
Probabilities with intensities and utilities without intensities	II Risk-Avoidance Rules	68	2	70
Probabilities without intensities and utilities with intensities	III Dominance, Lexicographic, Addition-of-Utilities Rules	46	3	49
Probabilities and utilities without intensities	IV Simon, Reversed Simon Rules	103	6	109
Total		219	12	231

But since this piece of information was not mentioned in the argumentation, no fitting decision rule could be found in the appropriate class. Thus the cases where no fitting rule could be found lacked some necessary additional information.

Now that we have found that our approach seems to be very capable of detecting decision rules that predict the suggested choice of the decision-maker, we are able to focus on the argumentation employed by politicians. The seven argumentation rules were able to describe almost perfectly the 231 choices of politicians. However, these arguments were based on severe reductions of information, which occurred during the structuring and the evaluation.

One of these simplifications, already encountered in the case studies (Chapters 4 through 7) concerned the reduction of complex value problems to simple value problems. This was managed by unsystematically comparing utilities of diverse single dimensions or by indicating holistic utilities to outcomes relating to various different dimensions instead of the systematic comparison of each of the utilities of the relevant aspects. Another simplification

Table 8.6:
Example of an Argument for Which No Fitting Decision Rule Could Be Detected

Strategies	Outcomes	
	O_{11}	O_{21}
	a_{111}: Serious national problems	a_{211}: No serious national problems
	a_{112}: No chaos in Indonesia	a_{212}: Enormous chaos in Indonesia
S_1*: Ask the Security Council to send troops to Indonesia	$U(a_{111})$=- $U(a_{112})$=+ p=certain	
S_2: Do nothing		$U(a_{211})$=+ $U(a_{212})$=- p=certain

Source: Official of foreign affairs, Feb. 1948, Memo, Archives of the Ministry of Foreign Affairs, record no. GS 999.224, VN vol. 12.

Symbols: S_i strategy i. S_i* the chosen strategy. O_{ij} outcome j under strategy i. A_{ijm} aspect m under outcome j and under srategy i. $U(a_{ijm})$ utility of aspect m under outcome j and stragey i. P probability of O_{ij}.

encountered in Chapters 4, 5, 6 and 7 concerned the omission of uncertainty or the reduction of uncertainty to quasi certainty by indicating extremely high chances and/or extremely low chances and treating them as quasi certain or zero.

Given these simplifications, it can be assumed that the choices based on this reduced information are in principle less than optimal. In Chapter 9 these reductions of information, which can also occur in combination, will be examined in detail and we will investigate to what extent these choices are in agreement with the Dominance Principle as a normative criterion of correct choices. We will now investigate whether the decision-makers and the general population actually recognized the rules that have been identified.

ARE THE RULES OBVIOUS TO THE GENERAL POPULATION?

In order to investigate whether the expected argumentation rules are also recognized by people in general, a new study was carried out. Since politicians could not be asked about the argumentation rules—most of the original decision-makers were now dead, and politicians in office do not normally cooperate with such studies—some of the problem structures of arguments indicated by politicians for specific choices were presented to a sample of the Dutch population.

The questions of interest were: first, do people in general arrive at the same choice of strategies as the politicians, given the same description of the problem? If the majority of subjects chooses the same strategies as the politicians, this indicates that they understand the politicians' problem structure and that they are able to draw the same inferences from the given data regarding which strategy to choose. Second, do people in general recognize the expected argumentation rule when they are presented with the same description of the problem as provided by the politicians? If the majority of subjects explain in their own words their choice relating to a specific decision problem in terms of the argumentation rule we had expected according to our approach, this would indicate that the rules we derived are generally understood by human decision-makers.

In the following sections, the research design is presented and then the decision problems are described. Subsequently, the data collection and the coding of the verbal protocols are explained, and in the last section the results are presented.

Research Design

Thirteen decision problems were selected from our foreign policy data collection. The number of examples from each class of decision rules was based on their frequency of occurrence in our data set. The assignment of the number of decision problems relating to each rule was based on structural characteristics of the decision problems. For some rules, several slightly differing structures were selected within the subset of data relating to a specific argumentation rule. This was done in order to test whether subjects recognized these structures as similar. From Class IV, Simon's and the Reversed Simon Rules, six cases were selected; from Class II, the Risk-Avoidance Rules, five decision problems were selected; and from Class III, the MAUT models, only two cases were taken. The Class I rules, SEU and MAUT-SEU Rules, were excluded from the experiment because of their infrequent occurrence. Within each class several different examples were chosen; these will be discussed with the results.

The next step was to choose the form for presentation of the problems to the subjects. In think-aloud experiments (e.g., Huber 1982; Svenson 1989; Ericsson and Simon 1984), abstract and concrete presentations were used. Based on the results of a pilot study in which we explored both modalities, it was discovered that when presented with concrete problems, subjects frequently preferred to discuss political details or speak in terms of norms rather than explain their choice in terms of the decision-making concepts, that were the basis for detecting the argumentation rule they used. It seemed that their attitude toward the political problem influenced the way they explained their choice. For example, in the abstract they agreed with an argument for starting military action in Indonesia (100 percent), but in concrete form with exactly the same problem description, they did not make this choice. Given the fact that with concrete decision problems subjects behaved differently, we will not discuss concrete problem specifications any further. For more details we can refer to Gallhofer, Saris and Schellekens (1988). This means that we had to make a translation from a concrete to an abstract decision problem.

Description of the decision problems

The first problem to be solved was the transformation of concrete forms into abstract ones without losing the essential characteristics of the problem. An example (Table 8.7) illustrates the procedure followed. Table 8.7 shows a decision problem with two strategies; Strategy 1 leads with certainty to two outcomes, and strategy 2 leads to four outcomes: two outcomes are likely to occur, and the two others have only a small chance of occurrence. The utilities of the outcomes are indicated only in terms of "good" and "bad," and the probabilities indicate intensity statements. The decision-maker chose the second strategy, leading probably to a positive outcome. In our approach a version of the Risk-Avoidance Rules was expected to account for the choice.

In order to transform this decision problem into abstract form, we first indicated the strategies by a number and assigned capital letters to outcomes. The various outcomes were labeled with different letters even if they related to the same aspect or dimension. In order to reduce further the complexity of the representations, outcomes of a strategy were combined if the utilities and probabilities were the same. This was done three times with the outcomes in Table 8.7. For strategy 1, outcomes A and B became A; for strategy 2, outcomes C and D became B, and E and F became C.

With respect to the sequence of presentation of strategies, the presentation of the decision-maker was followed. In our data, decision-makers most frequently presented the rejected strategy or strategies first, and then the chosen one. The abstract form of the decision problem reads as follows:

Strategy 1 leads with certainty to outcome A. Outcome A is negative.

Strategy 2 probably leads to outcome B. Outcome B is positive.

But there is also a very small probability that outcome C will occur.

Outcome C is negative.

In the same way, all decision problems were translated from concrete to abstract.

Data collection

Instead of conducting a think-aloud experiment, we chose a self administered, computer-assisted interviewing technique, the so-called tele-interview approach (Saris and De Pijper 1986; De Pijper and Saris 1986). The subjects were 59 members of households based on a random sample of the Dutch population: 21 percent were younger than 20, 39 percent were between 20 and 40, 29 percent

Table 8.7:
Concrete Representation of a Decision Problem

Strategies	Outcomes		
	A: No continuation of the negotiations B: No observance of the cease-fire order by the republic	C: Elimination of the republic D: Implementation of the treaty of Linggadjati	E: No elimination of the republic F: No implementation of the treaty of Linggadjati
Strategy 1			
Conclude military action and nego-tiate with the help of the United States	$U(A) = -$ $U(B) = -$ p=certain		
Strategy 2*			
Occupy the seat of the republican government and later accept the help of the United States		$U(C) = +$ $U(D) = +$ p=probable	$U(E) = -$ $U(F) = -$ p=very small

Symbols: U utility of an outcome. P probability of an outcome. * the chosen strategy.

were between 40 and 60, and 11 percent were above 60; 48.6 percent were male and 51.4 percent female; 25 percent had only a low level of education, 47 percent had a medium educational level, and 28 percent had had higher education. These data indicate that the respondents were not typical politicians but people of different education levels and different ages.

The subjects received the information on the decision problem on their computer screens at home and were asked to make a choice. The next question—an open-ended one—required that respondents explain their choice, taking both the rejected strategy or strategies and the one chosen into account. When performing this task, the information on the decision problem could always be recalled to the screen. The choice of this technique to record their thoughts corresponds with the retrospective verbal protocol technique (Ericsson and Simon 1984; Svenson 1989) and was especially appropriate for the second purpose of our study, namely, to see whether subjects explained their choices in terms of the expected argumentation rules. In order to determine the decision rule on the basis of their answers, a coding procedure was required.

Coding the verbal protocols to detect the rule

A coding instrument was developed based on verbal protocols from a pilot study. Since the explanations of the choice were (like think-aloud protocols) not formulated by well-formed sentences and punctuation marks, this instrument had to make use of semantic rather than grammatical units. The text analysis instrument used to derive the politicians' argumentations was not applicable because it focused on the construction of decision trees.

The coding instrument split the argumentation rules into elementary units, such as parts relating to the rejected or chosen strategy or to a comparison of both. Within these units, segments relating to probability and utility statements had to be detected. In addition, the coding instructions specified which units were minimally necessary to detect a specific rule and which elements in addition would give a maximal formulation of a specific argumentation rule. For more detailed information on this instrument, we refer to Appendix C.

Two coders independently coded 767 protocols relating to the 13 decision problems presented to 59 subjects (first experiment). The intercoder reliability between the individual codings was very high (Scott's π: 0.90). Although coder reliability was already reasonably high, in order to solve the differences in opinion between the coders, they compared results, and if they differed they tried to reach agreement by discussion. In general this leads to such improvements that no further corrections are possible (Gallhofer and Saris 1988).

Results

The first question we wanted to answer with this study was whether the subjects from our sample arrived at the same choice as the politicians, given the same description of the decision problem. The results show that when the information was presented in abstract form almost all subjects (99 %) chose the same strategy as the politicians. We therefore concluded that people understood the arguments and that the descriptions of the problems were so clear without a choice rule that nearly everybody would make the same choice.

The final question is whether people used the rules we expected them to use to derive this conclusion. We will answer this question for each class of decision problems separately, but before doing so we have to make a general remark. So far, we have suggested that the decision-maker used the decision rule that was expected on the basis of the classification of the decision problem. Perhaps this is the case, but it is not necessarily so. A decision-maker can also use a rule that requires less information in order to determine the choice. We have, however, hypothesized that the person who formulates an argument does not give the information about the intensity of probabilities and utilities for nothing. We believed that he would expect this information to help convince the audience. Nevertheless, the audience can say that it is already convinced with a weaker decision rule, that is, a rule that requires less information.

Given this possibility, we will indicate for each abstract decision problem what kind of weaker decision rule could also have been chosen to predict correctly the chosen strategy. After that, we will present the results with respect to the rules that were suggested by the respondents in our experiment.

Class II decision rules

Five decision problems relating to the Risk-Avoidance Rules were presented to the respondents in abstract form. We selected five slightly different problem structures for which we expected Risk-Avoidance Rules to be used, based on the use of all the information indicated by the decision-makers. The abstract forms of the problem structures are presented below.

1. Strategy 1 leads to outcome A. A is negative.
   Strategy 2 probably leads to outcome B. B is positive. However, there is also a small chance that A will occur.

2. Strategy 1 leads to outcome A. A is negative.
   Strategy 2 probably leads to outcomes B and C. B is positive and C is acceptable.

3. Strategy 1 leads to outcome A. A is negative.
   Strategy 2 probably leads to outcome B. B is positive. However, there is a small chance that C will occur. C is negative.

4. Strategy 1 probably leads to outcome A. A is positive. There is also a small chance that B will occur. B is negative.
   Strategy 2 probably leads to outcome C. C is negative. There is also a small chance that D will occur. D is positive.

5. Strategy 1 probably leads to outcome A. A is negative. There is also a small chance that B will occur. B is positive.
   Strategy 2 leads with certainty to outcome C. C is negative.
   Strategy 3 leads with certainty to outcome D. D is positive.

In the first three decision situations, the decision problems are very similar in the sense that one strategy will lead with certainty to a negative outcome, the political decision-maker chose strategy 2, and we expected this decision to be based on the Negative Risk-Avoidance Rule. In the fourth decision situation, strategy 1 is chosen and we expected in this case an argument based on the Positive Risk-Avoidance Rule. In the fifth case, we also expected the Positive Risk-Avoidance Rule to account for the choice, but it should be clear that the situation is much simpler in the last case since there is one strategy that leads with certainty to a positive result. Since it is conceivable that respondents may produce other argumentation rules based on the presentation of this problem, it seems useful to determine whether other rules that are correct exist.

For the first three presentations the Reversed Simon Rule is also correct, since only one strategy leads possibly to positive outcomes. We did not predict this rule here, because this rule does not make use of all relevant information (i.e., intensity statements of probabilities), although this information is not necessary to make the choice. Another correct rule for the first and second decision problems would be what we call the Dominance Principle. Subjects would have to state that strategy 2 is better because of the positive outcome B, while the negative outcomes of the two strategies are the same and therefore equally negative. Therefore, even the SEU model would also be correct for the first and second decision problems. Simon's Rule is correct only for the fifth problem, because in this case alone is there one strategy that leads to positive outcomes only. Here too, probability statements with intensities are not necessary to make a choice, but since the politicians indicated them, we expected the Risk-Avoidance Rule. Only for the fourth case could no alternative correct model be found. In Table 8.8 the results of the study are summarized for this class of rules.

The Negative Risk-Avoidance Rule was recognized by only 51 percent of the subjects in examples 1, 2, and 3. This result falls somewhat short of our expectations. The main reason is that subjects did not always make use of probabilities with intensities as presented in the information; they often reduced them to "possible," which is also sufficient to solve these problems. Thus the Reversed Simon Rule was very frequently used as an alternative correct rule. Furthermore, the formulation of a Dominance Rule occurred frequently and, as mentioned, a SEU-type Rule was even used. Given the use of a large variety of less expected but correct rules, there is little room for the use of incorrect rules. Only in 11 percent of the cases was an incorrect rule suggested by the respondents.

The Positive Risk-Avoidance Rule was recognized by 60 percent of the subjects in example 4, while 40 percent suggested a wrong rule. Among the wrong rules, Simon's Rule and the Dominance Principle were frequently used. The subjects who used Simon's Rule had treated the high probability of the positive

Table 8.8:
Relationship between Expected Argumentation Rules and the Rules Used by Subjects for Risk-Avoidance Rules

	Rules used by subjects					
Expected rules	Same as expected		Alternative correct rule		Wrong rule		N
	%	abs.	%	abs.	%	abs.	abs.
Example 1, 2, 3	51	90	38	67	11	20	177[*]
Example 4	60	35	—	—	40	24	59
Example 5	10	6	86	51	4	2	59

[*] The expected rules are grouped according to the seven problem structures the subjects considered fundamentally different. Depending on the number of structures grouped together, n varies. Fifty-nine respondents took part in the experiments.

outcome as certain, which Tversky and Kahnemann (1986) call a "pseudo-certainty" effect. When using the Dominance Principle, they may have weighted the positive outcome by the probability without being explicit about it.

The Positive Risk-Avoidance Rule in decision problem 5 was only recognized by 10 percent of the subjects. However, the percentage of correct rules produced by the subjects was a considerable 86 percent. For this structure, 52 percent of the correct rules consisted of Simon's Rule, which means that subjects resolved the problem without using the probabilities with intensities indicated by the political decision-makers, and this is adequate to arrive at the proper choice. This last result is analogous to the results of alternative correct rules obtained for the Negative Risk-Avoidance Rule, which was also sufficient to resolve the problem structures without probabilities with intensities.

The overall picture seems to be that our respondents in the main are able to recognize the rule we expected, but if they have to make a choice between a stronger and a weaker rule that can produce the same choice, they often prefer the weaker rule. It is, however, not clear when this is done and by whom. For example, the reason people in the first three examples very frequently chose a Risk-Avoidance Rule and people in the last example chose mostly Simon's Rule remains unclear.

Class III decision rules

Two decision problems in class III were presented to the respondents. The abstract form for which we expected the Dominance Rule to apply is as follows:

Strategy 1 and strategy 2 both lead to outcome A. Outcome A is negative.

Strategy 1 also leads to outcome B. Outcome B is very negative.

Strategy 2 also leads to outcome C. Outcome C is less negative than outcome B.

Based on this information (utilities with intensity statements, probabilities without intensity statements but indicated as certain), we predicted a Dominance Rule, which corresponded with the choice of strategy 2 by the political decision-maker.

Given this problem structure, the SEU model could be applied, but in a very trivial way, since both probabilities can be considered as one. Respondents would then have to indicate that they had combined values with probabilities. Simon's Rule, the Reversed Simon Rule, and the Risk-Avoidance Rules are not appropriate. The Lexicographic Rule is also incorrect, because no importance of outcomes is mentioned.

The second example from this class was an example where we expected the Lexicographic Rule to apply. This problem has been formulated in the following way:

Strategy 1 leads to outcomes A and B. A is positive, B is negative.

Strategy 2 leads to outcomes C and D. C is positive, D is negative.

A and D are the most important outcomes in this situation.

Table 8.9:
Relationship between Expected Argumentation Rules and the Rules Used by Subjects for Class III Decision Problems

Expected rules	Rules used by subjects						N
	Same as expected		Alternative correct rule		Wrong rule		
	%	abs.	%	abs.	%	abs.	abs.
Dominance Rule	90	53	—	—	10	6	59
Lexicographic Rule	61	36	—	—	39	23	59

Because the importance of the outcomes is indicated, we predicted the Lexicographic Rule, which leads to the choice of strategy 1. No other rules are appropriate here; the Lexicographic Rule does not accord with the SEU model, nor can the Dominance Principle or the other rules mentioned in this study handle importance criteria.

As Table 8.9 shows, subjects recognized the Dominance Rule most; 90 percent of them used the expected rule. They did not use an alternative correct rule in this case. With regard to the wrong rules, some used a Reversed Simon Rule, which means that they simplified the utilities. They used the Risk-Avoidance Rules to a lesser extent, which implies that they transformed both utilities and probabilities. In some cases their explanations were unclassifiable. The Lexicographic Rule was recognized by 61 percent of the subjects. Since there were no other correct rules, 39 percent of the subjects used inappropriate rules. Among these rules, the transformation of the information into a Dominance structure was very common. Otherwise, the problem was mostly solved by the subjects' own heuristics.

Class IV decision rules
One abstract decision problem relating to Simon 's Rule was presented:

Strategy 1 leads certainly to outcome A. A is negative.

Strategy 2 leads possibly to outcome A or B. A is negative and B is positive.

Strategy 3 leads possibly to outcome B or C. B and C are both positive.

Simon's rule predicts the choice of strategy 3. A correct rule would also be the Dominance Principle, since the outcomes of strategy 3 are better than the outcomes of the other alternatives. The SEU model would also be correct, because all outcomes of strategy 3 are better than the outcomes of the other strategies. Under the assumption that different outcomes can occur, the chance of a better outcome would be higher with strategy 3 than with the others. The Risk-Avoidance Rule is also correct, because there is more chance of positive outcomes with strategy 3 than with the others. The Reversed Simon Rule is of course not correct, because, although we can in this way eliminate strategy 1, this rule does not lead to the choice of a single strategy in this case.

Two decision problems of the Reserved Simon type were presented to the respondents:

1. Strategy 1 leads to outcome A. Outcome A is negative.
   Strategy 2 possibly leads to outcome A or B. B is positive.

2. Strategy 1 leads to outcome A. A is negative.
   Strategy 2 possibly leads to outcome B. B is negative.
   Strategy 3 possibly leads to outcome C or D. C is positive, D is negative.

In the first problem, the political decision-maker chose strategy 2, and in the second, he chose strategy 3. Since values and probabilities were without intensities and only one strategy possibly led to a positive outcome, the Reversed Simon Rule was expected to predict the choice. The Risk-Avoidance Rule would be correct, since, assuming that different outcomes could occur, there is more chance of a positive outcome if there is some chance than if there is no chance at all. Our approach did not predict this rule because the original decision-maker did not indicate probabilities with intensities. The Dominance Principle and the SEU model are correct only for the first presentation, where it is known that the negative outcomes are the same for both alternatives. Simon's Rule is not correct because of the absence of a strategy that leads to positive outcomes only.

Finally, three decision problems relating to both Simon's and the Reversed Simon Rules were presented. They had the following forms:

1. Strategy 1 leads to outcome A. A is negative.
   Strategy 2 leads to outcome B. B is positive.

2 and 3:
   Strategy 1 leads to outcome A. A is positive.
   Strategy 2 possibly leads to outcome B or C. B is negative and C is neutral.

The only difference between these two problems is the sequence of presentation of the alternatives. The utilities and probabilities of these problem structures are all without intensities. In the first example, the political decision-maker chose strategy 2 and in the second example, strategy 1. We expected in both cases that Simon's Rule and the Reversed Simon Rule would be able to predict the choice, since when all the available information is used, the choice can be derived by formulating that one either selects the first strategy to lead only to positive outcomes or one rejects all strategies that lead to negative outcomes while there remains an available strategy offering a positive outcome. Unexpectedly, the Dominance Principle is also correct, because a positive outcome is always better than a negative or a neutral one. The SEU model would also be

Table 8.10:
Relationship between Expected Argumentation Rules and the Rules Used by Subjects for Class IV Decision Rules

Expected rules	Rules used by subjects						
	Same as expected		Alternative correct rule		Wrong rule		N
	%	abs.	%	abs.	%	abs.	abs.
Simon's Rule	46	27	46	27	8	5	59
Reversed Simon Rule 1, 2	63	74	28	33	9	11	118*
Simon + Reversed Simon Rules 1, 2 , 3	70	124	25	45	5	8	177*

* The expected rules are grouped according to the seven problem structures the subjects considered fundamentally different. Depending on the number of structures grouped together, n varies. Fifty-nine respondents took part in the experiments.

correct if a respondent indicated that in some way he had combined values and probabilities of 1 (first example) or that there were more possibilities and the chance of a better outcome would be higher with strategy 1 (examples 2 and 3). The Risk-Avoidance Rule would also be correct, because the chances of obtaining positive outcomes differ for the strategies (namely, certain against certainly not), although this kind of reasoning seems very unlikely.

Not very surprisingly, the examples in which Simon's and the Reversed Simon Rules can predict the choice were those most recognized by the subjects (70 percent; see Table 8.10). The most frequently used alternative correct rule was the Dominance Principle, but Risk-Avoidance and SEU were also used. There are only very few incorrect rules suggested. The wrong rules consisted mainly of unclassifiable statements.

The Simon structure was recognized only by 46 percent of the respondents, which is rather surprising, since it is a very clear structure. A large part of the alternative correct rules were of the Reversed Simon type, which means that subjects did not explicitly mention that the chosen strategy led only to a positive outcome. Among the other correct rules were the Risk-Avoidance Rule and the Dominance Principle. Indeed, a larger range of different rules is possible in this case and was used, with only very few incorrect rules specified.

Finally, for the example for which we expected the Reversed Simon Rule to predict the choice, this rule was indeed suggested by the majority of the respondents (63 percent). As an alternative rule the Dominance Principle was frequently suggested, and the same was true for the Risk-Avoidance Rules. In this case also, the wrong rules were minimal.

Explanation of Differences between Expected Choice Rules and Those Used

Since for the abstract presentations the relationship between the predicted choice rules and the rules used by our subjects was not perfect, we tried to explain the differences between the choice rules of the subjects and those predicted in terms of background variables of the subjects. These variables were age, education, sex, and interest in the topic. It turned out that only education had an effect.

The result of a one-way analysis of variance for the thirteen abstract decision problems showed that the average number of identical rules of subjects with a lower education level (5.0) was significantly different ($\alpha = .01$) from subjects with a medium (8.25) or higher education level (8.07). There was, however, no significant difference between subjects with a medium and higher education. Subjects with a lower education, therefore, use fewer rules identical to those expected. As a result, we investigated the question of whether or not people with a lower education level have a preference for a specific decision heuristic in order to cope with a task. Analysis of variance showed that the average use of the Dominance Principle by subjects with a low education level (4.25) was significantly different ($\alpha = .01$) from that of subjects with a medium education level (2.25) and subjects with a high education level (1.85). There was again no significant difference between subjects with medium and higher education. This means that Dominance is a very fundamental structure, especially to the less educated subjects, and they are more inclined to create it than other subjects, by restructuring the information presented.

CONCLUSIONS

In this chapter it has been demonstrated that, given the available information on the decision problem, we could almost always predict a fitting decision rule in the appropriate class that produced the politicians' choice. Since the politicians never explicitly mentioned the argumentation rules used, experiments were carried out to find out whether or not people in general recognize the expected argumentation rules. The results of these studies showed that when the decision problems were presented in an abstract form, almost all the subjects chose the same strategy as the politicians. The structures were clear and there was no doubt about the conclusion one should draw, although this conclusion is not necessarily correct in terms of Dominance and the SEU model as standards for optimal choices (see, e.g., the structures of Reversed Simon Rule 2, Risk-Avoidance Rules 3, 4, 5, and the Lexicographic case). In other words, logically compelling choices are recognized as such by people in general.

When subjects were presented with concrete political decision problems, it depended on their attitude toward the political topic whether or not they chose the same strategy as the politicians. Concrete situations are therefore not suitable for research on drawing inferences from given problem structures.

The study also showed that subjects were generally able to distinguish the different problem structures. The results for both abstract and concrete presentations were similar. This implies that most of the problem structures that we detected with our approach were also fundamentally meaningful to the subjects.

Furthermore, in clear situations, the majority of the subjects specified the same rule as the one we expected. But if information was available that was not strictly necessary to derive the correct choice, they often ignored this information and used a simpler rule. This phenomenon could be due to the fact that, unlike the politicians, the study subjects had not generated the information themselves. Therefore it is possible that the subjects in the experiments searched only for the information necessary to make their choice. Furthermore, in the original arguments, the politicians could not be sure that other citizens agreed with them completely, and so to forestall criticism they would bolster their argumentation. Thus the findings of these experiments do validate to a considerable extent the expectation of the choice rules suggested by our approach.

Another form of simplification can be found in the frequent use of the Dominance Principle. We expected a Dominance Rule only once, but subjects frequently transformed the problem structures in such a way that they could arrive at a choice using the Dominance Principle. People with a lower education level used relatively more Dominance than subjects with a higher education. These results support Montgomery's hypothesis (1983) that human beings are in search of a Dominance structure. Given that politicians approximate the more highly educated subjects in our sample, it is reasonable to assume that the politicians would also have recognized the argumentation rules we expected.

Our overall conclusions are that in most situations the majority of subjects explained their choice in terms of the expected rule. If we take into account permissible simplifications, 85 percent of the subjects chose a correct rule out of the seven specified by us. This implies that our approach is a valid way to detect decision rules based on argumentation.

Chapter 9

The Quality of the Arguments*

In the previous chapters we have seen that politicians use arguments based on a set of six decision rules and that the simpler rules, those requiring the least information, are used most frequently. We have also shown that nonpoliticians, when confronted with the same information, agree with the choices of the politicians. This means that the arguments seem clear to the general population, but it does not mean that the arguments are correct. In this chapter we would like to study the quality of the arguments. First we will introduce a correct rule; then we will set out to demonstrate that the decision rules identified in the data are not necessarily correct. Finally, we will study the question of how far the arguments used satisfy the principles of proper argumentation.

CORRECT AND INCORRECT DECISION ARGUMENTS

In order to say that an argument is correct or incorrect, one has to have a criterion. A quite commonly accepted criterion would be that one should choose a strategy that leads to a better result than any other strategy, but how we determine what is better depends on the situation. If there is no uncertainty, we have only to compare the utility $U(O_1)$ with $U(O_i)$. If $U(O_1)$ is better for all i then S_1 leads to a better result. If S_1 leads to several consequences, one has to evaluate the sum of all utilities in a similar way.

In the case of uncertainty, the SEU concept can be used, but for practical purposes this concept is too complicated because it requires too much computation. Apart from that, it was shown that probabilities with intensities and utilities with intensities do not occur simultaneously in practice. This means that one does not need such a complex definition.

* An earlier version of this chapter was first published in *Acta Psychologica* 56 (1984): 247–265. Elsevier Science granted us permission to use the tables in this chapter.

Given this situation, we suggest the use of the Dominance Principle as the criterion. This principle posits that one should choose the strategy that leads to a result that is at least as good as any other strategy and possibly better. We call this the Dominance Principle because it is not applied to aspects of an outcome but to the outcomes themselves. It will be clear that this principle is not applicable in multiattribute utility problems with uncertainty, but we have mentioned that only very few cases are formulated in this way by political decision-makers. The advantage of this principle is that it can be easily used, in situations both of certainty and of uncertainty. It can easily be verified that in all cases where this principle can be applied, this rule will lead to the same choice as the SEU decision rule but for this principle no calculations are necessary. With this principle in mind, we will now demonstrate that the observed decision rules are correct only under specific conditions.

Example 1, Risk-Avoidance Rules:
Suppose a decision-maker indicates that he chooses the strategy with the lowest probability of a negative outcome. If the utility of the negative outcome of the chosen strategy was very negative and the utility(-ies) of the negative outcome(s) of the rejected strategy(-ies) were less negative, it would be very doubtful whether the lower probability is the proper criterion for the decision. In this case it is not so certain that the result (even the expected utility) of the chosen strategy would be greater than that of the rejected one(s).

It appears, therefore, that the Risk-Avoidance Rules are sound argumentation rules only when the utilities of the outcomes of the various strategies are more or less equal, in which case the choice of the strategy with the highest probability of a positive outcome or the lowest probability of a negative outcome is correct, since it satisfies the Dominance Principle.

Example 2, MAUT Models:
The Dominance and Addition-of-Utilities Rules are correct argumentation rules since they prescribe a choice of the strategy that leads with certainty to outcomes as good as or better than the outcomes of other strategies (which corresponds with the Dominance Principle). The Lexicographic Rule, however, is not necessarily a correct argumentation rule since it prescribes a choice of strategy in which the most important aspect of the outcome has the highest utility, regardless of the utilities of the other aspects of the outcome. It is clear that one can think of a situation where the second aspect of a strategy that is not chosen is preferable to that of the chosen strategy. But if the strategies are comparable on all aspects, the Lexicographic Rule also leads to a correct argument, in the sense of the Dominance Principle.

Example 3, Reversed Simon Rule and Simon's Rule:
The Reversed Simon rule prescribes rejecting all strategies that lead with certainty to negative outcomes and choosing the strategy that offers the possibil-

ity of a positive outcome. This rule only produces a correct choice in the sense of the Dominance Principle if the utilities of the negative outcomes are approximately the same. If the utilities of the negative outcomes of the chosen strategy were more negative than those of the rejected strategies, the expected utility of the chosen strategy might be smaller than that of the rejected ones. Simon's Rule prescribes selection of the strategy that leads only to positive outcomes. Here again the rule can only be necessarily correct in the sense of the Dominance Principle if the positive outcomes of the rejected strategies have approximately the same utilities and are not considerably higher than those of the chosen one.

These examples show that it is not necessarily the case that the rules used and recognized by most people provide a basis for a correct argument. Only if certain restrictions are satisfied can these rules be used in an acceptable argument. We have also shown that the Dominance Principle can suggest which conditions lead with certainty to a correct argument.

RESTRICTIONS AND SPECIFICATIONS

The case studies made it clear that political decision problems can best be characterized as complex value problems with uncertainty, but previous chapters also showed that decision-makers reduced information in order to make problems manageable. This reduction of information can be obtained in two different ways: through restrictions and through specifications.

By "restrictions" we mean simplifications *implicitly* indicated by the structure of the decision tree, relating to the representations of probabilities or utilities of outcomes. An example of a restriction with respect to probabilities is when for several strategies only one outcome (O_{ij}) can occur, given the choice of strategy (S_i), which is indicated in the tree structure by a single branch where $P_{ij}=1$. Restrictions with respect to utilities are frequently indicated by outcomes: e.g., for several strategies the same outcome (O_{i1}) could be specified, which means that $U(O_{i1})=U(O_{j1})$. Sometimes the outcomes relate to the same subject, for instance, defeat or no defeat. When it is claimed that under a specific strategy (S_1) the outcome (O_{11}) involves a defeat and under S_i this consequence will not occur then it can be concluded that $U(O_{11})< U(O_{i1})$.

By "specifications" we mean statements relating to probabilities or utilities that are *explicitly* indicated by the decision-maker; for example, that the probability of a positive outcome is higher under a specific strategy (S_1) than under the other(s) ($P_{1+} > P_{i+}$, $i \neq 1$) or that the utilities of the outcomes of one strategy are superior to the utilities of the outcomes of the alternative strategies ($U(O_{1j}) > U(O_{ij})$, $i \neq 1$; for all j).

Using the uncertainty and complexity of the utilities as the characteristics for classifying the decision problems, the necessary restrictions and/or specifications will be indicated in order to formulate a correct argument. In this approach we will use what we have called the Dominance Principle as the rule to guarantee a correct argument.

CLASS I: SIMPLE UTILITY PROBLEMS WITHOUT UNCERTAINTY

The restriction introduced into the structuring of the problem representation in the arguments of this class is as follows:

Restriction I: $P_{i1} = 1$ for all S_i

This class of decision problems is quite simple. Using the Dominance Principle, one only needs to specify that $U(O_{11})$ is better than all others in order to be sure that one has to choose S_1. This can be formulated in two different ways:

Specification I.1: $U(O_{11}) > U(O_{i1})$ for all $i \neq 1$
Specification I.2: $U(O_{11}) > 0$ and $U(O_{i1}) < 0$ for all $i \neq 1$

Specification I.1 specifies a rank order of the utilities (utilities with intensities), so the Dominance Rule leads to the conclusion that S_1 should be chosen. Specification I.2 specifies whether the utilities are positive or negative (utilities without intensities), implying that Simon's Rule or the Reversed Simon Rule could be anticipated. In both cases the argumentation rule implied in the argument accords with the Dominance Principle insofar as a strategy is chosen that is better that any other strategy. Table 9.1 summarizes the frequency of occurrence of these two types of arguments. The table shows that specifications in agreement with Simon's Rule or the Reversed Simon Rule are much more frequent than the ordering required in I.1. It should be mentioned, however, that the choice is rather arbitrary, and I.1 is more general. In practice, this argument is used only if all outcomes have positive utilities or if the outcome contains only one aspect that is considered systematically across strategies; otherwise the decision-makers prefer the simpler, second formulation.

CLASS II: SIMPLE UTILITY PROBLEMS WITH UNCERTAINTY

In Class II, the degree of certainty that a particular strategy will lead to a particular outcome may vary. Although there are other possibilities, we found three kinds of arguments in our data: uncertainty exists for only one strategy (Category II.A), for all strategies except one (Category II.B), or for all strategies (Category II.C).

Category II.A: Uncertainty for Only One Strategy

In this category, the following restrictions are present:

Restriction II.A: $P_{i1} = 1$ for all $i \neq 1$

This restriction is often combined with restriction II.A.1:

Restriction II.A.1: $U(O_{i1}) \leq U(O_{11})$ for all $i \neq 1$

Table 9.1:

Frequency of Occurrence of the Arguments in Class I

Class	Restriction	Specification	Rule	Accords with the Dominance Principle	Frequency
I.1	I: $P_{i1} = 1$ for all S_i	I.1: $U(O_{11}) > U(O_{i1})$ for all $i \neq 1$	Dominance	Yes	10
I.2	I: $P_{i1} = 1$ for all S_i	I.2: $U(O_{11}) > 0$ and $U(O_{i1}) < 0$ for all $i \neq 1$	Simon/ Reversed Simon	Yes	30

The latter restriction on the utilities is clear from the description of the decision problem if all strategies lead either to the same outcome as S_1 or a worse outcome than S_1, and where S_1 may also lead to another outcome. If this second outcome for S_1 is specified as being better than $U(O_{i1})$, then it is clear that strategy S_1 should be chosen. The specification found in practice is often the following:

Specification II.1: $U(O_{i1}) < 0$ for all i , but $U(O_{12}) > 0$

Combined with restrictions II.A and II.A.1, this specification provides sufficient information for the choice of S_1 according to the Reversed Simon Rule, because all strategies except S_1 lead with certainty to a negative outcome, while S_1 may lead to a positive outcome (O_{12}). This argument also accords with the Dominance Principle, as can be readily verified.

Sometimes specification II.1 is combined with specification II.2:

Specification II.2: $P_{12} > P_{11}$

This further specification is unnecessary, since one should choose S_1 anyway whenever $P_{12} > 0$. It is possible that the decision-makers indicate these probabilities because they want to reinforce their argument for S_1, stressing that the most attractive outcome (O_{12}) is also the most likely if S_1 is chosen. Given this information, we can use the Risk-Avoidance Rules to describe the choice proposed in the argument, a decision that is also in accordance with the Dominance Principle. It can also occur that restriction II.A.1 is not given in the structuring of the problem. In such cases, this restriction has to be specified explicitly in order to use the same argument. This means that restriction II.A is combined with specification II.3, which is identical to restriction II.A.1:

Specification II.3: $U(O_{i1}) \leq U(O_{11})$ for all $i \neq 1$

Table 9.2:
Frequency of Occurrence of the Arguments in Class II.A

Class	Restriction	Specification	Rule	Accords with the Dominance Principle	Frequency
II.A.1	II.A: $P_{i1} = 1$ for all $i \neq 1$ II.A.1: $U(O_{i1}) \leq U(O_{11})$ for all $i \neq 1$	II.1: $U(O_{i1}) < 0$ for all i but $U(O_{12}) > 0$	Reversed Simon	Yes	22
II.A.2	II.A: $P_{i1} = 1$ for all $i \neq 1$ II.A.1: $U(O_{i1}) \leq U(O_{11})$ for all $i \neq 1$	II.1: $U(O_{i1}) < 0$ for all i but $U(O_{12}) > 0$ II.2: $P_{12} > P_{11}$	Risk-Avoidance	Yes	11
II.A.3	II.A: $P_{i1} = 1$ for all $i \neq 1$	II.1: $U(O_{i1}) < 0$ for all i but $U(O_{12}) > 0$ II.3: $U(O_{i1}) \leq U(O_{11})$ for all $i \neq 1$	Reversed Simon	Yes	4
II.A.4	II.A: $P_{i1} = 1$ for all $i \neq 1$	II.1: $U(O_{i1}) < 0$ for all i but $U(O_{12}) > 0$ II.2: $P_{12} > P_{11}$ II.3: $U(O_{i1}) \leq U(O_{11})$ for all $i \neq 1$	Risk-Avoidance	Yes	5
II.A.5	II.A: $P_{i1} = 1$ for all $i \neq 1$	II.1: $U(O_{i1}) < 0$ for all i but $U(O_{12}) > 0$	Reversed Simon	No	16
II.A.6	II.A: $P_{i1} = 1$ for all $i \neq 1$	II.1: $U(O_{i1}) < 0$ for all i but $U(O_{12}) > 0$ II.2: $P_{12} > P_{11}$	Risk-Avoidance	No	3

If specification II.3 is combined with specification II.1, the Reversed Simon Rule again leads to the choice of S_1, and this decision accords with the Dominance Principle. If specification II.3 is combined with specifications II.1 and II.2, the Risk-Avoidance Rules can explain the choice as before, a choice that also accords with the Dominance Principle.

Furthermore, restriction II.A is sometimes only combined with specification II.1. In this case, the Reversed Simon Rule can also describe the choice of S_1, but it is unclear whether the decision accords with the Dominance Principle, since nothing is known about the relationship between $U(O_{i1})$ and $U(O_{11})$. If specification II.2 is added, the choice can again be explained by the Risk-Avoidance Rule, but the decision is still not necessarily in accordance with the Dominance Principle because nothing is known about the relationship between $U(O_{i1})$ and $U(O_{11})$, which are negative.

In this section we have specified six different ways of presenting arguments. Table 9.2 summarizes the frequency of occurrence of these arguments.

Category II.B: Uncertainty for All Strategies except One

In this category, uncertainty is introduced for all strategies except one. This restriction is formulated in restriction II.B:

Restriction II.B: $P_{i1} < 1$ for all $i \neq 1$, but $P_{11} = 1$

This restriction is often combined with restriction II.B.1:

Restriction II.B.1: $U(O_{11}) \geq U(O_{i1})$ for all $i \neq 1$

These restrictions are not enough, however, to make a correct decision. Sometimes they are combined with specification II.5:

Specification II.5: $U(O_{11}) > 0$ and $U(O_{i2}) < 0$ for all $i \neq 1$

The combination of these restrictions with specification II.5 describes a decision problem where one strategy leads with certainty to an outcome that is at least as good as a particular outcome that might result under any other strategy, while the other outcomes of the other strategies are less favorable. The choice of S_1 obviously accords with Simon's Rule and with the Dominance Principle.

Sometimes specification II.5 is combined with specification II.6 with respect to the probabilities:

Specification II.6: $P_{i2} < P_{11}$, $i \neq 1$

In this case the Risk-Avoidance Rule also leads to the choice of S_1, although this information is not strictly necessary in order to prescribe the choice. Here, the decision-maker probably wanted to strengthen the argument for choosing S_1, stressing the disadvantages of the other strategies in comparison with S_1. In this case, too, the choice proposed is in agreement with the Dominance Principle.

Table 9.3:
Frequency of Occurrence of the Arguments in Class II.B

Class	Restriction	Specification	Rule	Accords with the Dominance Principle	Frequency
II.B.1	II.B: $P_{i1} < 1$ for all $i \neq 1$, but $P_{11} = 1$ II.B.1: $U(O_{11}) \geq U(O_{i1})$ for all $i \neq 1$	II.5: $U(O_{11}) > 0$ and $U(O_{i2}) < 0$ for all $i \neq 1$	Simon	Yes	3
II.B.2	II.B: $P_{i1} < 1$ for all $i \neq 1$, but $P_{11} = 1$ II.B.1: $U(O_{11}) \geq U(O_{i1})$ for all $i \neq 1$	II.5: $U(O_{11}) > 0$ and $U(O_{i2}) < 0$ for all $i \neq 1$ II.6: $P_{i2} < P_{11}$ for all $i \neq 1$	Risk-Avoidance	Yes	3
II.B.3	II.B: $P_{i1} < 1$ for all $i \neq 1$, but $P_{11} = 1$	II.5: $U(O_{11}) > 0$ and $U(O_{i2}) < 0$ for all $i \neq 1$ II.7: $U(O_{11}) \geq U(O_{i1})$ for all $i \neq 1$	Simon/ Reversed Simon	Yes	4
II.B.4	II.B: $P_{i1} < 1$ for all $i \neq 1$, but $P_{11} = 1$	II.5: $U(O_{11}) > 0$ and $U(O_{i2}) < 0$ for all $i \neq 1$ II.6: $P_{i2} < P_{11}$ for all $i \neq 1$ II.7: $U(O_{11}) \geq U(O_{i1})$ for all $i \neq 1$	Risk-Avoidance	Yes	3
II.B.5	II.B: $P_{i1} < 1$ for all $i \neq 1$, but $P_{11} = 1$	II.8: $U(O_{11}) > 0$ while $U(O_{i2}) < 0$ for all i	Simon	No	5
II.B.6	II.B: $P_{i1} < 1$ for all $i \neq 1$, but $P_{11} = 1$	II.6: $P_{i2} < P_{11}$ for all $i \neq 1$ II.8: $U(O_{11}) > 0$ while $U(O_{i2}) < 0$ for all i	Risk-Avoidance	No	4

As before, restriction II.B.1 is not always obvious from the structuring of the problem representation. If this is the case, specification II.7 has to be added, which is identical to restriction II.B.1:

Specification II.7: $U(O_{11}) \geq U(O_{i1})$ for all $i \neq 1$

If specification II.7 is combined with specification II.5, both Simon's Rule and the Reversed Simon Rule lead to S_1; again, this choice is in agreement with the Dominance Principle. If specification II.7 is combined with specifications II.5 and II.6, the Risk-Avoidance Rules can describe the choice; again, this choice accords with the Dominance Principle.

Finally, there is the possibility that specification II.5 is not given, but specification II.8 is given instead:

Specification II.8: $U(O_{11}) > 0$ while $U(O_{i2}) < 0$ for all i

In such cases, Simon's Rule leads to the choice of S_1, but this choice does not necessarily accord with the Dominance Principle since nothing is known about $U(O_{i1})$. Further, the addition of specification II.6 does not bring the choice into accord with the Dominance Principle, but then the Risk-Avoidance Rules can describe the choice. Table 9.3 summarizes the frequency of occurrence of the arguments of category II.B.

Category II.C: Uncertainty for All Strategies

The last category in this class (II.C) is characterized by the fact that no restrictions on the probabilities are introduced. But since the arguments would be too complicated in the absence of restrictions, some restrictions are introduced on the utilities. The first type of restrictions is denoted by II.C.1:

Restriction II.C.1: $U(O_{12}) \geq U(O_{ij})$ for all j and $i \neq 1$

This restriction states that for S_1 outcome O_{12} is at least as good as any other outcome for the other strategies. Sometimes II.C.1 is combined with specification II.5:

Specification II.5: $U(O_{11}) > 0$ and $U(O_{i2}) < 0$ for all $i \neq 1$

In combination with specification II.5, the argument is complete because it states that S_1 is always better than any other strategy. The Reversed Simon Rule leads to the choice of S_1. As an alternative specification, specification II.9 may be used:

Specification II.9: $U(O_{1j}) > 0$ for all j

In this case Simon's Rule leads to the choice of S_1.

A specification with respect to the probabilities can be used to reinforce the

Table 9.4:
Frequency of the Occurrence of the Arguments in Class II.C

Class	Restriction	Specification	Rule	Accords with the Dominance Principle	Frequency
II.C.1	II.C.1: $U(O_{12}) \geq U(O_{ij})$ for all j and all $i \neq 1$	II.5: $U(O_{11}) > 0$ and $U(O_{i2}) < 0$ for all $i \neq 1$	Reversed Simon	Yes	9
II.C.2	II.C.1: $U(O_{12}) \geq U(O_{ij})$ for all j and all $i \neq 1$	II.9: $U(O_{1j}) > 0$ for all j	Simon	Yes	6
II.C.3	II.C.1: $U(O_{12}) \geq U(O_{ij})$ for all j and all $i \neq 1$	II.5: $U(O_{11}) > 0$ and $U(O_{i2}) < 0$ for all $i \neq 1$ II.9: $U(O_{1j}) > 0$ for all j II.10: $P_{1+} > P_{i+}$ for all $i \neq 1$	Risk-Avoidance	Yes	3
II.C.4	II.C.2: $U(O_{1+}) \geq U(O_{i+})$ for all $i \neq 1$ II.C.3: $U(O_{1-}) \approx U(O_{i-})$ for all $i \neq 1$	II.10: $P_{1+} > P_{i+}$ for all $i \neq 1$	Risk-Avoidance	Yes	18
II.C.5	None	II.10: $P_{1+} > P_{i+}$ for all $i \neq 1$	Risk-Avoidance	No	18
II.C.6	None	II.9: $U(O_{1j}) > 0$ for all j	Simon	No	4

argument in favor of S_1 if it is indicated that a positive outcome is much more likely to result from the choice of S_1 than from the choice derived from the other strategy or strategies:

Specification II.10: $P_{1+} > P_{i+}$, for all i and $i \neq 1$

In this case the Risk-Avoidance Rules lead to the choice of S_1. In all three cases, the choice is in agreement with the Dominance Principle if $P_{11} > 0$, as can easily be verified.

Instead of restriction II.C.1, restrictions II.C.2 and II.C.3 are sometimes used:

Restriction II.C.2: $U(O_{1+}) \geq U(O_{i+})$ for all $i \neq 1$
Restriction II.C.3: $U(O_{1-}) \approx U(O_{i-})$ for all $i \neq 1$

If these two restrictions are combined with specification II.10, the Risk-Avoidance Rule leads to the choice of S_1, and this choice is in accordance with the Dominance Principle, as can also be verified. In addition, there are situations where no restriction can be derived from the structuring of the problem representation but where specifications II.10 or II.9 are given. In such situations the Risk-Avoidance Rule or Simon's Rule leads to the choice of S_1. However, it is not clear whether this choice accords with the Dominance Principle. Table 9.4 summarizes the frequency of occurrence of the different arguments of category II.C.

CLASS III: COMPLEX UTILITY PROBLEMS WITHOUT UNCERTAINTY

In this class of problem representations, restriction III is always made, indicating that only one outcome results from the choice of any particular strategy S_i:

Restriction III: $P_{i1} = 1$ for all i

Furthermore, restriction III.1 is often made as follows:

Restriction III.1: $U(a_{11m}) \geq (Ua_{i1m})$ for all m and all $i \neq 1$

where $U(a_{ijm})$ indicates the utility of the mth aspect of the jth outcome of strategy i.

As these restrictions together specify a structure that is in accord with a Dominance situation, it is not surprising that the rule that can predict the choice also accords with the Dominance Principle.

In cases where restriction III.1 is not made, the choice can be in accordance with the Dominance Principle only if it is indicated that the sum of the part-worths of S_1 over all attributes is larger than the sum of the part-worths of all the other strategies, which is indicated by specification III.1:

Specification III.1: $\sum_{m} U(a_{11m}) > \sum_{m} U(a_{i1m})$ for all $i \neq 1$

Thus, if specification III.1 is made, an Additive Multi-Attribute Utility Rule can explain the choice, and assuming that attributes are value-wise independent, this is again in accordance with the Dominance Principle.

On the other hand, two other specifications are sometimes made:

Specification III.2: attribute 1 is the most important one
Specification III.3: $U(a_{111}) > U(a_{i11})$ for all $i \neq 1$

Table 9.5:
Frequency of Occurrence of the Arguments in Class III

Class	Restriction	Specification	Rule	Accords with the Dominance Principle	Frequency
III.1	III: $P_{i1} = 1$ for all i III.1: $U(a_{11m}) \geq U(a_{i1m})$ for all m and all $i \neq 1$	None	Dominance	Yes	13
III.2	III: $P_{i1} = 1$ for all i	III.1: $\sum_m U(a_{11m}) > \sum_m U(a_{i1m})$ for all $i \neq 1$	Addition-of-Utilities	Yes	13
III.3	III: $P_{i1} = 1$ for all i	III.2: attribute 1 is the most important one III.3: $U(a_{111}) > U(a_{i11})$ for all $i \neq 1$	Lexicographic	No	4

In this case, use of the Lexicographic Rule is implied by the simple statement that one attribute is the most important one. The choice specified by this rule is not necessarily in accordance with the Dominance Principle since the other attributes could have very negative values. Table 9.5 summarizes the frequency of occurrence of the different arguments in Class III.

CLASS IV: COMPLEX UTILITY PROBLEMS WITH UNCERTAINTY

In this class no restrictions are made with respect to probabilities, but occasionally restrictions regarding utilities are specified through the way the problem is structured.

Restriction IV.1: $U(a_{11m}) > U(a_{12m})$ for all m, and
$U(a_{12m}) > U(a_{ijm})$ for all j, m and $i \neq 1$

This restriction clearly identifies one dominant strategy, S_1. This means that the

Table 9.6:

Frequency of the Occurrence of Arguments in Class IV

Class	Restriction	Specification	Rule	Accords with the Dominance Principle	Frequency
IV.1	IV.1: $U(a_{11m}) > U(a_{12m})$ for all m and $U(a_{12m}) > U(a_{ijm})$ for all j, m and $i \neq 1$	none	Dominance	Yes	4
IV.2	IV.1: $U(a_{11m}) > U(a_{12m})$ for all m and $U(a_{12m}) > U(a_{ijm})$ for all j, m and $i \neq 1$	IV.1: $P_{11} > P_{i1}$ for all $i \neq 1$ where O_{i1} is the most favorable outcome of strategy S_i for all $i \neq 1$	SEU	Yes	2
IV.3	None	IV.2: $P_{11} > P_{i1}$ for all $i \neq 1$ IV.3: attribute 1 is the most important one IV.4: $U(a_{111}) > U(a_{i11})$ for all $i \neq 1$	Lexicographic	No	2

Dominance Rule can describe the choice and that this decision is of course in accordance with the Dominance Principle.

A specification that is sometimes given is IV.1:

Specification IV.1: $P_{11} > P_{i1}$ for all $i \neq 1$

where O_{i1} is the most favorable outcome of strategy S_i for all $i \neq 1$

If specification IV.1 is combined with restriction IV.1, then the decision to choose S_1 can be prescribed on the basis of the full SEU model , since intensities of both utilities and probabilities are given. If no restrictions are made, specification IV.2 is given with regard to probabilities of outcomes under alternative strategies. Two other specifications (IV.3, IV.4) are also made for the utilities:

Specification IV.2: $P_{11} > P_{i1}$ for all $i \neq 1$

Specification IV.3: attribute 1 is the most important one

Specification IV.4: $U(a_{111}) > U(a_{i11})$ for all $i \neq 1$

This complex utility problem is not easily solved. In this case, the choice rule proposed (such as the Lexicographic Rule) will not necessarily prescribe a choice that accords with the Dominance Principle. The frequency of occurrence of the different structurings of Class IV problem representations is indicated in Table 9.6.

CONCLUSIONS

In this chapter we have shown that 163 out of 219 proposed decisions were correct in the sense that the choice is in accordance with the choice suggested by the Dominance Principle. One should be aware of the fact that this high degree of correctness stems from the restrictions imposed on the decision situations.

Another interesting result is that in all the choices that accord with the Dominance Principle, the probabilities of the outcomes under the various strategies are not of importance for the argument.

For the arguments in Classes I and III, this is automatically true, since they assume certainty. For the correct decisions in Classes I and III, the decision-makers indicate that the preferred strategy leads to outcomes that are certainly as good as or better than the outcomes of any other strategy. These choices are in accordance with the Dominance criterion, and Dominance corresponds with the Dominance Principle.

In Class II, the Dominance Principle decisions are all decisions where the chosen strategy leads with certainty to an outcome at least as good as that which any other strategy could optimally reach, while there is also a chance that it could obtain a better outcome. In Class II situations, the probabilities that are specified have the function of reinforcing the argument, since they indicate that for the chosen strategy the most attractive outcome is also the most likely and/or for the rejected strategies, the less favorable outcomes are more likely.

In all these situations, the argument is clear, and, given the way the pattern is structured, correct beyond doubt. Our conclusion is that all correct arguments have a Dominance structure, since only the occurrence of outcomes is important but not the size of the probabilities. These empirical findings support Montgomery's theory that the decision process consists of a search for Dominance (Montgomery 1989).

In the other 56 cases, where it is unclear whether the preferred choice is in accordance with the Dominance Principle, the arguments are less convincing, as it is apparent that some information is lacking in the problem representation. In Class I, such cases do not occur. In Classes II.A and II.B, for 28 out of the 83 cases, the restriction that the chosen strategy must lead with certainty to better outcomes is not introduced. In these cases an explicit trade-off has to be made between the various utilities and probabilities to ensure that the choice is correct, but this is not done. The decision-makers' choices still conform to simple rules, like the Risk-Avoidance, Reversed Simon or Simon's Rule, which would ensure correspondence with the Dominance Principle only when employed in conjunction with the restrictions mentioned above. In these cases, the restrictions that would make the choices convincing are not given. In Class II.C, the restrictions that the utilities of the chosen strategy are better or at least equal are missing in 22 cases, which means that the choices do not correspond with the Dominance Principle. With respect to Classes III and IV, there is sometimes no simple solution because of the complex value structure. In six cases, the decision-makers relied on a Lexicographic Rule, and this does not provide a particularly strong argument.

This survey suggests that although the decision-makers used simpler argumentation rules than the Dominance Principle, in the majority of cases, such arguments are convincing because of the restrictions introduced in the way the problem is structured; these restrictions bring the prescriptions made on the basis of these rules into correspondence with the Dominance Principle.

Since there are still some essential questions left in the understanding of political arguments, we will try to answer them in the subsequent chapters. They relate mainly to the choice of the problem description by the decision-maker. There are many ways of formulating a decision problem, as we have mentioned. Two questions can therefore be raised: Why does a politician specify two specific options and not others, three specific outcomes and not others? Why are the utilities and probabilities specified in the way we have seen (suggesting that a specific rule should be applied)? These questions will be addressed systematically in the subsequent chapters.

Chapter 10

Explanation of the Individual Decision-Makers' Argumentations

In this chapter we will investigate whether or not there are specific external and internal characteristics that produce different types of argumentations.

One of the topics to be investigated concerns the kind of strategies specified. The case studies in Part 1 showed that in general decision-makers used very few strategies for making a choice. The relevant figures for the entire data collection of 231 individual argumentations are as follows: in 75 percent of the argumentations (174 cases) they considered only two strategies; in 20 percent of the argumentations (46 cases) they specified three strategies; and only in 5 percent of the argumentations (11 cases) did they consider four or more strategies. The question thus is, are there some external or internal factors that help decision-makers to reduce the number of strategies they need to consider?

Since only two strategies were followed in 75 percent of the argumentations, it seemed useful to classify them with respect to their substantive content rather than to analyze their frequency. One substantive classification of strategies views them in terms of conflict and cooperation with respect to other nations involved (see, e.g., Callahan, Brady, and Hermann 1982). To give an idea of such a classification, we can illustrate it with the following example. Suppose that a decision-maker considered the following three strategies when thinking about improving his country's trading position with another nation:

S_1: Do nothing
S_2: Ask for a meeting
S_3: Threaten them with countermeasures

S_1 could be considered neutral with respect to the other nation, since nothing happens; S_2 cooperative; and S_3 conflictive. Decision-makers could consider where only two strategies have been generated several combinations of neutral, conflictive, and cooperative strategies.

Our investigation centers on the question of whether there are conditions under which decision-makers consider and choose more neutral or cooperative strategies and whether there are other factors that contribute to the generation and selection of more conflictive strategies. Another way of looking at the substance of the strategies is in terms of the status quo and deviations from it. This classification is inspired by Lindblom (e.g., Lindblom 1982), who suggested that decision-makers consider a limited range of strategies, all of which differ only incrementally from the status quo. If the examples just mentioned were classified in this way, it would look something like this: S_1 ("do nothing") is a case of ongoing inactivity, which is the status quo strategy. S_2 ("ask for a meeting") could be considered something slightly different from the status quo because effort is involved, but it is minimal. S_3 ("threaten with countermeasures") can be classified a new strategy because it deviates strongly from the status quo. It is clear that decision-makers can generate several combinations of strategies. We must therefore investigate whether or not there are factors that contribute to the generation and selection of more status quo strategies, or more strategies that slightly deviate from the status quo, or more new strategies.

A topic dealt with in Chapter 12 relates to consequences. The case studies in Part 1 showed that decision-makers considered relatively few outcomes. An inspection of the entire data set showed that in 138 cases (59 percent), decision-makers considered no more than three outcomes for each strategy; in 72 cases (32 percent), they considered no more than five outcomes for each strategy; and in 21 cases (9 percent) they considered only one outcome for each strategy. We will not engage in a frequency analysis of the specification of consequences but will concentrate on their substance. The substance of outcomes can refer, for instance, to a short or long-term time frame with respect to the realization of consequences. Examples of short-term consequences are "receiving a favorable answer," having asked some question, or "getting access to some territory," having demanded access. A consequence relating to a longer time frame could focus on "finally achieving a peace agreement," having initiated preliminary negotiations to fix the place and the agenda for the peace negotiations and then started with the negotiations. The achievement of long-term goals requires several actions across time. We will try to find out under what conditions, if any, the consequences focus on a short- or a long-term time frame.

The substance of outcomes can also be viewed in terms of topics that relate to specific governmental departments, such as defense, economic/financial, legal, internal, foreign affairs and overseas territories. For instance, if the outcomes refer mainly to achieving influence in the international system, they can be considered foreign affairs, whereas if they refer mainly to social stability in the country, they can be considered internal. Others might focus mainly on trade agreements, which we would call economic/financial, and so forth. On the basis of this last categorization of consequences, we will investigate whether or not there are factors that encourage decision-makers to focus more on one specific aspect of consequences than on others.

The last topic to be considered relates to argumentation rules. Chapter 8 showed that only six rules were needed to describe the choices made in 219 argumentations. Are there factors that encourage decision-makers to choose one or more argumentation rules rather than others? There have been several theoretical and empirical efforts to detect such relevant factors and conditions (e.g., Snyder, Bruck, and Sapin 1962; Rosenau 1966; Brecher, Steinberg, and Stein 1969; East, Salmore, and Hermann 1978; Callahan, Brady, and Hermann 1982; Wilkenfeld et al. 1980). We draw from these studies most of our theoretical concepts relating to situational, organizational, external actors', and personal characteristics.

SURVEY OF THE LITERATURE

The main source of the theoretical concepts we use to explain different types of argumentations is the schemes or frameworks developed for studies of a national government's decision-making process in terms of an input-process-output perspective (e.g., Snyder, Bruck, and Sapin 1962; Brecher, Steinberg, and Stein 1969) and for studies in the field of comparative foreign policy behavior relating to various governments (e.g., Rosenau 1966, Hermann et al. 1973; Wilkenfeld et. al. 1980). These frameworks and studies focus on the external verbal and nonverbal behavior of national governments as implementation of decisions. Although we are studying the argumentations of individual decision-makers and not the outputs in terms of implemented decisions, these schemes are relevant to our study since they indicate a variety of factors that can influence decision-makers during their argumentations before they make their choice.

The framework devised by Snyder and colleagues consists of a listing of potentially relevant factors that could explain different choice behaviors of foreign policy decision-makers. It distinguishes four sets of factors (Snyder, Bruck, and Sapin 1962, 212). The first is called the "organizational/individual" factor, and relates to the personal characteristics and the roles, rules, and functions of the decision-makers in the agencies. The second factor concerns the "internal setting" of the nation-state of the decision-makers, and deals with resources, groups, elites, public opinion, and cultural values. The third factor, the "external setting," encompasses the international system. The authors distinguished decision-makers on the basis of the parties they were dealing with: allies, neutrals, enemies, and international organizations. Bilateral or multilateral relationships and the relevant internal factors of other nations might also have an impact on decision-making behavior. The fourth factor relates to "situational properties," and emphasizes that the particular event or problem that has triggered the decision-making activity, together with the perceived variables of the other settings, might have some influence. Snyder and colleagues were the first to stress the importance of situational, organizational, external actor, and personal characteristics as well as the organizational, internal, and external contexts that can affect decision-making. They did not, however, indicate clear relationships between these variables and the choices made.

Another attempt to identify important characteristics was made by Rosenau (1966). Rosenau's framework, in a comparative study of behaviors among nations, distinguishes personal, organizational, internal, and external variables besides other characteristics. Rosenau posited that the variables that would be most important for a country's foreign policy depended on the type of nation, defined by its size, development, and political accountability. For small, developed countries with an open political system, such as the Netherlands, he theorized that role variables were the most important ones, but he acknowledged that this was mere speculation. Another concept introduced by Rosenau is the variable of "issue areas" into which decisions or actions can be classified. Foreign policy makers may disagree on the importance of issue areas such as territorial matters, status, human resources, and nonhuman resources. However, Rosenau did not have much to say about the relationship between the variables and the characteristics of actions.

Brecher and colleagues (1969) made further efforts to improve the understanding of explanatory variables and concentrated on the relationship between the environment and the decision-makers' perception of the environment. In this framework, a distinction is made between an "operational environment" and a "psychological environment." The former refers to a set of potentially relevant variables that may affect foreign policy decision-making, but this "objective" environment influences the choice of policy options only to the extent that decision-makers are able to perceive it. The perceptions of the operational environment, which they call the "psychological environment," depend on personality characteristics, historical legacy, and so forth. These authors also considered situational, organizational, and external actor characteristics to be important. Like Rosenau, they stressed the importance of issue areas in which decisions can be classified but introduced a slightly different classification, comprised of four substantive issue areas: military-security, political-diplomatic, economic-developmental, and cultural-status. Like the other authors already mentioned, the Brecher group failed to specify the relationships between the variables and the characteristics of the choices made, but Brecher did apply this framework to several case studies (e.g., Brecher 1972, 1974; Brecher and Geist 1980) in order to be able to make concrete propositions.

The last two frameworks we consider important to our research, IBA, developed by Wilkenfeld and colleagues (1980), and CREON (see Hermann et al. 1973; East, Salmore and Hermann 1978; Callahan, Brady, and Hermann 1982; Hermann, Kegley, and Rosenau 1987) were developed to allow systematic empirical research to be carried out on foreign policy behavior, expanding on the earlier frameworks mentioned.

The IBA (Interstate Behavior Analysis) framework postulated that four distinct groups of variables would determine foreign policy behavior, that is, the actions or reactions of nations that can be equated with events (Wilkenfeld et al. 1980). IBA comprises a psychological component relating to the decision-makers' values; the second component is the political component, pertaining to public opinion; the third component is the societal component, comprising economic indicators of nations; the fourth group of variables deals with the interstate component, such as international trade; and the fifth component, the global component, refers to membership in international organizations, economic structure, governmental structure, and so forth. Wilkenfeld and his associates tested this framework by relating each cluster of independent variables to the dependent variable of foreign policy behavior and finally by testing the framework as a whole.[1] We will make use of some of their findings in our study.

Those participating in the CREON (Comparative Research on the Events of Nations) project (e.g., Hermann et al. 1973; East, Salmore, and Hermann 1978; Callahan, Brady, and Hermann 1982; Hermann, Kegley, and Rosenau 1987) have tried to develop multivariate theories of foreign policy behavior by exploring the interrelationships between independent variables with each other and with the dependent variable of foreign policy actions. These characteristics relate not only to outcome properties of behavior but also to the predecisional context and the decision-making process. The explanatory variables belong to the following variable clusters: personal characteristics of political leaders, such as beliefs, motives, decision styles; bureaucratic aspects of governmental decision-making, such as decision structures; political features of regimes, comprising internal coherence, accountability to constituencies, and so forth; national attributes of societies, pertaining to population size, military power, economic capacities, and so on; transitory qualities of the situation, referring to situational characteristics such as crisis or noncrisis, whether or not the action is an initiative or a reaction to a stimulus, problem complexity, and the like; and properties of the international system, pertaining to distributions of goods, resources, and so on. In our study we will also make use of findings of the CREON project.

Having briefly reviewed the main theoretical efforts to explain foreign policy decisions and behavior, we can state that despite their diversity, each framework includes situational, organizational, and personal characteristics and characteristics of the external actors.

SELECTION OF EXPLANATORY VARIABLES

Table 10.1 summarizes the explanatory variables we have selected and indicates the literature from which they derive. The specific classification into five broad categories, that is situational, organizational, external actor, social context, and personal characteristics, was divised by the authors of this book, whereas in the frameworks discussed earlier the variables might be classified under other headings.

The first item in the situational characteristics category in Table 10.1 is issue areas. This concept was considered important in all the frameworks mentioned above, apart from Snyder's. For each situation, it will also be determined whether or not there was a preceding event stemming from an external actor, that is, a verbal or nonverbal deed addressed to the nation under study that could be considered the stimulus for the decision. If it was preceded by a prior event, then the argumentation is considered reactive, and if no event occurred, it is seen as an initiative. A further distinction will be made between cases where the decision-makers perceive the situation as a crisis and those where they do not. These three situational concepts seem to be very important, since they were mentioned in all five frameworks. Further situational characteristics are the perception of the presence or absence of control over the future and the perception of satisfaction or dissatisfaction with the status quo. The concept of control over the future was encountered only in the CREON project, while satisfaction and dissatisfaction with the status quo has been introduced by the authors of this book.

The organizational characteristics include the departmental affiliation of the decision-maker and his function in the government. Table 10.1 shows that all frameworks deal with these concepts. As external actor characteristics, we use

Table 10.1:
Summary of Selected Explanatory Variables

		Considered in:				
	Snyder	Rosenau	Brecher	CREON	IBA	Our study
Situational characteristics						
Issue areas	No	Yes	Yes	Yes	Yes	Yes
Presence or absence of prior events	Yes	Yes	Yes	Yes	Yes	Yes
Reaction to prior event(s) or initiative	Yes	Yes	Yes	Yes	Yes	Yes
Crisis or noncrisis	Yes	Yes	Yes	Yes	Yes	Yes
Perception of control over the future	No	No	No	Yes	No	Yes
Perception of satisfaction or dissatis-faction with the status quo	No	No	No	No	No	Yes
Organizational characteristics						
Departmental affiliation	Yes	Yes	Yes	Yes	Yes	Yes
Function in the government	Yes	Yes	Yes	Yes	Yes	Yes
External actor characteristics						
Type of other nation	Yes	Yes	Yes	Yes	Yes	Yes
Size of the nation	Yes	Yes	Yes	Yes	Yes	Yes
Social context characteristics						
Sequence number of argumentation in the decision-making process	No	No	No	No	No	Yes
Agreement or disagreement with other decision-makers	No	No	No	Yes	No	Yes
Personal characteristics						
Individual cognitive style	No	No	No	Yes	No	Yes

the type of other nation, in other words, whether it is an ally or not, and its size.[2] These concepts were also used in all frameworks. The social context variables relate to the sequence number of the individual argumentation during the argumentation process and whether or not the decision-maker's argumentation produced disagreement among other decision-makers involved. The sequence number concept seemed to us to be useful in order to determine whether it contributes to the use of different argumentation rules, and therefore we have introduced it, while disagreement and agreement with other decision-makers is also encountered in that part of the CREON project that looks at the process. Finally, the only personal characteristic we use relates to the individual cognitive style of the decision-maker, a concept also mentioned in the CREON project.

RESEARCH METHODOLOGY

In this section we will first introduce the text analysis of the various variables. Then the coding reliabilities will be studied and the research design will be outlined. Readers who are not interested in these methodological issues can continue with the subsequent chapters without problems.

Text Analysis of the Strategy Classifications

Conflict and cooperation

One of the dependent variables we use is strategies, alternatively classified in two ways with respect to their substance. One of these classifications referred to conflict and cooperation according to the revised version of the World Event/ Interaction Survey (WEIS REV) classification system (Callahan, Brady, and Hermann 1982, 320–324). This classification scheme distinguishes between 20 conflictual actions and 16 cooperative ones, including both verbal and nonverbal actions. Table 10.2 summarizes the cooperative categories and Table 10.3 gives an illustration of conflictive categories.

The following examples illustrate the coding:

"Reduce the armed forces"	: Cooperative, decrease force.
"Put 100 million guilders at their disposal"	: Cooperative, positive proposal.
"Grant access to our territory"	: Cooperative, grant access.
"Recognize this government"	: Very cooperative, nurture relationship.

The following examples illustrate the coding of conflictive strategies:

"Propose spending a maximum of 1 million guilders on defense, although NATO asked for 10 million"	: Conflictive; proposal.
"Demand that the case be settled in an international court"	: Conflictive; demand.
"Threaten the Security Council to withdraw from Indonesia"	: Very conflictive; threaten.
"Invade the seat of the Republican government"	: Very conflictive; force.

Table 10.2:
Summary of the Classification of Cooperative Categories (WEIS REV)

Categories

Positive Comment:	Comment on situation, explain policy desired by actor or target, abstain on vote
Consult:	Make or arrange official visit, participate in meetings
Approve:	Praise, hail, applaud, endorse, support
Positive request:	Ask for information desired by target
Positive proposal:	Offer proposal, suggest or urge action or policy desired by target
Negotiate:	Participate in substantive talks, negotiate on specific issue or interest area
Positive intention:	Explain future action desired by target
Agree:	Accept proposal, agree to meet or negotiate, agree to future action (does not include the signing of formal agreements or the transfer of resources)
Offer:	Offer an explicit proposal for future action desired by target (of a contingent if-then nature)
Yield:	Surrender, submit, retreat, evacuate
*Grant:	End negative sanctions, conflict action, threat of conflict action; express regret, apologize, release
*Reward:	Give or receive economic, technical or military aid unilaterally
Decrease military capability:	Reduce military spending, troop levels; reduce readiness for military action
Implement agreement:	Implement a previous agreement
*Nurture relationship:	Increase economic, military, technical or cultural exchanges bilaterally (includes the signing of formal agreements involving the transfer of resources)

---

* Coded as "very cooperative" by us.

Callahan, Brady, and Hermann (1982; 320) coded neutral action as cooperative, but we found it useful to consider this a separate category. The neutral strategies comprise the following two categories:

1. Do nothing

2. Delay a verbal or non-verbal action

Table 10.3:
Summary of the Classification of Conflictual Events (WEIS REV)

Categories

Negative comment:	Comment on situation, explain policy not desired by actor or target
Accuse:	Charge, criticize, blame, disapprove, denounce, denigrate
Deny:	Deny accusation, attributed action, or policy
Negative request:	Ask for information not desired by target
Negative proposal:	Offer proposal, suggest or urge action or policy not desired by target
Protest:	Make formal or informal complaint
Demand:	Order, command, insist, demand compliance
Negative intention:	Explain future policy not desired by target
Reject:	Turn down proposal, vote against, protest, demand, threaten, refuse, oppose, harden position
Warn:	Warn of future situation or action not desired by target; warn against action by target not desired by actor (a less specific noncontingent category than threaten)
*Threaten:	Threaten to take future action against the target with or without sanction
*Demonstrate force:	Mobilization of armed forces, movement, exercise, display; nonmilitary demonstration sponsored by government
Neglect relationship:	Cancel or postpone event, meeting, boycott, or walkout; reduce routine international activity; recall officials; halt negotiations; break diplomatic relations
*Expel:	Expel organization, group, or personnel
*Seize:	Seize position or possessions, detain or arrest personnel
*Force:	Forceful or violent use of military resources and equipment to achieve objectives; military engagement, nonmilitary destruction
Increase military capability:	Increase military spending, troop levels; develop weapons; authorize action, increase call-ups
*Aid opponent:	Give aid to opponents of target outside the borders of the target, such as granting asylum to opponents of target
*Subvert:	Aid insurgents in their own country; make nonverbal attempts to influence internal politics of target

* Coded as "very conflictive" by us.

Examples of neutral strategies are: "wait and see," "postpone a military action," "delay an answer," and so forth.

Status quo

The second classification of strategies refers to the status quo and deviations from it. The following three categories were used:

1. Status quo

2. Something slightly different from the status quo

3. Something new

The status quo strategy is defined as the continuation of some ongoing activity or a state of inactivity. For example, if negotiations have already started and the continuation of negotiations is still considered a possible strategy, then this strategy belongs to the status quo category. If a nation is inactive and is approached by another state to do something, for example, to participate in some organization, and the decision-maker considers the strategies of "delaying the answer," "not reacting at all," or "not participating," then these three strategies are also classified under the "status quo," since they amount to no-change solutions.

In a case where, for instance, the status quo consists of holding hostages, a promise to release them after certain conditions are fulfilled or to enter into negotiations on this question could be considered "something slightly different from the status quo." If the status quo consists of no activity and the decision-maker has to react to some demand or condition such as to grant access to foreign troops as observers, then "doing something slightly different" might entail granting access to ten soldiers as observers for a fixed amount of time. The third category, "doing something new," would mean, in the case of hostages being held, releasing them. In the case of the observers, something new would be to explicitly refuse access or to grant them access.

Text Analysis of the Outcome Classifications

Time frame of outcomes

As another dependent variable, we use outcomes. The classification of consequences was related to their substance and was also twofold. One scheme refers to the time frame for the realization of outcomes. The short time frame for the realization of consequences does not require a wide range of strategies. They can be achieved by means of a single action. Contrary to short-term outcomes, long-term consequences require more actions to be taken if they are to be achieved. Even if decision-makers do not always indicate these actions explicitly, they frequently refer to the long-term perspective in some way. An example of a coding of the time frame of consequences is as follows:

"If we take military action (strategy) we might reestablish law and order (short-term outcome). But it is also possible that we will not reestablish law and order (short-term outcome) and that we will finally have to evacuate (long-term outcome)."

Departmental Topics

The other classification of outcomes tries to discern the substantive topics that relate to specific governmental departments. The following categories were distinguished: defense, economic/financial, legal, internal, foreign affairs, and overseas territories.

The substance of defense consequences focuses on military violence inflicted by external actors, the results of one's own military activities, military alliances, and weaponry. Examples are, for instance:

"It will lead to a military success."
"The NATO treaty will be ratified by the parliament."
"We will receive no permission to acquire this submarine."

Economic/financial outcomes refer to consequences comprising the acquisition and allocation of resources, such as trade, aid, investment, and economic alliances. The following are examples of economic consequences:

"The result will be that our foreign trade will improve."
"Consequently our financial position worsens."
"It leads to the preservation of the gold standard."

Legal consequences refer to justice, arbitration, laws, and other judicial matters, for instance:

"We received justice from the arbitration court."
"It resulted in a different interpretation of the sea law."

Internal consequences relate exclusively to the fatherland and focus mainly on social stability, for example:

"We would have mass demonstrations."
"It would not lead to the assimilation of other ethnic groups."

Foreign affairs outcomes refer to relations with other nations, international organizations in general, and influence on other nations or international organizations. The following examples illustrate this category:

"We did not receive any support from the United States."
"We reached an agreement with country x."
"They might understand our point of view."

The overseas territories category comprises all those outcomes that exclusively relate to the colonies. Thus if defense, economic, legal, internal, and foreign affairs consequences only relate to the colonies and not to the fatherland they were classified in this category. Some examples will make this clear:

"The result will be a Japanese occupation of the East Indies."

"The material losses in the East Indies will be high."

"There will be an internal uproar on all islands."

"A possible consequence is that the republican regime will gain increased support from the Security Council."

Text Analysis of the Situational Variables

In this section we will indicate how each of the explanatory variables mentioned in Table 10.1 was operationalized and clarify the concepts by examples.

Issue areas

For the situational characteristic of issue areas, Brecher's classification was used (Brecher, Steinberg, and Stein 1969, 87–88). Brecher and colleagues distinguish four substantive categories of problem areas: economic-developmental, security-military, cultural-status, and political-diplomatic.

Brecher and associates (1969, 87–88) define these categories as follows: "The *economic-developmental issue area* comprises all those issues which involve the acquisition and allocation of resources, such as trade, aid and foreign investment."

As the context unit (Holsti 1969), that is, the largest body of text that has to be searched for the issue concept, we took a paragraph within a particular argumentation text. The recording unit (the specific segment of text into which the concept is classified; see also Holsti 1969) was variable and consisted of one or more full sentences. These units were used for the extraction of most of the concepts; where no other unit is indicated, these units were applied.

Examples of our data classified in the economic-developmental category include:

The improvement of trade by participation in international economic organizations.

Negotiations about war reparations.

The granting of financial aid to less developed countries.

The security-military issue is defined by Brecher and his associates (1969, 88) as follows: "The *security-military issue* comprises all issues which focus on questions pertaining to violence, including alliances and weaponry, and those which are perceived by the foreign policy elite as constituting a security threat." Examples include:

The defense of the fatherland and/or the colonies against external agression.

Participation in defense organizations like NATO.

The next issue area relates to the cultural-developmental category, defined as follows by Brecher and his colleagues (1969, 88): "The *cultural-status issue area* consists of those foreign policy issues involving cultural, educational, and scientific exchanges. It also contains status issues which relate primarily to self-image, namely, the decision maker's perception of their state's legitimate place in the global and/or subordinate system." In the data sample we studied, this category was not present.

The last concept of substantive issue areas, the political-diplomatic category, is defined as follows by Brecher and colleagues (Brecher 1969, 88): "The *political-diplomatic issue area* covers the spectrum of foreign policy interaction to each of the three levels of the external environment—global, subordinate, and bilateral—except for those dealing with violence, material resources, and cultural and status relations." For example:

Argumentations about future legal relations with former colonies.

The starting or reopening of diplomatic relations with another nation.

Prior events

Another variable refers to the presence or absence of an event prior to the argumentation. An event is defined, as usual in the event-data approach, as an "actor-action-target" theme (e.g., Callahan, Brady, and Hermann 1982). The actor can be a nation-state, an international organization, or an alliance. The action can be verbal or nonverbal, and the target is always the Netherlands. Again, a paragraph within a particular argumentation text was used as context unit, and the recording unit was the actor-action-target theme, which might be mentioned in one or more full sentences. Examples of such themes would be:

"The United Nations is threatening to interfere in Indonesia."

"Our allies have urged us to reestablish diplomatic relations with the Soviet Union."

"The republican government broke the cease-fire agreement at our demarcation line."

"The Germans proposed concluding a peace treaty with us."

Conflict and cooperation

Thereafter, the detected events were classified in terms of conflict and cooperation, according to the revised version of the World Event/Interaction Survey (WEIS REV) classification system (see Tables 10.2 and 10.3). In order to illustrate the coding, the examples of events just mentioned could be classified as follows:

"The United Nations is threatening to interfere in Indonesia": very conflictive, threat

"Our allies have urged us to reestablish diplomatic relations with the Soviet Union": conflictive, negative proposal, since this policy was not desired by the Netherlands

"The republican government broke the cease-fire order at our demarcation line": very conflictive, force

"The Germans proposed concluding a peace treaty with us": cooperative, positive
proposal since it was desired by the Netherlands

Reaction and initiative

Yet another situational characteristic refers to reactive or initiative argumentation. A reactive argument may be elicited by an event, but it may also be a part
or the result of a set of interchanges between governments, such as the implementation of an agreement or abiding by a vote in an international organization.
In order to determine reactive behavior precisely, we use the operationalization
developed by M. Hermann (Hermann 1982, 248). Hermann proposed that coders
should answer the following six questions in order to ascertain whether or not
behavior is reactive:

1. Was the argument elicited, that is, is the argument a response to the behavior of
   another government or external entity which explicitly requested a response from the
   actor?

2. Does the argument relate to a public vote by a government representative in an
   international organization?

3. Does the argument involve an actual agreement to, announcement of, or transfer of a
   loan, credit or other foreign assistance?

4. Does the argument involve an actual agreement to, announcement of, or execution of
   an economic transaction?

5. Is the argument a denial, a rejection of or agreement to a prior proposal or a protest of
   a prior activity directed at the acting government by another government or external
   entity?

6. Does the argument involve negotiation, consultation, or a response dictated by a
   treaty?[3]

In accordance with Hermann's guidelines, the coders coded the argument as
reactive if any of these questions could be answered yes, and otherwise as an
initiative. Here are two examples of initiatives:

Arguments containing own plans or proposals to establish diplomatic relations with
some other nations.

Arguments to build European economic organizations.

Crisis

The next situational characteristic mentioned in Table 10.1 relates to the perception of crisis. We decided to use Brecher's definition (e.g., Brecher 1977,
44–45; Brecher and Geist 1980, 16), which states that if a decision-maker
perceives the situation as threatening to the core values of his country, with a
limited decision time available and an increased probability of war, then he
perceives the situation as a crisis. If one of these components is absent, then the
situation is not perceived as critical. Another prominent crisis definition is

Hermann's (Hermann 1972, 187), which characterizes a crisis situation as one that threatens high priority goals of the decision-making unit, with only a short decision time available, and which takes the members of the decision-making unit by surprise. However, we found Brecher's definition more suitable because, in our opinion, neither surprise nor short decision time are basic characteristics of crisis, while an increased probability of war does seem to be typical of crisis.

Following Brecher, we operationalized a decision-maker's perception of a threat to basic values with respect to the military-security issue in three ways:

1. If a decision-maker indicated during his argumentation that the interests of his nation were threatened with respect to the military-security issue, then this characteristic was present. As "basic values," the survival of the population, independence as international actor, maintenance of territorial integrity, and the autonomy of the political system were suggested (see also Brecher 1977, 66–67).

The following statements are examples of the presence or absence of perceptions of threat:

"In conclusion I would like to state that the German occupation of Antwerp does not at all threaten our status of neutrality" (no perception of threat).

"We now run the risk that under the auspices of the Security Council the United States will take over Indonesia" (perception of threat).

Sometimes, however, decision-makers did not mention these perceptions explicitly, so they had to be measured indirectly on the basis of the argumentation tree. This was done as follows, and constitutes the second measurement of threat:

2. If a decision-maker indicated, on the basis of his argument, that in pursuing his strategy (the status quo) only negative outcomes would occur or the probability of negative outcomes was very high, then he perceived the situation as threatening to the interests of his nation.

An example of this second measurement of perception of threat can be found in Table 7.1 where the commander of the troops indicated that "doing nothing" would lead with certainty to the loss of Indonesia.

3. If the same decision-maker produced several arguments relating to the same decision situation and if he had mentioned the first time that there were threats to the interests of his nation while omitting it in the following arguments because it seemed evident, then the situation was coded as perception of threat.

The second component of Brecher's crisis definition relates to the perception of limited time. This was measured in three ways:

1. Each paragraph (context unit) in the document was searched for one or more sentences (recording unit) which contained statements of some time limit for the

decision. This indication could be quite vague, such as "we cannot delay our answer indefinitely," or indicated with a more precise indication of a time limit, which did not necessarily need to be short, such as "we still have some weeks to work out a solution, but then we have to react."

Sometimes, however, there were no direct indications of time limits made in the document at all, so we had to proceed as follows:

2. The time intervals between the arguments of several decision-makers relating to the specific decision were established, and if they occurred within a limited period, such as two or three months, and a final decision was made at the end of this period, then we considered these situations as perceptions of limited time.

3. If the same decision-maker produced several arguments relating to the same decision situation and if he had mentioned the first time that there was a time limit, while omitting this in the following arguments because it seemed evident, then the situation was coded as perception of time limit.

If there was no time limit indicated at all, as in the first two cases, the situation was classified as "absence of time limit."

The third characteristic that relates to crisis situations, according to Brecher, is the perception of increased likelihood of war. This characteristic was measured in two ways:

1. Each paragraph of a document was searched for statements consisting of one or more sentences (recording unit), which would indicate that the decision-makers considered war more likely than in former times.

The following are examples of such statements:

"The German invasion of Antwerp increases the chances that we will have to enter the war."

"I foresee that we will have to resort to military measures during the next weeks."

In addition, a second coding rule was devised for cases where the decision-maker did not repeat a likelihood of war in a later argument with respect to the same subject:

2. If the same decision-maker produced several arguments relating to the same decision situation and had mentioned the first time that there was an increased likelihood of war while omitting it in the following arguments because it seemed evident, then the situation was coded as perception of increased likelihood of war.

Control over the future

The next situational characteristic is perception of control over the future. M. Hermann (1982, 244–247) posits that the maintenance of control over a nation's future is a basic tenet of most governments. However, our operationalization of this concept differs from her measurement of the degree of autonomy a government tries to maintain. In our analysis this concept simply denotes that the decision-maker is able to find a strategy that leads with certainty or a high probability to a desired outcome. The text analysis was based on the decision-maker's argumentation tree and was conducted as follows:

Each chosen strategy (context unit) was searched for probabilities of positive outcomes (recording unit).
If the chosen strategy led with certainty or with a high probability to positive outcomes, then there was control over the future. If the probability of a positive outcome was low, uncertain or absent, then the decision-maker had no control over the future.

The arguments presented, for example, in Tables 7.3, 7.4, and 7.5 are examples of lack of control over the future. The arguments presented in Tables 7.1 and 7.10 are examples of control over the future.

Satisfaction with the status quo

The last situational characteristic we measured is called perception of satisfaction with the status quo. To our knowledge, this variable has not been mentioned anywhere previously in the theoretical literature. We thought, however, that it was relevant to establish whether a decision-maker was satisfied with what his nation had or was (the status quo) or whether he was dissatisfied and wanted action taken to improve this situation.

Each paragraph in a document (context unit) was searched for statements that indicated that the decision-maker either wanted to maintain the situation, which were coded as satisfaction with the status quo, or whether he indicated that his country needed to improve the situation, implying that he was dissatisfied with the status quo.
These statements could consist of one or more full sentences (recording unit).

An example of satisfaction with the status quo would be if a decision-maker were to state that his government had to devote all their efforts to maintaining their status of neutrality, a status that had proved to be very satisfactory in the past. An example of dissatisfaction with the status quo would be utterances such as "the way things are going nowadays in Indonesia is very unsatisfactory; we will have to reestablish law and order."

Text Analysis of the Organizational Characteristics

In the analyses we will make use of two organizational characteristics as independent variables.

Departmental affiliation

One of these characteristics, called the departmental affiliation of the decision-maker, relates to the following categories:

1. Foreign affairs official

2. Finance or Economics official

3. Overseas territories official

4. Defense official

5. Official from another department

The measurement of this variable was straightforward. Given the name of the decision-maker, his affiliation could be established on the basis of the heading of the document.

Function of the decision-maker

The second organizational variable defines the organizational role or function of the decision-maker. Three categories were discerned: key minister, minister, and adviser.

The notion of "key minister" needs some clarification. It comprises those ministers who play a critical role in the decision-making unit. The role of the prime minister, the deputy prime minister and the minister of finance are considered important in all kinds of decisions, because of their central role in government. Dutch governments are mostly coalition governments, and the prime minister and deputy prime minister are the leaders of their party in the cabinet. The minister of finance provides the financial means for all endeavors and can therefore be considered to be an important decision-maker. With respect to other ministers, their importance depends on the issue area of decision. Since all decisions studied relate to foreign policy, the minister of foreign affairs also always has a key position. If the issue is security-military, the ministers of defense and maritime affairs are in a key position, and if it also relates to the colonies, the minister of overseas territories is involved as well. From this it follows that arguments relating to economic-developmental issues bring the minister of economic affairs into a key position, and if they refer to the colonies, too, the minister of overseas territories is also involved. The "adviser" category comprises officials from several departments or even experts from outside government who are asked to give their views.

Text Analysis of the External Actor Characteristics

Type of the other nation

Two explanatory variables were used as external actor characteristics. One relates to the type of other nation. This variable contains two categories: ally, and nonally. The measurement of this variable is quite straightforward. Based on the name of the external actor to whom an initiative or a reaction is directed, it can be established whether or not he is an ally of the Netherlands.

Size of the other nation

The second characteristic of an external actor refers to his size. On the basis of population size and economic capabilities, we distinguished three categories: large power, medium power, and small power. The United States and the Soviet Union are examples of large powers; Britain, France, and Germany are examples of medium powers; and Belgium and Luxemburg are examples of small powers.

Measurement of Social Context Characteristics

Two relevant explanatory social context variables were discerned in which the individual arguments could take place.

Sequence number of the argument
The score of this variable is based on the number of arguments given in the same decision case by the same decision-maker. For example, in the case study in Chapter 7 the minister of foreign affairs gave three arguments.

Agreement
The second variable relates to the perception of agreement or disagreement with other decision-makers in the same decision case. This characteristic was measured as follows:
In each particular argumentation text, the paragraphs were searched for indications that a specific decision-maker agreed or disagreed with others, or anticipated agreement or disagreement. For example:

> " I agree with the minister of foreign affairs that we are now closer to war than ever before."

> " I disagree with colleagues who think that negotiations are the only viable alternative."

If no statements explicitly expressed agreement or disagreement and there were no indications from earlier arguments in the sequence of the same decision-maker that there was disagreement, then it was coded as "agreement."

Measurement of Personal Characteristics

Individual cognitive style
The last independent variable we used relates to personal characteristics of the decision-makers, that is, the individual cognitive style. Since it was not possible to measure directly the individual cognitive style of a decision-maker on the basis of the argumentation documents, it was decided to study a subset of decision-makers who produced several arguments relating to different issues and at different times. This characteristic was operationalized in the following way: given the name of the decision-maker, the data were searched for the number of arguments he contributed. If he had produced five or more arguments, his decision-making style was selected for study.

Table 10.4:
Intercoder Reliabilities for the Various Characteristics

		Scott's π
Situational characteristics	Issue areas of arguments	.89
	Presence or absence of prior events	.91
	Nature of prior events in terms of conflict or cooperation	.84
	Reactive or initiative argumentation	.87
	Perception of threat to basic values	.83
	Perception of limited time	.81
	Perception of increase in likelihood of war	.85
	Crisis/noncrisis argument	*
	Perception of presence or absence of control over the future	.79
	Perception of satisfaction or dissatisfaction with the status quo	.80
Organizational characteristics	Departmental affiliation of the decision-maker	.98
	Function of the decision-maker	.96
External actor characteristics	Type of other nation	1.00
	Size of other nation	.91
Social context characteristics	Sequence number of argumentation in the decision-making process	**
	Agreement or disagreement with other individual decision-makers	.82
Personal characteristics	Individual cognitive style	**
Strategies	Conflictive/cooperative/neutral	.89
	Status quo and deviations from it	.84
Outcomes	Short term/long term	.95
	Departmental classification	.77

*Crisis was composed on the basis of coded perceptions of threat, limited time, and increase in likelihood of war, and needed no extra coding.

**These variables did not require coding since scores could be derived by a frequency count.

Assessment of the Coding Reliability of the Various Variables

Two coders first individually coded each variable. They then came together and compared their results and, where differences in categorization occurred, they tried to reach a common solution, which was used for the subsequent analysis.

Table 10.4 summarizes the results for the intercoder reliability. In general, the scores of Scott's pi are quite high. Almost all scores are above .80, but depending on the difficulty of the concept, they vary slightly. Given that the coders corrected each other, the joint coding has an even higher reliability, as we showed in Chapter 3.

Data Analysis

Thanks to the very satisfactory results of the coding reliabilities, we were able to test the relationship between the independent and the dependent variables. First, some plausible bivariate relationships suggested in the literature were studied, but as expected, these relationships were too simple, and therefore theoretically plausible multivariate relationships were tested. On the basis of significance tests it could be decided whether interactions were present or not. Using Loglinear analysis, in fact, no interactions could be detected. However, the absence of interactions could also have been due to the relatively small sample size. Therefore, we used Loglinear analysis mainly for the selection of variables and then concentrated on cross-table analyses to test the propositions made in Chapters 11 through 13.

CONCLUSIONS

In this chapter we have discussed the literature that proposes that specific characteristics explain foreign policy decisions. We then made a selection of variables to explain the different types of argumentation encountered in our studies in terms of the strategies, consequences, and choice rules used. These explanatory variables consist of situational, organizational, external actor, social context, and personal characteristics.

Next the text analysis approach to identifying these characteristics was laid out in detail. We also showed that the coding to detect the various variables was conducted with very high reliability by pairs of coders.

In Chapter 11 we will introduce the propositions made for the specifications and selection of strategies, present the results of the tests, and draw some conclusions. Chapter 12 will deal in a similar way with the specification of consequences, and Chapter 13 relates to the explanation of the use of argumentation rules.

NOTES

1. The dependent variables, the foreign policy actions or events, which are the outputs of decisions, are classified according to situational characteristics such as crisis and noncrisis, the level of conflict or cooperation, and so forth.

2. The size of one's own nation is also important, as will be seen later, but it is a constant and not a variable.

3. We have replaced "action" from the original text with "argument" to make it more appropriate for our purposes.

Chapter 11

Factors in the Specification of Strategies

In this chapter we will present an empirical study of the factors that might influence the specification of strategies by individual decision-makers in their arguments. In this study we look at the problem in two different ways:

1. We have previously classified the different strategies on a scale of very cooperative to very conflictive, and we will try to explain what factors influence the specification and choice of conflictive or cooperative strategies.

2. We have previously classified the different strategies as preserving the status quo, doing something slightly different, and doing something new, and will try to explain what factors influence the specification and choice of strategies that preserve the status quo and those that deviate from it.

We will use as our starting point factors that have been mentioned in the literature. From this survey we will derive certain propositions that we will consequently test with the empirical material we have collected as described earlier. For the measurement instruments employed, see the previous chapter.

FACTORS MENTIONED IN THE LITERATURE

In the literature there are several explanations offered for foreign policy actions. These explanations mainly refer to situational and external actor characteristics. Although we do not want to explain foreign policy action, we expect the same factors to determine the specification and choice of strategies by the decision-makers.

One simple explanation (Rosenau and Hoggard 1974; Rosenau 1966) stresses the importance of the situational characteristic of a decision issue. Different issues might generate different kinds of actions. In situations where decision-makers are dealing with diplomatic matters, they might be more cooperative than where they are dealing with economic or security issues.

According to another well-known explanation, which is substantiated by empirical findings (Phillips 1978; Wilkenfeld et al. 1980; Ward 1982), foreign policy actions can be primarily explained by the prior behavior of other nations toward a particular state. This means that the specification and choice of strategies would be a reciprocal phenomenon: cooperative actions of other nations would lead to a cooperative answer, and conflictive actions would lead to a conflictive answer.

This explanation thus assumes a simple "behavior-begets-behavior" model, which means that the prior behavior of another nation in the main determines the nature of the strategies considered and the nature of the strategy chosen. But the adherents of this model also suggest looking at other factors in order to get a more complete explanation. It is clear that the behavior-begets-behavior model relates to the situation of reaction to another nation. But there are also situations where a nation can itself take an initiative to improve its situation, in which case the nature of the specification and selection of strategies might be quite different. In our opinion it will depend on the decision-maker's satisfaction with the status quo; if he is satisfied with the status quo but still wishes to improve the position of his nation, he might be more careful than if he is dissatisfied with the status quo and wants to change it fundamentally. It follows that most of the situational characteristics mentioned in Table 10.1 are assumed to influence the specification and selection of conflictive and cooperative strategies.

As far as organizational characteristics are concerned, we did not encounter in the literature special assumptions relating to the specification and selection of strategies. However, when making propositions, we will make use of a decision-maker's function in government as a possible explanatory condition.

The next characteristic mentioned in Table 10.1 relate to the external actor. There is a view (Rosenau 1966; East and Hermann 1974; Papadakis and Starr 1987) that assumes that the physical size of a nation is determinant of its actions. Small nations are viewed as being more reactive in their foreign policy actions, while larger nations are thought to take more initiatives. Small states are also characterized as avoiding actions that tend to alienate the more powerful states on whom they are dependent. Their actions are mainly characterized as cooperative. Other findings (East 1975) corroborate the notion of a more reactive mode of decision-making but challenge the idea of cooperative behavior of small nations. East found that they engaged in higher levels of conflictive behavior than larger nations. The postulated relationships between the size of a nation-state, the size of the external actor to whom actions are addressed, and the actions of the first nation-state will have to be taken into account. But in our opinion, the type of other nation (mentioned as an external actor characteristic in Table 10.1) plays a role too.

Social context and personal characteristics were not mentioned in the literature as being of particular influence for the generation and selection of strategies.

THE SPECIFICATION AND CHOICE OF COOPERATIVE AND CONFLICTIVE STRATEGIES

As we have mentioned before, we expect quite a different process when a government is taking an initiative than when it is reacting to an action of another nation. Therefore we will make an explicit distinction and start with the situation of reaction.

The Situation of Reaction to Another Nation

In a reactive situation, we postulated that the decision-makers might be influenced by the prior action of another nation. But since we did not expect a simple action-reaction pattern, we postulated also that the size of the other nation and its type—whether it is a large or medium power, an ally or not—might affect the consideration and selection of different strategies.

Table 11.1 sets out the type of nation, its size, the external actor's prior actions, and the kind of specification and selection of strategies we expect in a specific situation. Based on these assumptions, the following proposition can be formulated:

Proposition I:

Generally, cooperative prior actions will produce cooperative strategies in response, but in situations where the prior behavior is conflictive, the size of the other nation and its type will play a role. If a conflictive stimulus comes from an ally which is a large or medium power, the response will be cooperative in order to preserve the alliance commitments on which one's own nation depends. If the conflictive stimulus comes from a small ally and one's own nation is a large or medium power, the answer might be conflictive since there is less dependence on small allies. But if one's own nation in this case is a small power, the answer is likely to be cooperative because of a greater dependence on allies.

If a conflictive stimulus comes from a nonally, the specified and selected strategies will generally reflect his prior behavior. But if one's own nation is a small power and the nonallies are large or medium powers, cooperative reactions might still occur since the small power might not want to annoy the nonallies excessively.

This proposition deviates from the behavior-begets-behavior model inasfar as it supposes that in the event of a conflict, the sizes of the other and one's own nation and the type of other nation may also play a role.

More variables could be introduced here (for example, issue area and function), but to avoid making the theory too complex, these characteristics will be specified in the following passages as possible, alternative explanations. In addition to size and type, it was assumed that certain issue areas might produce more conflictive answers than others. In diplomatic matters, for instance, decision-makers might respond more cautiously than with security or economic issues.

Table 11.2 shows the issue areas together with the external actors' prior actions and the kind of specification and selection of strategies we expect.

Proposition II formulates the relationships:

Proposition II:

If the stimulus of an external actor is cooperative, in general, the response will also be cooperative. But if the stimulus is conflictive, the issue area involved may play a role.

If the issue area is diplomacy, more cooperative answers can be expected than if the issue areas relate to security or economy. The latter issue areas are considered to be more important, and therefore the specification and selection of strategies will reflect more strongly the prior actions of the other nation.

Table 11.1:
Influence of Type of Other Nation and Prior Actions of External Actor on the Generation and Choice of Cooperative or Conflictive Strategies

Type of other nation	Size of external actor	Prior actions of external actor	Strategies
Ally	Large/medium	Cooperative	Cooperative
Ally	Large/medium	Conflictive	Cooperative
Ally	Small	Cooperative	Cooperative
Ally	Small	Conflictive	Cooperative/Conflictive
Nonally	Large/medium	Cooperative	Cooperative
Nonally	Large/medium	Conflictive	Cooperative/Conflictive
Nonally	Small	Cooperative	Cooperative
Nonally	Small	Conflictive	Conflictive

Table 11.2:
Influence of Issue Areas and Prior Actions of External Actor on the Generation and Choice of Cooperative or Conflictive Strategies

Issue areas	Prior actions of external actor	Strategies
Diplomacy	Cooperative	Cooperative
Security/economy	Cooperative	Cooperative
Diplomacy	Conflictive	Cooperative/conflictive
Security/economy	Conflictive	Conflictive

Here again, no simple behavior-begets-behavior model is postulated, and it is assumed that in the case of conflictive events the issue area at stake may play a role.

It was also thought that the condition of issue areas could be substituted by the condition of a decision-maker's function, which might produce distinct response strategies. For example, ministers who have higher responsibilities than advisers might react more cautiously than advisers.

Table 11.3 shows a decision-maker's function together with the external actors' prior actions and the kind of specification and selection of strategies we expect. Proposition III formulates the relationships:

Proposition III:

If the prior actions of another nation are cooperative, in general, the response will also be cooperative. However, if the prior actions are conflictive, the function of the decision-maker may play a role.

It is expected that ministers will be more cautious because of their greater responsibility, while advisers might feel freer to reflect in their specification and selection of strategies the prior actions of the other nations.

Results

In the first test of the effects of the different variables by means of Loglinear modeling it turned out that in combination with the variable "ally," the variable "size of the other country" no longer had any effect. In the same way, it was found that neither issue area nor function of the decision-maker had a significant effect on the specification of the strategies with respect to whether they were more or less conflictive. This means that a part of Proposition I and Propositions II and III are rejected on the basis of our data.

Proposition I posited that cooperative prior actions would generally provoke

Table 11.3:

Influence of Decision-Maker's Function and Prior Actions of External Actor on the Generation and Choice of Cooperative or Conflictive Strategies

Function of the decision-maker	Prior actions of external actor	Strategies
Minister	Cooperative	Cooperative
Adviser	Cooperative	Cooperative
Minister	Conflictive	Cooperative/conflictive
Adviser	Conflictive	Conflictive

cooperative strategies in response, but in situations where the prior behavior was conflictive, the size of the other nation and its type would play a role. It turned out that size had no significant effect, and so it was omitted from the cross-table analysis. Table 11.4 summarizes the three-dimensional analysis relating to Proposition I with the type of other nation and the external actor's prior actions, which did have significant effects in the Loglinear analysis. The table clearly shows that when dealing with allies, there is a tendency to specify mainly co-operative strategies, almost irrespective of their prior actions, in order to preserve alliance commitments. This result contradicts the assumptions made in Proposition I insofar as it was assumed that in cases of conflictive prior actions of an ally, the size of this nation might produce different responses, but this was not the case. But it was also assumed that if one's own nation was a small power, it would tend to respond cooperatively because of its greater dependence on allies, an assumption supported by these findings.

As for nonallies, the responses summarized in Table 11.4 are quite different. The decision-makers here react to the prior action. When very conflictive actions

Table 11.4:
Relationship between an External Actor's Prior Action and the Specified Strategies when Reacting to Another Nation

Type of other nation	External actor's prior action	Very conflictive		Conflictive		Neutral		Cooperative		Very cooperative		Total
		%	abs.	%	abs.	%	abs.	%	abs.	%	abs.	abs.
Ally	Very conflictive	0		10	(1)	10	(1)	80	(8)	0		10
	Conflictive	0		29	(33)	11	(13)	60	(68)	0		114
	Cooperative	0		20	(13)	13	(8)	67	(43)	0		64
Nonally	Very conflictive	48	(17)	14	(5)	8	(3)	22	(8)	8	(3)	36
	Conflictive	19	(27)	23	(32)	21	(30)	33	(47)	4	(6)	142
	Cooperative	26	(9)	6	(2)	9	(3)	56	(19)	3	(1)	34
Total												400

The ally subtable showed no significant relation: $\chi^2 = 3.075$, df = 4, prob. = 0.54; the nonally subtable had a significant relation: $\chi^2 = 25.52$, df = 8, prob. = 0.00 and contingency coefficient CC = 0.328.

occur, the responses considered are mainly very conflictive also. In this case it seems that decision-makers feel there is no necessity to appease the other nation. Here the ideas of the behavior-begets-behavior model are supported. These results are also in agreement with the key assumptions of Proposition I, which assumed the behavior-begets-behavior model.

Since we know the proposed strategy, we can also see whether the relations were different for the proposed strategy as summarized in Table 11.5. The table shows that when allies are conflictive, decision-makers choose cooperative answers in 66 percent of the cases, but conflictive (23 percent) and neutral answers (11 percent) also occur. Being dependent on the ally, the decision-maker does not dare annoy him too much, and even when conflictive answers are chosen, they probably do not lead to disastrous consequences. When allies are cooperative, the answer is, of course, even more frequently cooperative (97 percent).

When reacting to very conflictive nonallies (Table 11.5), the chosen answer is very conflictive in 79 percent of the cases. If nonallies are conflictive, there is an overreaction in 20 percent of the cases where a very conflictive strategy is

Table 11.5:
Relationship between an External Actor's Prior Action and the Proposed Strategy when Reacting to Another Nation

Type of other nation	External actor's prior action	Very conflictive		Conflictive		Neutral		Cooperative		Very cooperative		Total
		%	abs.	%	abs.	%	abs.	%	abs.	%	abs.	abs.
Ally	Very conflictive	0		25	(1)	0		75	(3)	0		4
	Conflictive	0		23	(12)	11	(6)	66	(35)	0		53
	Cooperative	0		3	(1)	0		97	(28)	0		29
Nonally	Very conflictive	79	(11)	14	(2)	0		7	(1)	0		14
	Conflictive	20	(12)	20	(12)	19	(11)	38	(22)	3	(2)	59
	Cooperative	8	(1)	0		8	(1)	76	(10)	8	(1)	13
Total												172

Both subtables showed significant relations. For the ally subtable $\chi^2 = 10.45$, df = 4, prob. = 0.03 and the contingency coefficient CC = 0.329; for the nonally subtable $\chi^2 = 30.30$, df = 8, prob.= 0.00 and CC = 0.508.

chosen, another 20 percent of the answers are conflictive, and also 38 percent of the chosen strategies are cooperative. This can only be explained by looking at the consequences of the acts. Finally, cooperative actions lead mainly to the choice of cooperative strategies. A comparison of allies and nonallies in the table shows that when dealing with nonallies, decision-makers are inclined to choose conflictive answers, but in the case of allies, they are in general more careful, and conflictive answers are less numerous, although a weak action-reaction relation was found. These results for the proposed strategies are very similar to those for the specified strategies (Table 11.4) and the remarks made about deviations from Proposition I apply here also.

The Choice of Cooperative or Conflictive Strategies when Taking the Initiative

In situations of initiative, where no other nation has taken prior action, it was assumed that the presence or absence of satisfaction with the status quo might play a central role, since decision-makers might behave differently if they are satisfied with the status quo but still wish to improve their situation than if they are dissatisfied with the status quo and want to improve their position. However, even in this case, we would expect the size of the other nation toward whom the action is directed together with the type of other nation (whether it is an ally or not) to play a role, in the sense that these variables will determine whether the strategies specified are cooperative or conflictive. This is similar to the situation where a nation is reacting to prior behavior of another state.

Table 11.6 sets out the type of other nation, its size, a decision-maker's satisfaction with the status quo, and the kind of specification and selection of strategies we expect. Proposition IV formulates the relation.

Proposition IV:

In situations where a decision-maker initiates an action and is satisfied with the status quo but still seeks to improve it, cooperative strategies will, in general, be specified and selected because he does not want to endanger his satisfactory position.

In situations of dissatisfaction with the status quo, it is assumed that the size and type of the other nation will play a role. If a decision-maker is dissatisfied with the status quo and his initiative is directed toward an ally which is a large or medium power, he will specify and select cooperative strategies in order to preserve the alliance commitments on which his own nation depends.

If he is dealing with a small ally and he himself belongs to a medium or large power, his initiative may be more conflictive, since there is less dependence on the small allies and he may hope to further his interest more quickly by taking this kind of initiative. But if his own nation is a small power, the initiative is likely to be cooperative because of greater dependence on allies.

If dissatisfied decision-makers direct initiatives toward nonallies, they will generally be more conflictive.

If their own nation is a small power, cautious initiatives can also be expected toward nonallies that are large or medium powers, so as not to annoy them too much.

Table 11.6:
Influence of Type of Other Nation, Size of External Actor and Satisfaction with the Status Quo on the Generation and Choice of Cooperative or Conflictive Strategies

Type of other nation	Size of external actor	Satisfaction with the status quo	Strategies
Ally	Large/medium	Satisfied	Cooperative
Ally	Large/medium	Dissatisfied	Cooperative
Ally	Small	Satisfied	Cooperative
Ally	Small	Dissatisfied	Cooperative/conflictive
Nonally	Large/medium	Satisfied	Cooperative
Nonally	Large/medium	Dissatisfied	Cooperative/conflictive
Nonally	Small	Satisfied	Cooperative
Nonally	Small	Dissatisfied	Conflictive

In this case also, issue areas can play a role. This relationship is specified in a separate propositon (Proposition V). Table 11.7 shows the issue areas together with a decision-maker's satisfaction with the status quo and the kind of specification and selection of strategies we expect. Proposition V formulates the relationships.

Proposition V:

In situations where a decision-maker initiates an action and is satisfied with the status quo but wants nevertheless to improve it, cooperative strategies will generally be specified and selected.

When he is dissatisfied with the status quo and wants to change it, the issue area will play a role. If the issue area is diplomacy, more cooperative strategies will be specified and selected than if the issue areas are security or economy, where more crucial values are at stake.

Results

First, Loglinear modeling was again used as a general test of all the variables mentioned in a specific proposition. This led to the selection of variables being cross-tabulated. Here, too, the size of the other nation specified in Proposition IV has been omitted from the cross-table analysis because this variable had no effect at all. In Proposition V the variable issue area was suggested, but this variable had no significant effect. This leaves the test of Proposition IV without the size of the other nation as a variable.

Table 11.7:
Influence of Issue Area and Satisfaction with the Status Quo on the
Generation and Choice of Cooperative or Conflictive Strategies

Issue area	Satisfaction with the status quo	Strategies
Diplomacy	Satisfied	Cooperative
Security/economy	Satisfied	Cooperative
Diplomacy	Dissatisfied	Cooperative
Security/economy	Dissatisfied	Conflictive

Table 11.8 summarizes the three-dimensional results of the analysis. The table shows that when taking an initiative toward an ally, it does not matter whether the decision-maker is satisfied with the status quo or not. He specifies mainly neutral and cooperative strategies. When a nonally is involved, and the decision-maker is satisfied with the status quo yet still seeks to improve it, mainly neutral strategies are generated. It seems as though decision-makers proceed cautiously in order to obtain real improvement. However, when they are dissatisfied, the specification of conflictive and cooperative strategies increases and far fewer neutral options are specified. In this situation, decision-makers do not have so much to lose, since they are already dissatisfied, and therefore they dare to present moderately conflictive demands to nonallies or try to improve their situation by making moderately cooperative offers.

These results deviate somewhat from the assumptions made in Proposition IV, which posited that in a situation of satisfaction with the status quo there would be no difference in behavior toward allies and nonallies and the initiatives would be mainly of a cooperative nature. In the case of dissatisfaction, it was assumed that the size of the other nation and its type would play a role. However, it was assumed that if one's own nation is a small power, in a situation of dissatisfaction, one would mainly select cooperative alternatives in order to preserve alliance commitments. Nevertheless, our data also showed the use of neutral strategies.

When decision-makers were dissatisfied and dealt with nonallies, it was assumed they would generally be conflictive but that cautious initiatives might be taken in cases where a small nation was dealing with a medium or large power. Our data show the use of both kinds of strategies, but the size of the nation did not appear to play a role. We could not repeat the same analyses for the proposed strategies because of the small sample size.

Table 11.8:

Relationship between Satisfaction and the Specified Strategies when Taking an Initiative toward Other Nations

Type of other nation	Satis-faction with the status quo	All specified strategies										
		Very conflictive		Conflictive		Neutral		Cooperative		Very cooperative		Total
		%	abs.	%	abs.	%	abs.	%	abs.	%	abs.	abs.
Ally	Satisfied	0		0		32	(6)	21	(4)	47	(9)	19
	Dissatisfied	0		3	(1)	33	(13)	41	(16)	23	(9)	39
Nonally	Satisfied	11	(2)	11	(2)	56	(10)	17	(3)	5	(1)	18
	Dissatisfied	4	(2)	30	(17)	23	(13)	33	(18)	11	(6)	56
Total												132

The ally subtable showed no significant relation ($\chi^2 = 4.4$, df = 3, prob. = 0.22) while the nonally subtable had a significant relation: $\chi^2 = 9.5$, df = 4, prob. = 0.05, and the contingency coefficient CC = 0.34.

THE SPECIFICATION AND CHOICE OF STRATEGIES IN TERMS OF THE STATUS QUO AND DEVIATIONS FROM IT

Lindblom's hypothesis about strategies in terms of the status quo and deviations from it (Lindblom 1982) offers a different method of analysis. Although Lindblom suggests that decision-makers generally prefer strategies that only incrementally differ from the status quo, we expect them to be more specific with respect to the specification and selection of strategies, which means that new strategies and status quo strategies are also specified and selected.

It seemed plausible to make first a distinction between the situation where decision-makers are satisfied with the status quo and the situation where they are dissatisfied with the status quo. Further, it was assumed that the question of whether decision-makers are reacting to or initiating an action toward allies or nonallies (the type of other nation) might play a role.

Table 11.9 sets out the type of other nation together with the situation of initiative or reaction, the decision-maker's satisfaction with the status quo, and the kind of strategies we expect. From this the following proposition is derived:

Proposition VI:

In situations where decision-makers are satisfied with the status quo and are reacting to another nation, which means that they do not wish for change, they will specify mainly

Table 11.9:
Influence of Type of Other Nation, Reaction/Initiative, and Satisfaction with the Status Quo on the Generation and Choice of Strategies in Terms of the Status Quo and Deviations from It

Type of other nation	Reaction/initiative	Satisfaction with the status quo	Strategies
Ally	Reaction	Satisfied	*Sq/ssd
Ally	Reaction	Dissatisfied	Ssd/new
Ally	Initiative	Satisfied	Ssd/new
Ally	Initiative	Dissatisfied	Ssd/new
Nonally	Reaction	Satisfied	Sq/ssd
Nonally	Reaction	Dissatisfied	New
Nonally	Initiative	Satisfied	New
Nonally	Initiative	Dissatisfied	New

* "Sq" indicates the status quo strategy; "ssd" refers to someting slightly different from the status quo; and"new" refers to a new strategy.

the status quo strategy and strategies only slightly differing from the status quo. The type of other nation does not play a role. The selected strategy will be mainly the status quo.

When decision-makers are satisfied with the status quo but still wish to improve it by taking an initiative, the type of other nation does play a role. If allies are concerned, decision-makers will mostly consider either strategies that differ slightly from the status quo or new strategies. With nonallies they will specify and select more new strategies, since they want to improve their position.

In situations where decision-makers are dissatisfied with the status quo, we assume that initiative or reaction to another nation will play no role but the type of other nation will have some influence. When nonallies are concerned, they will specify and select new strategies, since they may have little to lose. With allies they will be more careful, considering mainly strategies which differ slightly from the status quo and new strategies, as in the situation of satisfaction and initiative. If the new strategies are not conflictive, then they will be chosen; otherwise, something slightly different from the status quo will be selected.

Results

Proposition VI posited that satisfaction and dissatisfaction with the status quo, combined with initiative or reaction and the type of other nation, will play a role in the specification of strategies in terms of the status quo and deviations from it.

Table 11.10:

Relationship between Type of the Other Nation, Reaction/Initiative, and the Specified Strategies when Decision-Makers Are Dissatisfied with the Status Quo

Type of other nation	Reaction	*Specified strategies						Total
		Sq		Ssd		New		
		%	abs.	%	abs.	%	abs.	abs.
Ally	Reaction	14	(20)	46	(63)	40	(55)	138
	Initiative	36	(14)	28	(11)	36	(14)	39
Nonally	Reaction	20	(38)	21	(39)	59	(109)	186
	Initiative	25	(14)	21	(12)	54	(30)	56
Total								419

*"Sq" indicates the status quo strategy; "ssd" refers to someting slightly different from the status quo; and "new" refers to a new strategy.
The ally subtable showed a significant relation: $\chi^2 = 8.4$, df = 3, prob. = 0.05, CC = 0.35; while the nonally subtable had no significant relation: $\chi^2 = 7.5$, df = 4, prob. = 0.12.

Since there were very few data on satisfaction with the status quo, testing the proposition was focused on the situation of dissatisfaction.

Table 11.10 presents the results of the cross-table analysis for the specification of strategies. The table shows that when reacting to allies, decision-makers mainly specify strategies that differ only slightly from the status quo. When taking an initiative toward an ally, they more frequently consider the status quo and new strategies. When dealing with nonallies, they mainly specify new strategies, irrespective of whether they are reacting or taking an initiative. The results regarding allies differ somewhat from the assumptions made in Proposition VI. It was posited that in situations of dissatisfaction with the status quo, reaction or initiative would play no role, and only the type of other nation would play a role. Where allies were concerned, it was assumed that, generally, strategies ranging from something slightly different from the status quo to new strategies would be considered. However, the data show that when decision-makers were dissatisfied and reacted, they usually considered something only slightly different from the status quo, whereas when they took an initiative, both the status quo and new options were specified. With respect to nonallies, the assumptions of Proposition VI are similar to the results of the analyses where the situation of reaction or initiative played no role, and where mostly new strategies were considered.

Table 11.11:

Relationship between Type of Other Nation, Reaction/Initiative, and the Proposed Strategy when Decision-Makers Are Dissatisfied with the Status Quo

Type of other nation	Reaction	*Specified strategies						Total
		Sq		Ssd		New		
		%	abs.	%	abs.	%	abs.	abs.
Ally	Reaction	8	(5)	65	(42)	27	(18)	65
	Initiative	10	(2)	32	(6)	58	(11)	19
Nonally	Reaction	9	(7)	28	(21)	63	(48)	76
	Initiative	14	(3)	24	(5)	62	(13)	21
Total								181

*"Sq" indicates the status quo strategy; "ssd" refers to someting slightly different from the status quo; and "new" refers to a new strategy.
The ally subtable showed a significant relation: $\chi^2 = 6.5$, df = 3, prob. = 0.05, CC = 0.41 while the nonally subtable had no significant relation: $\chi^2 = 3.5$, df = 3, prob. = 0.21.

The results for the proposed strategies are shown in Table 11.11. The table indicates clearly that when choosing a strategy in reaction to an ally, decision-makers seem to be cautious, mainly selecting a strategy that is only slightly different from the status quo. When they take the initiative, they usually prefer to choose a new option, since a change is desired. Strategies that deviate slightly from the status quo are only second in frequency. When dealing with nonallies, it does not matter whether the decision-makers are reacting to them or taking an initiative, as they mainly choose new strategies. Since they are dissatisfied with the status quo and are not bound by alliance commitments, it seems that they feel freer to announce the changes they want.

Since a decision-maker, when reacting to allies, prefers to choose a strategy that is only slightly different from the status quo, the question arises as to why this is so. Further analysis showed that these "ssd" strategies consisted of cooperative behavior practically regardless of the prior behavior of the allies. Decision-makers thus try to accommodate their allies by taking only very small steps, cautiously deviating from an unsatisfactory status quo. If they are taking the initiative, they most frequently choose new strategies, while "ssd" strategies are only second in frequency. Further analysis showed that the new strategies chosen were all cooperative, and only if there was no new cooperative strategy available did decision-makers choose a cooperative "ssd" strategy in order not to annoy the ally, though at some cost in terms of the desired change.

CONCLUSIONS

Theoretical arguments led us to anticipate that decision-makers would specify and select different strategies under different conditions. These conditions were the type of other nation, its size, an external actor's prior behavior, the issue area, the function of the decision-maker and satisfaction with the status quo. Of these conditions, four turned out to be of importance: first, whether the action was directed toward an ally or nonally; second, whether the situation was one where the decision-maker took the initiative or had to react to another nation; third, whether the prior behavior of the external actor was conflictive or not; and, fourth, whether the decision-maker was satisfied or dissatisfied with the status quo. The other conditions, the size of the other nation, the issue area, and the function of the decision-maker, did not have a significant effect, which means that Propositions II and III are rejected.

On the basis of the findings summarized in Table 11.12 Proposition I can be reformulated.

Proposition I:

In general, cooperative prior actions will produce cooperative strategies in response, but in situations where the prior behavior is conflictive, the type of other nation plays a role. If the conflictive action comes from an ally, the answer still will be mainly cooperative or neutral in order to preserve the good relationship. But if the conflictive stimulus comes from a nonally, the response will significantly resemble the nature of the prior action.

Table 11.12:

Summary of the Variables that Influenced the Generation and Choice of Cooperative or Conflictive Strategies when Reacting to an External Actor's Prior Behavior

Type of other nation	External actor's prior behavior	Strategies
Ally	Cooperative	Cooperative
Ally	Conflictive	Cooperative/neutral
Nonally	Cooperative	Cooperative
Nonally	Conflictive	Cooperative/conflictive

It should be clear, however, that this proposition does not always hold. If the advantages of the positive relationship with an ally are no longer considered to be relevant, the behavior may be quite different. We can see such cases in our data, though they are too few to be significant.

It is also possible that our data suggest this behavior toward allies because we studied a small power whose allies are mainly larger or medium powers. Without further research, it cannot be stated that Proposition I also holds for large or medium powers, although we assume it does. The formulation of strategies toward nonallies was more complex. The idea that one's own behavior reflects that of the other nation is logical, since the nation need not be especially friendly to nonallies. However, it is still possible, and it is indicated in the data, that a nation may react to a very conflictive act by a nonally with a cooperative strategy. The choice of strategy depends, of course, on the consequences the decision-maker anticipates from this act on his long-term relationship with the nonally. However, the data show this only occasionally and therefore do not allow for such a detailed analysis.

Proposition IV, which referred to the situation of initiative, also needs to be slightly reformulated. Table 11.13 summarizes the variables that were of influence.

Proposition IV:

If a decision-maker initiates an action toward an ally, satisfaction with the status quo plays no role. He will mainly use cooperative strategies in order not to disrupt the good relationship.

When he is dealing with a nonally and he is satisfied with the status quo, mainly neutral strategies will be employed, because he wants to be cautious so as not lose anything. If he is dissatisfied with the status quo, neutral strategies are ignored and both conflictive and cooperative strategies are considered. The use of a cooperative strategy would indicate that the decision-maker wants to improve his long-term relationship with the nonally.

Table 11.13:
Summary of the Variables that Influenced the Generation and Choice of Cooperative or Conflictive Strategies in the Situation of Initiative

Type of other nation	Satisfaction with the status quo	Strategies
Ally	Satisfied	Cooperative
Ally	Dissatisfied	Cooperative
Nonally	Satisfied	Neutral
Nonally	Dissatisfied	Cooperative/conflictive

Table 11.14:

Summary of the Variables that Influenced the Generation and Choice of Strategies in Terms of the Status Quo and Deviations from It

Type of other nation	Satisfaction with the status quo	Reaction/initiative	Strategies
Ally	Satisfied	Reaction	*Sq/ssd
Ally	Satisfied	Initiative	Ssd/new
Ally	Dissatisfied	Reaction	Ssd
Ally	Dissatisfied	Initiative	Sq/new
Nonally	Satisfied	Reaction	Sq/ssd
Nonally	Satisfied	Initiative	New
Nonally	Dissatisfied	Reaction	New
Nonally	Dissatisfied	Initiative	New

* "Sq" indicates the status quo strategy, "ssd" refers to something slightly different from the status quo, and "new" refers to a new strategy.

Proposition VI related to the specification and choice of strategies in terms of the status quo and deviations from it. This proposition could not be fully tested because we had insufficient arguments in the case of satisfaction. The test requires new data. Therefore we did not change the proposition on this point. On the other hand, the proposition needs to be slightly reformulated as a result of the testing (Table 11.14). For the reaction to allies and the initiative toward allies, slightly different strategies were postulated. The assumptions made in the proposition for the situation of satisfaction, although not tested, can still be maintained.

Proposition VI:

In situations where decision-makers are satisfied with the status quo and where they are reacting to another nation, which means that they do not wish for change, they will specify mainly the status quo strategy and strategies only slightly differing from the status quo. The type of other nation does not play any role. The selected strategy will be mainly the status quo.

When decision-makers are satisfied with the status quo but still wish to improve it by taking an initiative, the type of other nation does play a role. If it concerns allies, they will mostly consider strategies that differ slightly from the status quo or new strategies. If the new strategies are conflictive they will select something only slightly different from the status quo in order not to annoy the allies.

With nonallies, they will specify and select more new strategies, since they want to improve their position. When decision-makers are dissatisfied with the status quo and they are dealing with nonallies, they will specify mainly new strategies since they want a change, irrespective of whether they are reacting or taking an initiative.

When they are reacting to allies, they will mostly consider strategies that differ only slightly from the status quo in order not to disrupt the good relationship. When they are taking an initiative toward an ally, both the status quo and new strategies will be considered. If the new strategies are not conflictive, they will be chosen, since a change is desired.

To conclude this chapter, it should be stressed that none of these propositions excludes possibilities outside the specified range. We have the impression that decision-makers always consider the situation in more detail than we can in our overall analysis, and therefore, the relations we have found are not as strong as we had hoped. Exceptions to the rules of action we have specified will probably be in line with the basic philosophy behind decision-making, which is that strategies are considered with respect to the outcomes they are expected to produce. Thus there is a trend for decision-makers dealing with allies to choose cooperative strategies, and when they are dealing with nonallies, their behavior will either reflect the prior actions of the nonallies or, when taking the initiative, the choice of neutral or conflictive action depends on one's own nation's satisfaction with the status quo. The selection and choice of strategies is not an entirely fixed behavior pattern. If strategic considerations that take consequences into account suggest that a conflictive strategy will produce better results with an ally and that a cooperative strategy will produce better results with a nonally, then decision-makers are likely to act accordingly.

Chapter 12

Factors in the Specification of Outcomes

In accounting for the specification of outcomes, the literature mentions only situational and organizational characteristics. Brady (1982) suggested that variation in time frames for the realization of goals may be due to different situational conditions. In crisis situations, decision-makers may be inclined to pay most attention to immediate problems, while in noncrisis situations they should be more inclined to adopt a long-term perspective. These hypotheses, however, were not substantiated by results from the CREON project, which showed that decision-makers mainly adopt a short-time perspective. Other research reported by Brady (1975) did give some support to the idea that time frames were of some use in distinguishing crisis and noncrisis situations.

With respect to the substance of outcomes, the literature (Allison 1971; Allison and Halperin 1972; Halperin 1974; Brady 1975) suggested that individuals in governmental agencies try to advance the position of their department in order to enhance their own personal position: "where an individual sits in the process determines the stand that he takes" (Halperin 1974, 17). In the following passages we will formulate our propositions on the basis of suggestions taken from the literature and subject them to tests.

THE SPECIFICATION OF DIFFERENT TIME FRAMES FOR OUTCOMES

We also assume that in crisis situations fewer long-term consequences will be considered than in noncrisis situations. But as we did not expect such a simple pattern, it was postulated that the condition of the issue area at stake might lead to the specification of different time frames for consequences. Table 12.1 displays the situational characteristic of crisis together with issue areas and the time frame for outcomes. On the basis of our assumptions, the following proposition was formulated:

Table 12.1:
Influence of Crisis/Noncrisis and Issue Area Variables on the Specification of the Time Frame for Outcomes

Crisis	Issue area	Time frame for outcomes
Crisis	*Security	Short-term
Noncrisis	Diplomacy	Short-term/long-term
Noncrisis	Security	Short-term/long-term
Noncrisis	Economy	Long-term/short-term

*Crisis situations refer by definition (see Chapter 10) to security issues only.

Proposition I:

When decision-makers are faced with a crisis situation, they will mainly specify outcomes with a short-term time frame in order to resolve the immediate problem. However, when there is a noncrisis situation, the specification of long-term outcomes will increase, depending on the issue area involved. If the issue area is diplomacy or security, we expect fewer long-term outcomes than if the issue area is economy, since the latter involves more long-term planning, as an economy does not change overnight.

Results

Proposition I stated that in crisis situations it is mainly the outcomes with a short time frame that are considered, while in noncrisis situations whether or not more long-term outcomes are considered depends on the issue area. Table 12.2 summarizes the results from the cross-table analysis. The table shows, indeed, that in crisis situations it is mainly short-term consequences that are considered in order to resolve a problem. In noncrisis situations, the consideration of long-term outcomes increases. Proposition I postulated that if the issue was diplomacy or security, fewer long-term consequences would be mentioned than if the topic was economy. The data agree with the proposition. In noncrisis diplomatic or security issues, the consideration of long-term consequences increases, but these are considered less frequently than in the economic issue area.

THE SPECIFICATION OF THE SUBSTANCE OF OUTCOMES

We assume that if the proposition is correct, "where an individual sits in the process determines the stand that he takes" (Halperin 1974,17); a decision-maker's departmental affiliation must be reflected in some way in the substance

Table 12.2:
Relationship between Crisis, Issue Areas, and the Time Frame for Outcomes

Crisis	Issue area	Time frame for outcomes				Total
		Short-term		Long-term		
		%	abs.	%	abs.	abs.
Crisis	Security	88	(495)	12	(67)	562
Noncrisis	Diplomacy	66	(83)	34	(42)	125
Noncrisis	Security	65	(126)	35	(69)	195
Noncrisis	Economy	51	(214)	49	(205)	419
Total						1301

$\chi^2 = 163.97$, df. $= 3$, prob. $= 0.00$, CC $= .335$

of specified consequences. Nevertheless, the issue area of the decision might also be a condition. Since diplomatic issues are generally handled by Foreign Affairs officials, we concentrated on the security and economic issues when officials of several departments were involved. Table 12.3 displays the departmental affiliation of the decision-makers together with the issue areas and the substance of outcomes. This leads us to formulate the following proposition:

Proposition II:

When the issue area is security or economy, several other departments will also be involved, such as Finance, Overseas Territories, Foreign Affairs, and so forth, and the substance of outcomes is more likely to reflect the interests of the various governmental agencies. This means that when security or economic topics are being discussed, decision-makers will mention outcomes relevant to their own department as well as defense or economic/financial outcomes.

Results

Proposition II posited that the departmental affiliation of a decision-maker is more likely to be reflected if the issue area is security or economy than if the issue is diplomacy, because the former issues involve more governmental agencies, who may perceive the issue as an opportunity to advance their own interests.

Table 12.3:
Influence of Departmental Affiliation and Issue Area Variables on the
Specification of the Substance of Outcomes

Departmental affiliation	Issue area	Substance of outcomes
Defense officials	Security	Defense
Economics/Finance officials	Security	Defense/economic/financial
Foreign Affairs officials	Security	Defense/foreign affairs
Overseas Territories officials	Security	Defense/colonial
Interior officials	Security	Defense/internal
Justice officials	Security	Defense/legal
Defense officials	Economy	Economic/defense
Economics/Finance officials	Economy	Economic/financial
Foreign Affairs officials	Economy	Economic/foreign affairs
Overseas Territories officials	Economy	Economic/colonial
Interior officials	Economy	Economic/internal
Justice officials	Economy	Economic/legal

Table 12.4 displays the results of the analysis for the security issue. The table
does indeed show a trend for officials to specify substantive outcomes relating to
their own department more frequently than security outcomes, which is the topic
under discussion. Only 15 percent of the consequences specified by the ministers
and officials of Foreign Affairs relate to the security issue, while 39 percent of
the outcomes relate to foreign affairs. But since they also mention other consequences (for instance, 28 percent refer to overseas territories and 12 percent
refer to economic matters) one gets the impression that they are not only
safeguarding the interests of their own department but also trying to make a
sensible decision by considering more aspects of the problem. Only 13 percent
of the consequences specified by the officials of Finance and Economic Affairs
refer to the security topic, while 53 percent are economic/financial outcomes.
But these officials also considered other outcomes as relevant; 18 percent of the
consequences they specified concern foreign affairs and another 13 percent are
internal matters. In the case of officials of Overseas Territories, 48 percent of the
outcomes they mention relate to their departmental affiliation and only 6 percent
refer to defense, although foreign affairs (32 percent) and internal consequences
(16 percent) are also considered.

Table 12.4:

Relationship between the Departmental Affiliation of the Decision-Makers and the Substance of Outcomes They Considered for the Security Issue Area

Depart-mental affilia-tion	Substance of outcomes											
	Foreign affairs		Defense		Economic/ financial		Overseas territories		Legal		Internal		Total
	%	abs.	%	abs.	%	abs.	%	abs.	%	abs.	%	abs.	abs.
Ministers and officials of Foreign Affairs	39	(79)	15	(31)	12	(25)	28	(57)	0		6	(13)	205
Ministers and officials of Defense	10	(6)	57	(36)	8	(5)	24	(15)	0		1	(1)	63
Ministers and officials of Economic Affairs and Finance	18	(8)	13	(6)	54	(24)	2	(1)	0		13	(6)	45
Ministers and officials of Overseas Territories	32	(68)	6	(12)	3	(7)	48	(102)	1	(1)	10	(23)	213
Prime ministers and officials of General Affairs	28	(29)	19	(19)	7	(7)	30	(31)	0		16	(16)	102
Remaining ministers	34	(30)	6	(5)	4	(4)	40	(36)	0		16	(14)	89
Total													717

$\chi^2 = 158.43$, df = 25, prob. = 0.00, CC = .42

The prime minister and the other officials of General Affairs, with no specific departmental interests, since they are the coordinators of the other departments, anticipated a variety of different aspects of outcomes: 30 percent overseas territories, 28 percent foreign affairs, 19 percent defense, and 16 percent internal. The remaining ministers, representing a variety of departments, did not take a great part in the discussion as far as outcomes were concerned (n=89). Since their departments deal mainly with internal affairs such as justice, agriculture and the interior, one would expect, if they were to advance their own interests, an overwhelming amount of internal or legal consequences, but the table shows that this is not the case: 40 percent of the consequences relate to overseas territories, 34 percent to foreign affairs, and only 16 percent to internal outcomes. With respect to the security issue, our hypothesis is thus moderately confirmed.

Table 12.5 displays the relation between the departmental affiliation of the decision-makers and the substance of outcomes for the economic issue area. The table shows hardly any difference between the various groups of decision-makers. All considered a fair number of economic consequences, followed by foreign affairs consequences and internal outcomes. With respect to the economic issue area, we must therefore reject the hypothesis of increased departmental interests.

CONCLUSIONS

Theoretical considerations led us to expect that decision-makers would specify different outcomes under different conditions. The conditions were crisis,

Table 12.5:
Relationship between the Departmental Affiliation of the Decision-Makers and the Substance of Outcomes They Considered for the Economic Issue Area

Departmental affiliation	Substance of outcomes											
	Foreign affairs		Defense		Economic/ financial		Overseas territories		Legal		Internal	Total
	%	abs.	%	abs.	%	abs.	%	abs.	%	abs.	%	abs.	abs.
Ministers and officials of Foreign Affairs	41	(81)	0		45	(91)	1	(1)	6	(13)	7	(14)	200
Ministers and officials of Economic Affairs and Finance	38	(68)	2	(3)	47	(83)	1	(1)	5	(9)	7	(13)	177
Prime ministers and officials of General Affairs	33	(5)	0		34	(5)	0		0		33	(5)	15
Remaining ministers	26	(7)	0		44	(12)	0		15	(4)	15	(4)	27
Total													419

$\chi^2 = 23.68$, df = 15, prob. = 0.07, CC = .23

issue area, and the departmental affiliation of decision-makers. These conditions did indeed affect the specification of outcomes, as posited in Proposition I. When decision-makers were faced with a crisis situation, they mainly specified outcomes with a short-term time frame in order to resolve the immediate problem. However, when there was a noncrisis situation, the specification of long-term outcomes increased, depending on the issue area involved. If the issue area was diplomacy or security, fewer long-term outcomes were considered than if the issue area was economy, as in the latter case more long-term planning is necessary.

As for the advancement of the departmental interests of the various government officials, which may have been reflected in the substance of outcomes (Proposition II), the data produced little evidence of this. Only when dealing with the security issue did some decision-makers introduce a considerable number of consequences of direct concern to their own departmental affiliation. But alongside these specific outcomes, they enumerated a variety of other consequences, which seems to indicate that rather than safeguarding their departmental interests, they were simply trying to make a sensible decision by considering different aspects of the problem. We therefore suggest reformulating Proposition II as follows:

Proposition II:

The substance of outcomes a decision-maker specifies is generally not greatly influenced by the departmental affiliation of the decision-maker. Decision-makers try to solve the problem by anticipating different substantial consequences that might play a role. Only if the issue area is security do decision-makers feel the necessity to stress in some way consequences relating to their own agencies, because security matters are generally considered as being of the utmost importance, and if the defense consequences are not counterbalanced by others, their own agencies might be negatively affected.

Chapter 13

Factors in the Use of Argumentation Rules

The literature on the explanation of argumentation rules mentions situational and personal characteristics as possibly being of influence. Summarizing the literature with respect to the effects of crisis on decision-making, Holsti (1979) claimed that crisis can either diminish the cognitive abilities of decision-makers or enhance their ability to make rational and calculated choices. Brecher and Geist's findings (1980) on crisis and cognitive performance gave mixed results, and they concluded that the abilities of decision-makers were at least not wholly impaired. Another situational characteristic mentioned in the literature (e.g., Lentner 1972; Hermann 1974) that is supposed to have an impact on decision-making is an individual's belief in his ability to exercise control over the future. The presence of this characteristic can lead to a calculated choice, while its absence is supposed to produce less calculated choices. In crisis situations, furthermore, control over events is supposed to be reduced. The first observation we can make is that decisions are made in a different way in situations that are perceived as threatening to interests, with an increased probability of war, limited decision time (crisis) and reduced control over the future, than in situations not perceived as threatening. Personal characteristics such as an individual's cognitive style are also mentioned in the literature (e.g., Hermann 1974; Arroba 1977; George 1980) as having an impact on decision-making. Individuals differ in their way of processing and evaluating information, with some perceiving the environment as more complex than others.

Given these suggestions from the literature, we distinguished between crisis and noncrisis situations. In crisis situations, decision-makers can be expected either to be more careful and use more complex argumentation rules, which means that either they indicate utilities with intensities or probabilities (Classes II, III, Table 2.4) or they use simpler rules without indicating intensities of utilities or probabilities (Class IV, Table 2.4) because of diminished cognitive abilities. However, since we did not expect a simple relation here, we postulated that the condition of presence or absence of control over the future might be relevant.

Table 13.1 displays the situational characteristic of crisis together with control over the future and the kind of argumentation rules we anticipate. From this table the following proposition can be derived:

Proposition I:

In crisis situations, decision-makers will use more complex argumentation rules than in noncrisis situations if they think they have some control over the future. It is anticipated that they will mainly use rules from Classes II and III. If they have no control over the future, the simplest argumentation rules will be most frequently used (Class IV rules). In noncrisis situations, control over the future does not play a role; it is assumed that decision-makers will use a variety of rules.

Alternatively, it was postulated that the individual cognitive style of a decision-maker might determine the use of a particular argumentation rule.

Proposition II:

Depending on their cognitive style, certain individuals might have a preference for more complex rules, such as the rules of Classes II and III, while others prefer simpler rules such as the Class IV rules, independently of their perception of the situation.

Yet another possibility is that the function of the decision-maker within the government determines the use of a particular argumentation rule.

Proposition III:

Ministers who have greater responsibility than advisers might formulate the decision problem differently and use more complex rules (Classes II, III).

Table 13.1:
Influence of Crisis/Noncrisis and Control over the Future on the Use of Argumentation Rules

Crisis	Control over the future	Argumentation rules
Crisis	Control	Rules of Classes II, III
Crisis	No control	Rules of Class IV
Noncrisis	Control	Rules of Classes II, III, IV
Noncrisis	No control	Rules of Classes II, III, IV

Another factor not mentioned in the literature concerns the social context, which might produce a different use of argumentation rules. In this case, the complexity of the argument depends on the sequence of the argumentation. The first decision-maker might start with a simple argument, the next in sequence might provide a more complex argument because he has to take into account the remarks of the earlier decision-maker, and so on. This might be the case, especially, if there is disagreement among the decision-makers over strategies, the nature of outcomes, or their probability of occurrence. Table 13.2 shows the social context of the sequence of argumentation together with agreement among decision-makers and the kind of argumentation rules we expect. From this table the following proposition can be formulated:

Proposition IV:

Decision-makers generally use simpler rules (Class IV) when there is agreement about the problem formulation. If there is disagreement, more complex rules are used (Classes II, III) in an attempt to convince each other. Although disagreement can be anticipated by a decision-maker at the opening of the argumentation, arguments that come later in the sequence are expected to be more complex in the case of disagreement.

The transition from the use of a simple rule to a more complex one in the case of disagreement, as mentioned in Proposition IV, can be illustrated by the following example:

Suppose that the first decision-maker in the sequence rejected strategy S_1 because it might lead either to a positive outcome (O_{1+}) or to a negative outcome (O_{1-}). If the next

Table 13.2:
Influence of Agreement and Sequence Variables on the Use of Argumentation Rules

Agreement	Sequence	Argumentation rules
Agreement	Opening	Rules of Class IV
Agreement	In between	Rules of Class IV
Agreement	End	Rules of Class IV
Disagreement	Opening	Rules of Classes II, III
Disagreement	In between	Rules of Classes II, III
Disagreement	End	Rules of Classes II, III

decision-maker in the sequence disagrees with this conclusion, he could, for instance, state that the probability of O_{1+} is much higher than the probability of O_{1-}. In this way, probabilities with intensities are introduced, which indicates a transition to a more complex rule. But he could also restructure the problem and introduce several attributes for each outcome, which would also constitute a switch to a more complex rule.

Results

Proposition I posited that in crisis situations the use of more complex or less complex argumentation rules depended on the decision-maker's perceived control over the future, while in noncrisis situations it was assumed that decision-makers might use a variety of rules. Using Loglinear modelling as a general test, however, showed that control over the future had no significant effect at all, and it was therefore left out of the cross-table analysis.

Table 13.3 summarizes the two-dimensional analysis relating to Proposition I. The table shows that in crisis situations, decision-makers used slightly more complex rules (27 percent of Class III and 37 percent of Class II) than in noncrisis situations (17 percent of Class III and 28 percent of Class II). Proposition I postulated that this would occur when decision-makers thought they had some control over the future. The Loglinear analysis, however, showed that control did not play any role. We can thus conclude that in crisis situations, decision-makers try to look a bit more carefully at the problem by most frequently using the Risk-Avoidance Rules. In noncrisis situations, the simplest rules, that is, the satisficing

Table 13.3:
Relationship between Crisis and the Use of Argumentation Rules

Crisis	Argumentation rules used								
	Class IV		Class III		Class II		Class I		Total
	Simon, Reversed Simon Rules		Dominance, Lexicographic, Addition-of-Utilities Rules		Risk-Avoidance Rules		SEU model		
	%	abs.	%	abs.	%	abs.	%	abs.	abs.
Crisis	35	(31)	27	(24)	37	(32)	1	(1)	88
Noncrisis	54	(71)	17	(22)	28	(37)	1	(1)	131
Total									219

$\chi^2 = 7.5$, df = 3, prob. = .05, CC = .19

rules, are the most frequently used (54 percent, Class IV); they are also used in crisis situations, though to a lesser extent (35 percent, Class IV). Second in frequency are the Class II rules (28 percent), and third in frequency are the Class III rules (17 percent). Proposition I postulated that decision-makers would use the entire repertoire, which is essentially true, but there is a trend for the most simple rules to be most frequently used.

The testing of the other propositions, which postulated that either the individual cognitive style (Proposition II), the function of the decision-maker (Proposition III), or the social context (Proposition IV) could determine the use of argumentation rules, showed no significant relationship, and therefore these hypotheses had to be rejected. Since neither personal, organizational nor social context characteristics could explain the use of particular argumentation rules, we come to the conclusion that most of the decision-makers have the repertoire of rules from Classes II, III, and IV at their disposal and use these rules whenever it suits them. It seems that they employ different rules when they are having difficulty in convincing their audience.

ILLUSTRATION OF AN ARGUMENTATION PROCESS TO CONVINCE THE AUDIENCE

Although there were not enough sequential decisions to formulate a general argument about the effect of the social context and the sequence number (the test of Proposition IV showed no significant effect, which we attribute to the small number of available cases), we will give an example that can serve as an illustration of the possible context and sequence number effects. We use the process of argumentation employed by one decision-maker who tried to convince his audience by giving no less than eight arguments relating to the same decision problem, using six different argumentation rules sequentially and always drawing the same conclusion.

Table 13.4 displays these arguments, which were presented by the last Dutch governor general during the Indonesian struggle for independence. In the period from July to August 1947 the governor general repeatedly advised the Dutch government to "occupy the seat of the Indonesian republican government" (S_1). The alternative strategy was to "do nothing" (S_2). In his initial advice (Table 13.4), his argument (Drooglever and Van Schouten 1982, July 26, 1947, no. 46, 72–74) was as follows:

If we were to do nothing (S_2), the Republican government might capitulate (O_{21}), but it is also possible that the Dutch position will not improve (O_{22}). However, if we were to occupy the seat of the Republican government (S_1), it is possible that it will either capitulate (O_{11}) or even be liquidated (O_{12}).

The decision-maker structured the problem by indicating two outcomes for each strategy. Both utilities and probabilites were evaluated without intensities, and he selected the first strategy (S_1) he encountered that led to positive results only.

Table 13.4:
Different Arguments Given by the Last Governor General of the Dutch East Indies to Occupy the Seat of the Republican Government in 1947

Occasion of decision	Strategies				Argumentation rule
	S_1 (chosen) Occupy the seat, of the republican government		S_2 Do nothing		
First July 26	O_{11} Capitulation of the republic $U(O_{11})=+$ p_{11}=possible	O_{12} Liquidation of the republic $U(O_{12})=+$ p_{12}=possible	O_{21} Capitulation of the republic $U(O_{21})=+$ p_{21}=possible	O_{22} Dutch position not improved $U(O_{22})=-$ p_{22}=possible	Simon's Rule
Second July 29	O_{11} a_{111}: Liquidation of the republic a_{112}: Law and order re-established a_{113}: Not many international problems a_{114}: Not many national problems	O_{12} a_{121}: Liquidation of the republic a_{122}: Law and order re-established a_{123}: Many international problems a_{124}: Many national problems	O_{21} Armed forces not diminished, no cooperation for the reconstruction of the country, increased international involvement		Risk-Avoidance Rules
	$U(a_{111})=+$ $U(a_{112})=+$ $U(a_{113})$=acceptable $U(a_{114})$=acceptable p=high	$U(a_{121})=+$ $U(a_{122})=+$ $U(a_{123})=-$ $U(a_{124})=-$ p=low	$U(O_{21})=-$ p=certain		
Third July 31	O_{11} Restoration of law and order $U(O_{11})=+$ p_{11}=certain		O_{21} No restoration of law and order $U(O_{21})=-$ p_{21}=certain		Reversed Simon Rule and Simon's Rule

Table 13.4 (continued)

Occasion of decision	Strategies				Argumentation rule
	S_1 (chosen) Occupy the seat, of the republican government		S_2 Do nothing		
Fourth August 4	O_{11} Political reconstruction achieved $U(O_{11})=+$ $p_{11}=$higly probable	O_{12} Creation of a new untenable situation $U(O_{12})=-$ $p_{12}=$very small	O_{21} Republic respects the cease-fire order $U(O_{21})=+$ $p_{22}=$very improbable	O_{22} Creation of a new untenable situation $U(O_{22})=-$ $p_{22}=$very probable	Risk-Avoidance Rules
Fifth August 7	O_{11} Law and order reestablished, influence in the region maintained $U(O_{11})=+$ $p=$certain		O_{21} Law and order not reestablished, weakening of our position and, finally, loss of Indonesia $U(O_{21})=-$ $p=$certain		Reversed Simon Rule and Simon's Rule
Sixth August 10	O_{11} a_{111}: No defeat in Indonesia a_{112}: International troubles a_{113}: National problems $U(a_{111})=$very advantageous $U(a_{112})=$very serious $U(a_{113})=$very heavy $p_{11}=$certain		O_{21} a_{211}: Defeat in Indonesia a_{212}: No international troubles a_{213}: No national problems $U(a_{211})=$worst $U(a_{212})=$better $U(a_{213})=$better $p_{21}=$certain		Lexicographic Rule
Seventh August 12	O_{11} a_{111}: No defeat in Indonesia a_{112}: Temporary international problems a_{113}: Temporary national problems $U(O_{11})=$minor calamity $p_{11}=$certain		O_{21} a_{211}: Defeat in Indonesia a_{212}: No international problems a_{213}: No national problems $U(O_{21})=$greater calamity $p_{21}=$certain		Addition-of-Utilities Rule

Table 13.4 (continued)

Occasion of decision	Strategies		Argumentation rule
	S_1 (chosen) Occupy the seat, of the republican government	S_2 Do nothing	
Eighth August 26	O_{11} a_{111}: No defeat in Indonesia a_{112}: No deterioration of our international position a_{113}: No increase of amount of victims $U(a_{111})$=very positive $U(a_{112})$=quite negative $U(a_{113})$=less negative p_{11}=certain	O_{21} a_{211}: Defeat in Indonesia a_{212}: No improvement of our international position a_{213}: Great increase of amount of victims $U(a_{211})$=very negative $U(a_{212})$=quite negative $U(a_{213})$=very negative p_{21}=certain	Dominance Rule

Simon's Rule correctly describes this choice. The prime minister answered two days later that the government was still considering the matter and that they were worried about the national and international consequences (Drooglever and Van Schouten 1982, July 28, 1947, no. 64, 100). He therefore instructed the governor to wait for the cabinet decision, though if he felt it necessary, he was to feel free to offer further advice. On July 29, he gave more advice (Drooglever and Van Schouten 1982, July 29, 1947, no. 65, 100–102), which reads as follows:

If we do nothing (S_2), we certainly cannot reduce the armed forces, we will get no co-operation for the country's reconstruction, and we will be confronted with increased international involvement (O_{21}). However, if we occupy the seat of the Republican government (S_1), it is highly probable that the Republic will be eliminated (O_{11}: a_{111}), that law and order will be reestablished (O_{11}: a_{112}), and that the international and national troubles will be reduced to manageable proportions (O_{11}: a_{113}, a_{114}). Nevertheless, there is a small chance that we may liquidate the republic (O_{12}: a_{121}) and reestablish law and order (O_{12}: a_{122}) but still face severe international and national problems (O_{12}: a_{123}, a_{124}).

In this second argument the governor restructured the problem in such a way that two outcomes were considered for the chosen strategy and one outcome for the rejected option. He also took into account the international and national aspects of the problem, which worried the government, but did not use them systematically across strategies. For the rejected strategy, the national aspect was omitted. The utilities were evaluated without intensities, but he did indicate intensities for the probabilities. On the basis of this formulation, he selected the strategy with the highest probability of a positive outcome (S_1), which is correctly described by both versions of the Risk-Avoidance Rules. The government in The Hague studied this advice very seriously but came to the conclusion that, although it was sound in its Indonesian aspect, the international and national consequences could be very serious, and therefore the government cabled the governor that the occupation of the seat of the republican government was not a viable proposition (Drooglever and Van Schouten 1982, July 30, 1947, no. 87, 132).

Worried about the situation in Indonesia, the governor continued to urge the Dutch government to take action. On the third occasion (Drooglever and Van Schouten 1982, July 31, 1947, no. 92, 141–144), his argument was as follows:

If we continue to do nothing (S_2), law and order will certainly not be restored (O_{21}). But if we occupy the seat of the republican government (S_1), law and order will be restored (O_{11}).

This time, he considered only one outcome for each strategy and introduced certainty. Both utilities and probabilities were again evaluated without intensities, and he rejected the strategy that led only to a negative outcome (S_2), choosing instead S_1, which led with certainty to a positive outcome and which can be correctly described by the Reversed Simon Rule and Simon's Rule. When his complex argument (occasion 2) was rejected, he returned to a strong but simple argument. The minister of overseas territories, in reply to this advice, communicated to the governor that the government was not willing to give its permission, and even urged him to end the ongoing limited military action against the republican government in connection with the impending intervention of the United Nations Security Council in the matter (Drooglever and Van Schouten 1982, August 2, 1947, no. 134, 208–209).

Nevertheless, the governor made a fourth effort to convince the government in The Hague (Drooglever and Van Schouten 1982, August 4, 1947, no. 149, 223–225). The fourth argument reads as follows:

If we do nothing (S_2), it is very improbable that the Republic will respect the cease-fire order (O_{21}), but the chance is rather high that a new untenable situation will be created (O_{22}). However, if we occupy the seat of the republican government (S_1) it is highly probable that a political reconstruction will be achieved (O_{11}), while the risk of creating a new untenable situation is very small.

On this, the fourth occasion, the governor again considered two outcomes for each strategy and introduced uncertainty. The utilities were evaluated without intensities, but he used intensity statements for the probabilities. Since he selected the strategy with the highest probability of a positive outcome, both versions of the Risk-Avoidance Rules correctly describe his choice. Meanwhile, The Hague was busy appeasing the Security Council and did not reply to the governor. But the latter continued to urge The Hague to take measures in Indonesia.

On the fifth occasion, he cabled the following to The Hague (Drooglever and Van Schouten 1982, August 7, 1947, no. 186, 279–280):

If we do nothing (S_2), it is certain that law and order will not be reestablished, our position will weaken and finally we will lose Indonesia (O_{21}). But, if we occupy the seat of the Republican government (S_1), we will reestablish law and order and we will maintain our influence in this region (O_{11}).

This time, the governor again chose a very simple argument, restructuring the problem with one outcome for each strategy. The evaluation of utilities and probabilities was without intensities, and since he rejected the strategy that led with certainty to a negative outcome and chose the one that led with certainty to a positive outcome, the Reversed Simon Rule and Simon's Rule correctly describe his choice. The Hague replied very quickly, rejecting the advice and pointing out that the governor was mainly concerned with the Indonesian arena, while the government also had to take into account the national and the international arena (Drooglever and Van Schouten 1982, August 8, 1947, no. 198, 292–284).

However, the governor continued to press the Dutch government to give permission for action. From this time on he tried to convince The Hague by examining systematically the three aspects involved in the problem according to the government. On the sixth occasion (Drooglever and Van Schouten 1982, August 10, 1947, no. 221, 320–322), he communicated the following argument:

If we do nothing (S_2), we will be defeated in Indonesia (O_{21}: a_{211}), which is the worst outcome I can imagine. However, there will be no international trouble (O_{21}: a_{212}), nor will there be any national problems (O_{21}: a_{213}). If we occupy the seat of the Republican government (S_1), there will be no defeat in Indonesia (O_{11}: a_{111}), but there will be international and national trouble (O_{11}: a_{112}, a_{113}). The Indonesian question is, in my opinion, primary, not ancillary.

As the governor systematically made use of three aspects and indicated that the Indonesian aspect was the most important one, he selected the strategy (S_1), where the most important aspect had the highest value, irrespective of the utilities of the other aspects. The Lexicographic Rule describes his choice correctly. The Hague again answered promptly, rejecting his advice for the moment, perhaps because of the arbitrary choice of one aspect as the most important one, but keeping the possibility open for the future, if they could convince their own nation and the international arena that the situation in Indonesia had become untenable (Drooglever and Van Schouten 1982, August 12, 1947, no. 244, 363–364).

After he received the answer from the government, on the same day the governor made his seventh attempt to get permission for action (Drooglever and

Van Schouten 1982, August 12, 1947, no. 247, 366–367). This time, his argument was formulated as follows:

If we do nothing (S_2), we will be defeated in Indonesia (O_{21}: a_{211}). Although there will be no international or national problems (O_{21}: a_{212}, a_{213}). I consider this a greater calamity than occupying the seat of the Republican government (S_2), which avoids defeat in Indonesia (O_{11}: a_{111}) and for which I foresee only temporary international and national problems (O_{11}: a_{112}, a_{113}).

In this argument, the governor again formulated the problem with three aspects for each outcome. The probabilities were evaluated without intensities, but the utilities were indicated with intensities as a total value for all aspects. His choice can be correctly described by the Addition-of-Utilities Rule, although we cannot verify the computational activity. This argumentation did not convince The Hague, either. The minister of overseas territories replied that the governor underestimated the international consequences, which would not only be temporary but could lead to severe economic sanctions (Drooglever and Van Schouten 1982, August 14, 1947, no. 274, 408–409).

After some time had elapsed, the governor made one last effort to convince the Dutch government of the necessity of taking action against the republican government (Drooglever and Van Schouten 1982, August 26, 1947, no. 401, 639–640), in the following terms:

If we do nothing (S_2), we will be defeated in Indonesia (O_{21}: a_{211}), our international position will not improve (O_{21}: a_{212}), and there will be a great increase in the number of victims (O_{21}: a_{213}). If we occupy the seat of the Republican government (S_1), there will be no defeat in Indonesia (O_{11}: a_{111}), our international position will not deteriorate (O_{11}: a_{112}), and there will be no increase in the number of victims (O_{11}: a_{113}).

This time he evaluated each aspect separately with intensity statements, the probabilities were without intensities, and he chose the strategy where each aspect of an outcome had a value at least as good as, if not better than, that of the rejected strategy; this can be correctly described by the Dominance Rule. This was probably the strongest argument he could make. If the cabinet had accepted his structuring of the problem, the conclusion would inevitably have been in favor of the occupation. But the government did not agree that in the case of an occupation (S_1), the international position would not deteriorate (O_{11}: a_{112}). On the contrary, it feared severe international sanctions (Drooglever and Van Schouten 1982, August 27, 1947, no. 410, 657–660), since the Security Council had repeatedly called for a cease-fire and had also just decided to offer its good offices for the settlement of the dispute. The cabinet therefore summoned the governor to The Hague for internal consultation. On September 8 the governor seemed finally to have been convinced by the government to postpone the occupation and to collaborate first with the Security Council (Drooglever and Van Schouten 1982, September 8, 1947, no. 30, 57).

CONCLUSIONS

This chapter has shown that decision-makers can use argumentation rules quite arbitrarily. The only factor that has had some impact on the use of these rules is the situational characteristic of crisis. Although this relationship is not very strong, Proposition I needs to be reformulated:

Proposition I:

Decision-makers generally use the entire repertoire of argumentation rules. But in crisis situations, they try to look more carefully at the problem by using more complex rules (Class II and Class III). In noncrisis situations, there is a tendency to use the simplest rules (Class IV) more frequently.

The description of the governor general's arguments shows very clearly how a decision-maker, in one and the same situation, can vary his arguments constantly, using six different rules while each time arriving at the same conclusion. This high degree of flexibility is a result of slight variations in the description of the problem: variation in the structuring, that is, the number of outcomes and/or aspects, and the introduction of uncertainty or not, combined with adjusted evaluations of utilities or probabilites. This leads us to derive the second proposition:

Proposition II:

All decision-makers know these rules and may use them arbitrarily.

The arguments described also corroborate the results of the systematic study in this chapter, namely, that the rules are used rather arbitrarily, since we could hardly find any systematic factors of importance for the variation of the formulation. The only factor that seemed to matter in these examples was the reply obtained from other decision-makers. For the systematic study, this factor was too complex to be detected. From this finding follows the third proposition:

Proposition III:

Variation in the use of argumentation rules often occurs on the basis of a reaction to the arguments of another decision-maker.

Political Argumentation in Perspective

In Part 2 we studied the arguments of political decision-makers in order to detect general characteristics in their argumentations. We have conducted this study using the theoretical concepts and decision rules from decision theory, as we thought that this theory could help to select useful concepts and decision rules to derive conclusions from the descriptions of the decision problems. This approach turned out to be very successfull. In the following sections we will summarize what we think we have found and then formulate questions that remain for further research.

SIX TYPES OF ARGUMENTATION RULES

We found six types of argumentations that fit 219 of the total of 231 political arguments presented by politicians to their colleagues to convince them of their policy choice. These six argumentations can be classified according to the amount of information they require in order to derive a conclusion about a strategy. The classification is based on the use and lack of use of intensities to describe utilities and probabilities of possible outcomes. Table S.1 presents the classification of the six argumentations.

In cell 1 we did not mention any argumentation because the problem descriptions using utilities and probabilities with intensities hardly ever occur in practice, and when they do occur, they require decision rules that are too complex to be applied without decision aids. They require quantitative information and considerable calculation. Therefore, normally the rules in this class (SEU, etc.) do not play a role in political argumentation.

Argumentation in Class II

The rules of Class II (Table S.1) are called Risk-Avoidance Rules. They re-

Table S.1:
Six Different Argumentations Classified on the Basis of the Amount of Information about Utilities and Probabilities

	Utilities with intensities	Utilities without intensities
Probabilities with intensities		Positive Risk-Avoidance Rule
		Negative Risk-Avoidance Rule
	I	II
Probabilities without intensities	Dominance Rule	Simon's Rule
	Addition-of-Utilities Rule	Reversed Simon Rule
	Lexicographic Rule	
	III	IV

quire only probabilities with intensities, which means that the probability statements must at least indicate a rank order. The utility statements are supposed to be without intensities. The latter need be indicated only by positive or negative connotations in terms of "good" or "bad."

Arguments using the Positive Risk-Avoidance Rule should be formulated as follows:

1. Description : Description of the outcomes with intensities for probabilities but not for utilities
2. Rule   : If $P(O_{i+}) > P(O_{j+})$, then S_i must be chosen
3. Condition : $P(O_{i+}) > P(O_{j+})$
4. Conclusion : S_i must be chosen

Arguments using the Negative Risk-Avoidance Rule should be formulated as follows:

1. Description : Description of the outcomes with intensities for probabilities but not for utilities
2. Rule   : If $P(O_{i-}) < P(O_{j-})$ then S_i must be chosen
3. Condition : $P(O_{i-}) < P(O_{j-})$
4. Conclusion : S_i must be chosen

Argumentation in Class III

The Class III argumentations in Table S.1 call for utilities with intensities but no intensities for the probabilities.

Arguments that use the Dominance Rule can be summarized formally in the following way:

1. Description : Utilities with and probabilities without intensities
2. Rule : If $U(a_{ijm}) \geq U(a_{kjlm})$ for all k, l, m then S_i must be chosen
3. Condition : $U(a_{ijm}) \geq U(a_{kjlm})$ for all k, l, m
4. Conclusion : S_i must be chosen

Arguments that use the Addition-of-Utilities Rule can be summarized formally in the following way:

1. Description : The outcomes are described in aspects and at least the sum of the utilities for each strategy should be specified with intensities while the probabilities are specified without intensities.
2. Premise : If $\sum\limits_{j,m} U(a_{ijm}) > \sum\limits_{l,m} U(a_{klm})$ for all k then S_i must be chosen
3. Premise : $\sum\limits_{j,m} U(a_{ijm}) > \sum\limits_{l,m} U(a_{klm})$
4. Conclusion : S_i must be chosen

Arguments that use the Lexicographic Rule can be summarized formally in the following way:

1. Description : The outcomes are described with systematic aspects, the order of importance of these aspects is indicated and the utilities are given with and probabilities without intensities.
2. Rule : If $a_{.n}$ is the most important aspect and $U(a_{ijn}) > U(a_{kjn})$ for all k, j or if $U(a_{ijn}) = U(a_{kjn})$ and $a_{.o}$ is the second important aspect and $U(a_{ijo}) > U(a_{kjo})$ for all k, j, then S_i must be chosen
3. Condition : $U(a_{ijn}) > U(a_{kjn})$ for all k, j or $U(a_{ijn}) = U(a_{kjn})$ and $U(a_{ijo}) > U(a_{kjo})$ for all k, j
4. Conclusion : S_i must be chosen

Argumentation in Class IV

The Class IV argumentations are characterized by the fact that no intensities at all are specified (Table S.1, cell 4).

Arguments that employ Simon's Rule can be summarized formally in the following way:

1. Description : The utilities and probabilities are specified without intensities.
2. Rule   : If $U(O_{ij}) > 0$ for all j and $U(O_{kl}) < 0$ at least for one l, then S_i must be chosen
3. Condition : $U(O_{ij}) > 0$ for all j and $U(O_{kl}) < 0$ at least for one l
4. Conclusion : S_i must be chosen

Arguments that make use of the Reversed Simon Rule can be summarized formally in the following way:

1. Description : The utilities and probabilities are specified without intensities.
2. Rule   : If $U(O_{ij}) > 0$ for at least one j and $U(O_{kl}) < 0$ for all k, l, then S_i must be chosen.
3. Condition : $U(O_{ij}) > 0$ for at least one j and $U(O_{kl}) < 0$ for all k, l
4. Conclusion : S_i must be chosen

The advantages of these argumentations compared with the SEU argumentation is clear: they are much simpler and do not require any calculations. We have also seen that the Class IV type of argumentation requires the least information and occurs most frequently. The Class II type of argumentation requires probabilities with intensities and is the second most frequent type used. The Class III type of argumentation occurs less frequently than the II and IV Classes, since they require more information and a very systematic specification of consequences of the different strategies.

RULES ARE OBVIOUS WITHOUT EXPLICIT MENTION

The descriptions of the decision problems and the suggestion for a choice of a strategy can be found in texts of politicians, but the decision rule they used to derive their conclusion is not mentioned, even though this rule is an essential component of an argument. We have mentioned before that this could mean two things: either we have used a completely wrong approach, or these rules are so obvious both to the politicians who make the arguments and to their audience that they do not need to be mentioned.

If the latter possibility is true, then it must be possible to show three things:

1. The description of the problem suggests a decision rule that can predict the indicated choice with approximately 100 percent correctness.

2. Other people reading the problem description should make the same choice in 100 percent of the cases.

3. Other people reading the argument should be able to suggest the decision rule we anticipated.

In Chapter 8 these three points were scrutinized, and the first two were indeed confirmed with approximately 100 percent agreement. Only the third point did not lead to a perfect result. It was clear that all six types of argumentation mentioned were familiar or even obvious to a sample of the Dutch population, although people sometimes suggested different rules. The reason for this is that correct rules other than the rule we expected could also lead to the same choice. If such a rule required less information, then people often mentioned this rule while ignoring the extra information provided. This was more characteristic of the lesser educated than the more highly educated public.

We concluded from these findings that the decision rules were indeed obvious to the politicians and their audience. It would seem that such rules belong to the basic knowledge of people in general and, as in other fields of argumentation studies (e.g., Van Eemeren, Grootendorst, and Kruiger 1987), such knowledge is not mentioned explicitly if it is not absolutely necessary. Pólos and Masuch (1995) have shown how rules can be formulated by means of a different logic, assuming that the description contains sufficient information to specify the decision rule, which is then automatically applied to derive the choice. This led to the conclusion that the argumentations we have set out are the basic forms of argumentations that politicians use and understand when they argue about preferences for different actions in foreign policy.

QUALITY OF ARGUMENTATION

In Chapter 9 we looked at the question of whether the conclusions drawn in these arguments were always correct. We did this by determining whether the only certain decision principle, the Dominance Principle, could be applied to these choices and would lead to the same choice. The Dominance Principle is used because it says that one should choose the strategy that leads with certainty to better results than any other strategy. In this study, we found that the explicit formulations of the decision problems were not enough to derive a strategy corresponding with the Dominance Principle. This means that the anticipated argument did not lead to a choice in agreement with the Dominance Principle. However, if the implicit restrictions concerning utilities and probabilities were taken into account, 75 percent of the derived conclusions were in agreement with the Dominance Principle. This means that in 75 percent of the arguments, the specification, explicit and implicit, of the decision problem with utilities and probabilities was such that only one choice was possible: the choice preferred by the politician making the argument.

SIMPLIFICATIONS AND OVERSIMPLIFICATION

This strength of the logic of these arguments does not mean in itself that the arguments are very convincing. There are at least two sides to this: one is the logic used and the other is the completeness of the problem description. Further, on the basis of the case studies in Part 1, we showed that politicians simplify the decision problems considerably most of the time in order to make the argument simple and logically stronger. However, this simplification can also make the argument less convincing. On the basis of the case studies we have shown that, in fact, all politicians know that the problems they deal with are multiattribute problems with uncertainty but that hardly ever is an argument formulated in this way. This means that either the uncertainty and/or the multiattribute characteristics of the outcomes are ignored. This leaves a lot of space for other politicians to criticize an argument.

It is, however, difficult to think of a solution to the problem. The art of argumentation is to find a formulation that is as realistic as possible, introducing as much complexity as necessary, but on the other hand one that is as simple as possible so that everybody still can follow the argument without a problem. In this respect, the frequent occurrence of the Class IV argumentations without probabilities and utilities with intensities is an illustration of an oversimplification, in many instances. In Chapter 13 we showed a case where the decision-maker had been criticized explicitly for his oversimplifications and he then demonstrated his argumentation skills by presenting other more complex arguments leading to exactly the same choice.

CHOICE OF THE PROBLEM DESCRIPTION

There are many ways to formulate a decision problem, as we have outlined. Therefore, the questions were raised as to why a politician specifies two specific options and not others or three specific outcomes and not others, and why the utilities and probabilities are specified in the way we have seen, suggesting a specific rule that should be applied.

These topics were studied in Chapters 10 through 13, where we considered whether or not situational, organizational, external actor, and personal characteristics could lead to different types of argumentations. Chapter 11 studied the factors that might influence the specification and selection of strategies. It turned out that four conditions seemed to be of importance: whether the actions were directed toward an ally or nonally, whether the decision-maker took an initiative or was reacting to an external actor; whether the prior behavior of the external actor was conflictive or not, and whether the decision-maker was satisfied or dissatisfied with the status quo. These findings led to the formulation of three action rules:

Rule I   : When dealing with an ally, the generation and selection of strategies is mainly restricted to cooperative options.

Rule II   : When a decision-maker is dealing with a nonally and has to react to a prior action of this nonally, he specifies and selects mainly strategies that significantly resemble the nature of the prior action.

Rule III   : When a decision-maker initiates an action toward a nonally and is satisfied with the status quo, he mainly specifies neutral options. If he is dissatisfied with the status quo, neutral strategies are ignored and quite different strategies (conflictive or cooperative) are specified.

However, these relationships were not so strong as to exclude other possibilities. Exceptions to three rules are, in our opinion, in line with the strategic considerations of decision-making. Decision-makers consider consequences, and if they anticipate that a cooperative strategy toward a nonally or a conflictive strategy toward an ally will produce better results, then they prefer action in this way.

Chapter 12 investigated the conditions under which decision-makers specified different outcomes. Three conditions were of some influence: crisis, issue areas, and the departmental affiliation of the decision-maker. Based on the findings, the following rules can be formulated:

Rule IV : In crisis situations, decision-makers mainly specify consequences with a short time frame in order to resolve the immediate problem. Long-term consequences are more frequently considered in noncrisis situations when decision-makers are dealing with economic issues.

Rule V : The substance of outcomes reflects to some extent the departmental affiliation of the decision-maker when the issue area is security.

Here, too, the relationships were not so strong as to exclude possibilities outside of this range. The anticipation of long-term consequences is frequently very difficult, so decision-makers in noncrisis situations, when dealing with economic matters, preferred to consider clear, short-term outcomes. Besides safeguarding some departmental interests in terms of anticipated consequences, decision-makers tried to consider different aspects of the problem in order to make a reasonable decision.

Chapter 13 investigated factors that might explain the different use of argumentation rules. Based on the findings, the following rule can be formulated:

Rule VI : Decision-makers generally have the entire repertoire of argumentation rules at their disposal. They use these rules quite arbitrarily in order to convince their audience.
Only in crisis situations is there a trend to use slightly more complex rules.

Our overall conclusion is that although situational, organizational, and external actor characteristics have some influence on the type of argument decision-makers produce, these patterns are not fixed. Decision-makers may specify other strategies, consequences, and outcomes and may use a variety of rules based on strategic considerations. Rules I to VI suggest fixed behavior patterns based on allies, crises, and specific issues. On the other hand, there is room for strategic considerations and choices, as the relationships we found were not very strong. Apart from the weak trends found, the choices were made on the basis of the consequences perceived and evaluated for each strategy. Argumentation rules were used quite arbitrarily. All rules were known by the decision-makers and their audience, and therefore they did not have to be made explicit. The use of the rules probably depended mainly on the sequence of argumentation or the reaction to other decision-makers.

QUESTIONS THAT HAVE BEEN LEFT OPEN

One of the topics that remains unanswered in this book but is immediately suggested by our analyses relates to the collective choice problem. How do politicians as a group choose a strategy when different people have given arguments in favor of different strategies? Do they discuss the arguments, do they look for a compromise, or do they vote? In a subsequent volume, we will try to answer this question by the systematic analysis of data.

The last topic concerns the generalizability of our findings. In this volume it was demonstrated that decision-makers of other nations argue in the same way as their Dutch colleagues. Nevertheless, a systematic cross-national comparative study could strengthen the findings.

Appendix A

Guidelines for the Construction of Decision Trees

In this appendix, each step in the text analysis will be illustrated by a different example. The text quoted below is less clear than that analyzed in Chapter 3, and so may be of some help to readers who would like to use our text analysis approach for research purposes.

The text is that of a telegram from a Dutch official in Indonesia to the minister of foreign affairs in The Hague in 1947. In order to reestablish law and order in Indonesia, in July 1947 the Dutch undertook a so-called limited police action against the self-proclaimed Indonesian government seeking independence. Since the Dutch military measures did not prove effective enough to restore law and order, The Hague was on the point of giving in to the requirements of the Security Council of the United Nations. The Security Council wanted to intervene in the independence negotiations between the Dutch and Indonesia by establishing a so-called Good Offices Committee (GOC).

Telegram from the Chief of the Direction Far East to the Dutch Minister of Foreign Affairs, August 25, 1947

Par. 1:   In connection with the critical situation and as head of an office belonging to your department, I would like to bring the following unsolicited points to your attention in connection with the dilemma which has arisen from the advice of the governor and the reports from Lake Success [location of the United Nations] cabled by Van Kleffens:

Par. 2:   All the proposals from the Security Council would lead to the maintenance of the increasingly untenable state of affairs, both politically and economically, here in Indonesia.

Par. 3:   However, in the report from Foreign Affairs which we have just received, it is said that the aim of limitation has to be the collapse of the Djocja regime or its readiness to make concessions. Limitation cannot have been an aim in itself for it required certain calculations. Since our miscalculations have come to light, Foreign Affairs mentions in its own report two available options:

Par. 4:   To take strong military action quickly, as generally advised here.

Par. 5:   The way suggested by the United Nations and/or the Good Offices, preferred by the Dutch government.

Par. 6:   I am greatly concerned that the wrong way may have been chosen. In particular, Van Kleffens mentioned in his letter that from the very beginning the measures of the Security Council were inspired by "passion, fanaticism and prejudice." They want to sacrifice not only us but also the lives of the native population and the minorities to a combination of communist, coloured and Latin-American countries.

Par. 7:   Nevertheless, I wonder whether the various threats of the powers were not partially dictated by the wish to limit the problems they are facing now. These threats may also have been an undesired result of your report, by which we showed our hand and lost the trump of surprise. The same warning had also been issued by the Americans with respect to the limited action.

Par. 8:   In spite of the threats, there is no certainty that the Security Council could and indeed would apply sanctions, especially if the action, as advocated by Van Mook, was successful and destroyed the present Republican regime and ensured that it never reached power again in this form.

Par. 9:   The question is whether or not, ultimately, France will have to take our side in order not to prejudice irrevocably its own position in Indochina.

Par. 10:   For the Netherlands it is a question of life and death, whereas for the various other countries bringing the Indonesian question before the Security Council it cannot be other than a prelude to a Dutch evacuation, first from Java and Sumatra, and thereafter from Indonesia entirely. The responsibility for law and order in Indonesia would then rest in fact with the United States, Britain and the United Nations.

Par. 11:   However, were an action against Djocja, unexpectedly to provoke such severe sanctions that the Netherlands had to give way, as a last resort we could turn over the responsibility to the United States or the Security Council, perhaps by means of a trusteeship.

Par. 12:   Therefore I agree with the advice of Van Mook in his telegram [to occupy Djocjakarta]—which was actually redated without consulting my office—although I cannot disguise the fact that the circumstances are now much more unfavorable than they would have been had the advice been immediately pushed through.

Par. 13:   Because of some possible negative circumstances (the escape of the top leaders) the results might therefore fall somewhat short of expectations.

Par. 14:   Having considered the above thoroughly, I could not reach any other conclusion but that we should stand up for our rights and fulfill our moral obligations.

(Source: Chief of the Direction Far East, August 25, 1947, Telegram, in P. J. Drooglever and M. J. van Schouten, 1982, vol. 10, no. 390, 626–627.)

After reading the document carefully to gain insight into the structure of the discourse, the following must be registered:

1. The strategies the decision-maker considers available:

   S_1: To take strong military action quickly (Par. 4),
   which means the occupation of Djocjakarta (Pars. 11,12).

   S_2: To accept the Good Offices of the United Nations (Par. 5).

2. The course of action preferred by the decision-maker:

   S_1: The occupation of Djocjakarta.

3. A brief summary of the content of each paragraph with respect to the presence or absence of arguments relating to the available strategies:

   Par. 1: Introduction

   Par. 2: Results relating to the proposals of the Security Council (S_2), quite vaguely formulated *(relevant)*

   Par. 3: Discussion about the aim of the limited action in the past

   Par. 4: S_1

   Par. 5: S_2

   Par. 6: Relates to S_2 but considers past effects

   Par. 7: *Idem*

   Par. 8: Possible consequences of S_1. Will the Security Council apply sanctions? *(relevant)*

   Par. 9: Will France side with us? Question not answered

   Par. 10: Possible consequences of S_2 *(relevant)*

   Par. 11: Possible consequences of S_1 *(relevant)*

   Par. 12: Indicates that he prefers S_1, description of circumstances *(relevant)*

   Par. 13: Possible consequences of S_1 *(relevant)*

   Par. 14: Motivation for the choice of S_1 indicated by moral and legal goals

This step reveals the relevant paragraphs for the decision analysis: S_2: Pars. 2, 10; S_1: Pars. 8, 11, 12, 13.

Extraction of Concepts and Construction of Partial Decision Trees

In the following passage one possible way to code the text is shown.

Par. 2:

(O: All of the proposals from the Security Council (P: would lead) to the maintenance of the (U: increasingly untenable state of affairs, both politically and economically, here in Indonesia))

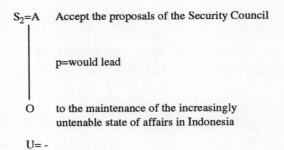

S_2=A   Accept the proposals of the Security Council

p=would lead

O   to the maintenance of the increasingly
     untenable state of affairs in Indonesia

U= -

Comment: The Dutch action is not explicitly indicated but can be assumed since it is mentioned explicitly in Par. 5. The reader should also be aware that an argumentation tree, even a partial structure, always starts with an action available to one's own nation and ends with outcomes. Note that the probability statement is derived by the modality of the verb phrase, which is signaling certainty.

Par. 10:

(UNDF: For the Netherlands it is a question of life and death)

(UNDF: whereas for the various other countries, bringing the Indonesian question before the Security Council) (P: cannot be anything other) (O: than a prelude to (U: the Dutch evacuation) first from Java and Sumatra, and thereafter from Indonesia entirely))

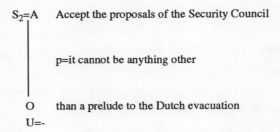

S_2=A   Accept the proposals of the Security Council

p=it cannot be anything other

O   than a prelude to the Dutch evacuation
U=-

Comment: From UNDF$_1$ it can be inferred that "evacuation" has a negative connotation. UNDF$_2$ suggests that it relates to S_2. After inspection of the subtrees, the tree of Par. 10 was taken as the essential one for S_2 since it contains the final outcome for the Netherlands. A combination of the two subtrees turned out to be problematic since there is no linguistic link between them.

Par. 8:

(UNDF: In spite of the threats) (P: there is no certainty))

(AO: that the Security Council could and indeed would apply sanctions)

(O: especially if the action, as advocated by Van Mook, was (U: successful))

(O: and (U: destroyed) the present Republican regime and (U: ensured it would never reach power again in this form))

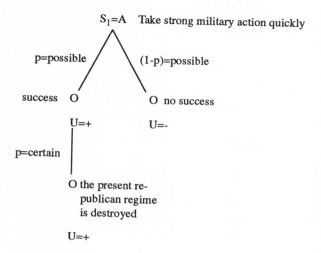

Comment: Here no probability is indicated for "success," but Par. 13 mentions that it is possible that they could be less successful. Therefore two branches are drawn.

Par. 11:

(O: However, were (A: an action against Djocja) to (P: unexpectedly) provoke such
(U: severe sanctions))

(A: that the Netherlands had to give way, as a last resort we could turn over the responsibility to the United States or the Security Council, perhaps by means of a trusteeship)

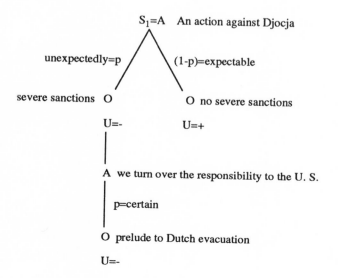

Comment: The final outcome is not mentioned here, but from Par. 10 we have the result of delegating responsibility.

Par. 12:

No subtree could be constructed. The decision maker only advises that action should be taken.

Par. 13:

(O: Because of some (P: possible) (U: negative) circumstances, the escape of the top leaders))

(U: (O: the results) (P: might) therefore fall somewhat short of expectations)

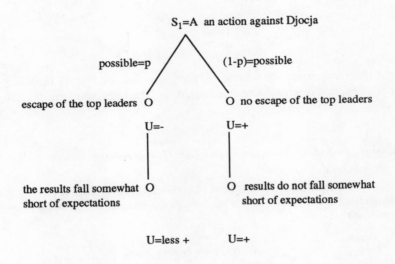

S_1=A an action against Djocja

possible=p   (1-p)=possible

escape of the top leaders O   O no escape of the top leaders

U=-   U=+

the results fall somewhat O   O results do not fall somewhat
short of expectations   short of expectations

U=less +   U=+

Comment: "Might" was interpreted as certain under the condition of the escape. One could also interpret this sentence as one possible outcome, since it does not change the meaning of the possibility of less success. This will be shown in the complete tree.

The alternative outcome "no escape of the top leaders" was not mentioned explicitly. But it can be inferred because of the statement of a "possible" escape of the top leaders, which implies that "no escape of the top leaders" is also "possible" (1-p).

Construction of the Entire Decision Tree

The combination of paragraphs 8, 11, and 13 produces the complete diagram of S_1. This is achieved mainly by using indications of the chronological sequence of the events. The coders started with the possible success or less success of the action and then brought in the possibilities of sanctions. Then under the condition of severe sanctions, they ended with the Dutch evacuation. The second strategy (S_2) is derived from paragraph 10. Figure A-1 shows the complete argumentation tree.

Figure A-1:
Complete Decision Tree

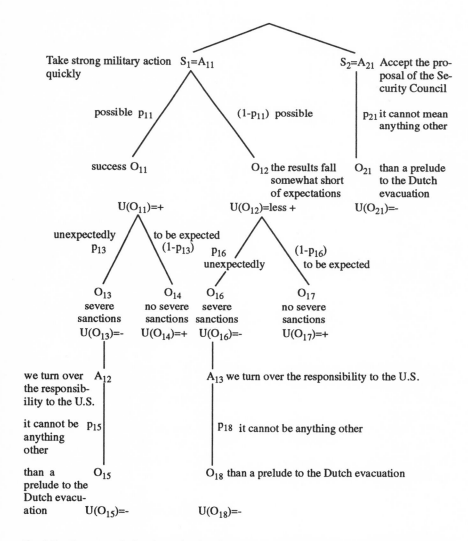

Symbols: S_i strategy i; A_{ij} alternative j under strategy i; O_{ij} outcome j under strategy i; $U(O_{ij})$ subjective utility of outcome j under strategy i; P_{ij} subjective probability of the O_{ij}'s.

Appendix B

Assessing Coding Reliability

In Chapter 3 we discussed the results of the reliability studies we had undertaken. In this appendix we will introduce some technical details about the computation of the various reliabilities so that readers interested in using our text analysis instrument could replicate parts of the reliability studies for their own research. In the following sections, the computation of the reliability measures with respect to the decomposition of segments of text into semantic units, concept assignment, and the construction of argumentation trees will be introduced.

Computation of Intercoder Reliability with Regard to the Determination of Semantic Units

An example will illustrate the agreement computation based on two alternative decompositions of semantic units:

Coder 1: ((I am absolutely not excluding the possibility)
  (that we might receive a (satisfactory) answer)
  (as a result of which the Dutch position could be (greatly consolidated) in the future peace treaty))

Coder 2: ((I am absolutely not excluding the possibility that we might receive a (satisfactory) answer)
  (as a result of which the Dutch position could be (greatly) consolidated in the future peace treaty))

In order to compute the agreement between these two coders, the parentheses notations of the codings are represented in linguistic tree structures. Figure B-1 displays the two alternative tree structures and the computation of the agreement measure.

The parentheses notation shows that the first coder discerned three main components, indicated in Figure B-1 by 1A, 1B, and 1C. The embeddings are placed at the second level of the tree where the "remaining parts" of the main categories are also indicated but not categorized. Component 1A has no embeddings. Since this structure consists partially of two levels, a dummy level is added to 1A.

Turning to the second coder's results, all units bracketed similarly to these of coder 1 receive the same label. In this case, coder 2 has distinguished two main categories. Because the first component is not equivalent to 1A, it receives a different level, 2D.

The structures in Figure B-1 have the same number of levels. If structures differ in the number of levels, dummy levels are added in order to match the one with the most levels. Subsequently, each level is assigned an equal partition of one (thus all levels summing up to 1), which is partitioned proportionally among the units of each level. The measure is computed by adding the weights of all identically coded units and dividing the result by 2. In the case of perfect agreement among coders, the measure yields 1, and in the case of no agreement, 0.

Figure B-1:
Representation of Two Alternative Tree Structures and Computation of the Agreement Measure

Coder 1

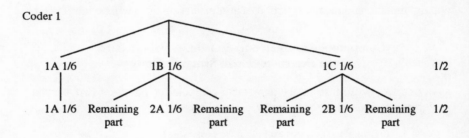

Coder 2

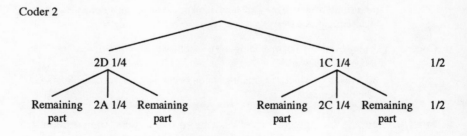

Measure = 1/2 (1/6 + 1/4 + 1/6 + 1/4) = .416

Computation of Intercoder Reliability with Regard
to the Concept Assignment

The second coding step consisted of assigning concepts to the semantic units. To assess the reliability of concept assignment, an association measure for nominal data was needed. We selected Scott's π, defined as the ratio of the above-chance agreement (Krippendorff 1970, 144).

If P_o is the observed proportion of agreement and P_e the expected proportion of agreement, then

$$\pi = \frac{P_o - P_e}{1 - P_e}$$

The numerator is a measure of the above-chance agreement observed and the denominator is a measure of the highest possible above-chance agreement.

$$P_o = 1/n \sum_{i=1}^{k} n_{ii}$$ where n is the total number of codings and n_{ii} is the number of codings assigned to concept i by both coders.

The proportion of expected agreement is defined by

$$P_e = 1/n^2 \sum_{i=1}^{k} (n_{i.} + n_{.i} / 2)^2$$ where $n_{i.}$ is the frequency with which concept i is used by the first coder and $n_{.i}$ is the frequency with which concept i is used by the second coder.

When the level of agreement equals chance expectancy, the value of π is zero; if perfect, it is one, and if less than can be expected by chance, its value becomes negative. The following example illustrates the computation:

Coder 1:   (UNDF: In spite of the threats) (P: there is no certainty)
            (AO: that the Security Council could and indeed would apply
            sanctions)
            (O: especially if the action, as advocated by Van Mook, was
            (U: successful))
            (O: and (U: destroyed) the present Republican regime and
            (U: ensured that it never reached power again in this form))

Coder 2:   (AO: In spite of the threats) (P: there is no certainty)
            (O: that the Security Council could and indeed would apply
            sanctions)
            (O: especially if the action, as advocated by Van Mook, was
            (U: successful))
            (O: and (U: destroyed) the present Republican regime and
            (U: ensured that it never reached power again in this form))

Table B-1:
Comparison of the Coding Results of the Two Coders

Concepts Coder 1		Concepts Coder 2				$n_{i.}$
	UNDF	AO	O	U	P	
UNDF	1					1
AO			1			1
O			2			2
U				3		3
P					1	1
$n_{.i}$	0	1	3	3	1	8

Note that only concepts can be used that consist of the same bracketed semantic units, which in this example is the case. Table B-1 summarizes the concept assignment of the two coders, facilitating the computation.

On the basis of Table B-1 the agreement measure can be computed as follows. The expected proportion of agreement is

$$P_e = 1/64 \left((1/2)^2 + (2/2)^2 + (5/2)^2 + (6/2)^2 + (2/2)^2 \right) = .27$$

This means that if the coders assigned concepts randomly, they should agree on about 27 percent.
The observed proportion of agreement is

$$P_o = 1/8 * 6 = .75$$

We now can compute π:

$$\pi = \frac{.75 - .27}{1 - .27} = .66$$

It is clear that the agreement is not perfect since the coders disagreed on two concepts.

Computation of Intercoder Reliability with Regard
to the Construction of Decision Trees

For the assessment of the coding reliability of the construction of decision trees, an ad hoc measure constructed for this purpose was used as the measure of agreement. The denominator of the agreement coefficient consists of the sum of

Figure B-2:
Representation of Two Decision Trees from Different Coders and
Computation of the Measure of Agreement

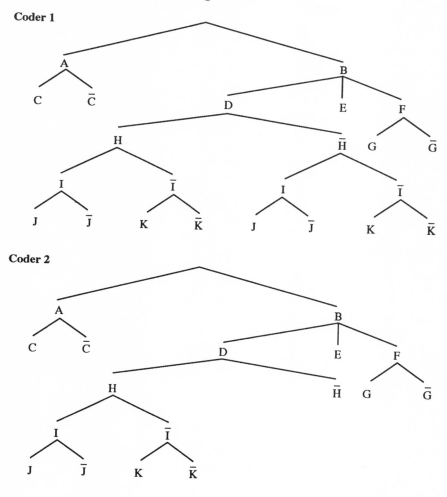

Labels of the branches	A B	C C̄	D E F	G Ḡ	H H̄	I Ī	I Ī	J J̄	J J̄	K K̄	K K̄
Number of identical branches	2 3	1 1	2 1 2	1 1	2 0	2 2	0 0	1 1	0 0	1 1	0 0
Maximal number of branches	2 3	1 1	2 1 2	1 1	2 2	2 2	2 2	1 1	1 1	1 1	1 1

Agreement coefficient   M = 24/34 = 0.71

the maximum number of branches for each node in the tree structure made by either of the coders. The numerator represents the sum of the branches that are identical for both coders, that is, in respect to the number of branches and their concepts. The measure of agreement is thus the ratio between the sum of the identical branches and the sum of the maximum number of branches:

$$M = \frac{\text{Number of identical branches}}{\text{Maximum number of branches}}$$

M can take on values ranging from 0 to 1. Figure B-2 illustrates the computation of the measure of agreement. The figure displays two argumentation trees from two different coders. Each node at the beginning and end of a branch with the same text unit and the same category received the same label. The figure further shows that each node represents a beginning and an end point of a branch. A node can therefore be characterized by having zero, one, or more branches. In cases where the maximum for both coders is zero this number is replaced by 1 in order to be counted as agreement (for example, J $\bar{\text{J}}$, K $\bar{\text{K}}$). Does and Overweel (1978) pointed out that however arbitrary this choice was, it worked satisfactorily. The argumentation trees in Figure B-2 have an agreement score of .71; greater differences between coders produce lower agreement scores.

Appendix C

Detection of Decision Rules from Interviews

The coding instrument we needed in order to analyze the verbal protocols had to be able to split the argumentation rules into elementary units and to indicate which units were minimally necessary to detect a specific rule and which elements in addition would give a maximal formulation of a specific argumentation rule. We therefore first split the protocols into six main conceptual components:

1. Statements about the chosen strategy (CHS)
2. Statements about the rejected strategy (-ies) (RS)
3. Comparisons between rejected and chosen strategy(-ies) (COMP)
4. Criterion statement (CR)
5. Normative statement (NR)
6. Undefined (UNDF)

For the first three statements, utterances about utilities (U) and probabilities (P) were identified. Criterion statements relate to choice principles such as maximization, threshold values, most important aspects, and so forth. Normative statements are statements in which subjects do not explain their choice in terms of the concepts mentioned but indicate an ethical principle: for example, one should always be loyal to one's allies. Such statements frequently occurred with presentations of concrete decision problems. Undefined relates to parts of protocols where subjects speak neither in terms of decision making nor in normative statements: for example, "I do not know what to say."

Having coded the text in this way, the utility and probability statements were classified as being with or without intensities. Finally, on the basis of a scheme summarizing the elements maximally and minimally required to detect the expected argumentation rules, the coders decided whether or not the protocol in question referred to one of these rules or to another known or unknown rule. The latter we called "own heuristic." To make all this less abstract, the coding for each decision rule we expect to find will be illustrated by an example.

Dominance Rule and Dominance Principle

In the summary scheme, it is indicated that the protocol should mention maximally a comparison (COMP) showing for which aspects of outcomes the chosen strategy (CHS) has the same utilities (U) as the rejected one(s) (RS) and for which aspects the chosen strategy is better. Thus in summary it should have a form roughly as follows:

(COMP: CHS (U: the same) as RS and CHS (U:better) than RS)

A concrete protocol illustrates this structure:

(COMP: Strategy 1 and strategy 2 (P: lead) to A, which is (U: negative))
(RS: Strategy 2 also (P: has) B which is (U: very negative),
(CHS: while choice 1 (P: has) C, which is (U: less negative); thus I choose the
(U: least negative) strategy))

Since subjects may express their arguments in an even shorter way, the minimal formulation that can still be identified as the Dominance Principle is, in our opinion, the indication that the chosen strategy is better than the rejected one(s):

(COMP: CHS (U: better) than RS)

The following is an example of a concrete protocol:

(COMP: because I shall always choose something which (P: is) (U: less negative),
    and C is
(U: less negative) than B)

In both examples, utilities are formulated with intensities and probabilities are formulated without intensities. The probabilities are indicated as certain and actually do not play a role, since they are the same for all strategies.

Simon's Rule

A complete protocol should indicate that the chosen strategy leads with certainty to positive outcomes while the rejected one(s) lead(s) possibly to negative outcomes or only possibly to certain positive outcomes. In summary, the following formulations are appropriate:

(CHS: (P: certainly) (U: positive)) and (RS: (P: possibly) (U: negative))
or
(CHS: (P: certainly) (U: positive)) and (RS: (P: possibly) some (U: positive))

Here is an example to illustrate one of these formulations:

(CHS: because strategy 1 (P: is entirely) (U: positive)) and
(RS: strategy 2 is (P: possibly) (U: negative))

A correct minimal formulation should at least indicate that the chosen altern-ative leads with certainty to positive results or that the rejected strategy(-ies) lead(s) possibly to negative or only possibly to positive outcomes. The structures are as follows:

(CHS: (P: certainly) (U:positive)
or
(RS: (P: possibly) (U: negative))
or
(RS: only (P: possibly) (U: positive))

The following is an example of a protocol:

(CHS: because choice 1 is (P: certainly) (U: positive)

Note that utilities and probabilites are indicated without intensities. In practice, subjects also express themselves in a more fragmentary way, omitting to state that the chosen strategy "only" leads to a positive outcome, for example, "because outcome C is positive" and so forth. Such statements were also classi-fied under the Simon Principle.

Reversed Simon Rule

The complete formulation should contain a reference to the rejected strategies, mentioning that they are certainly negative, while the chosen strategy could be expressed as possibly positive or only as possibly negative. The summary structures are approximately as follows:

(CHS: (P: possibly) (U: negative)) and (RS: (P: certainly) (U: negative))
or
(CHS: (P: possibly) (U: positive)) and (RS: (P: certainly) (U: negative))

Here is a concrete example:

(RS: if I (P: only expect) a (U: negative) effect, I do not like it)
(CHS: if I (P: can) expect a (U: positive) or a (P: negative), effect it is acceptable)

The minimal formulation must contain, in our opinion, either a reference to the chosen strategy, indicating that a positive result is possible or that a negative outcome is uncertain, or a reference to the rejected strategy(-ies), mentioning the certain negative outcomes.

This gives the following summary formulations:

> (CHS: (P: possibly) (U: positive))
>
> or
>
> (CHS: only (P: possibly) (U: negative))
>
> or
>
> (RS: (P: certainly) (U: negative))

Here are some examples:

> (CHS: because 2 also (P: can) lead to B, which is (U: positive))
>
> or
>
> (RS: because 1 (P: has only a chance) of leading to something (U: negative))

Here again, values and probabilities must be indicated without intensities.

Risk-Avoidance Rules

The complete formulation should contain a comparison of probabilities of either positive or negative results for the rejected and the chosen strategy. An alternative formulation would be to indicate for the chosen strategy a high chance of a positive result or a low chance of a negative result while indicating that it is different from the rejected strategy(-ies).

The summary structures are as follows:

> (COMP: (CHS: (P: smaller probability) of a (U: negative outcome) than RS)
>
> or
>
> (COMP: (CHS: (P: higher probability) of a (U: positive outcome) than RS)
>
> or
>
> (COMP: (CHS: (P: high/low probability) of a (U: positive/negative outcome) not with RS)

Here are some examples:

> (COMP: (CHS: I chose 2 because the negative outcome was (P: less probable) than with 1))
>
> or
>
> (COMP: (CHS: because the (P: probability is high) of obtaining (U: a positive result) B while (RS: with 1 it is not so))

The minimal formulations relate to the chosen or rejected strategy, indicating that the chance of a positive or negative result is high or low:

(CHS: (P: high) to obtain a (U: positive) outcome)
or
(CHS: (P: low) to obtain a (U: negative) outcome)
or
(RS: (P: low) to obtain a (U: positive) outcome)
or
(RS: (P: high) to obtain a (U: negative) outcome)

Here is an example:

(COMP: (CHS: because C has (P: the highest chance) of occurring and C is (U: positive)))

Note that utilities must be indicated without intensities and probabilities with intensities.

Lexicographic Rule

Normally, strategies should be compared, indicating that for the chosen strategy the most important outcome has a higher value than for the rejected strategy(-ies). Since our presentation of the information does not allow any systematic comparison of strategies, the maximal formulation should indicate only that for the chosen strategy the most important outcome is positive:

(CHS: (CRIT: most important outcome) (P: is) (U: positive))

Here is an example:

(CHS: because A is (CRIT: the most important outcome) and it (P: is) (U: positive))

In the minimal formulation, subjects should indicate that their choice was based on the importance of the outcomes:

(CHS: (CRIT: most important outcome))

For example:

(CHS: Because outcome A is (CRIT: most important))

It is clear that a criterion must be mentioned (most important outcome) but that utilities should not be indicated with intensities, as we have already explained. Probabilities should be indicated without intensities. Since they are the same for all strategies, they play no role in the choice.

Formulation of a SEU-type Rule

The necessary elements to detect the SEU model would consist of a comparison between the chosen strategy and the rejected one(s), combining in some way the utilities and probabilities indicated with intensities:

(COMP: (CHS: (P: higher probability) of (U: better) results than with RS))

The following example illustrates this rule:

(COMP: (RS: because I wanted to avoid the (U: negative) outcome A of 1 and since 1 (P: always leads) to A) (CHS: I prefer 2 because 2 has (P: a high chance) of a (U: better) result and only (P: a small chance) of A))

Formulation of Own Heuristics

The remaining coding category was own heuristics. We speak about own heuristics when subjects still mention some of the decision-making concepts but when, on the basis of the utilities and probabilities they indicated, we could not find an argumentation rule in the appropriate class to predict their choice, or when their argument does not fit the classification of argumentation rules into four groups according to the quality of utility and probability statements. Here is an example to illustrate this category:

(CHS: 2 offers (P: more possibilities))

(CHS: if a strategy has (U: positive) and (U: negative) outcomes and the (U: positive outcomes are more frequent) than the negative ones, I choose it, trying to diminish as much as possible the (U: negative ones)).

On the basis of the utilities and probabilities indicated (both without intensities), Class IV (Table 6.6) would be appropriate, but neither Simon's Rule nor the Reversed Simon Rule could produce this choice. The heuristics posits that the strategy where more positive outcomes could occur should be chosen.

References

LITERATURE

Allen, T. H. 1978. *New Methods in Social Science Research: Policy Sciences and Future Research.* New York: Praeger

Allison, G. T. 1971. *The Essence of Decision: Explaining the Cuban Missile Crisis.* Boston: Little Brown.

Allison, G. T., and H. M. Halperin. 1972. "Bureaucratic Politics: A Paradigm and Some Policy Implications." In R. Tanter and R. U. Ullman, eds., *Theory and Policy in International Relations,* 40–79. Princeton: Princeton University Press.

Akten zur Deutschen Auswärtigen Politik 1918 –1945, Serie D, vols.1, 2, 7. 1956. Baden-Baden: Imprimerie Nationale.

Arroba, T. 1977. "Styles of Decision-Making and Their Use: An Empirical Study." *British Journal of Guidance and Counselling* 5: 149–158.

Axelrod, R., ed. 1976. *Structure of Decision.* Princeton: Princeton University Press.

Baybrooke, D., and Ch. E. Lindblom. 1963. *A Strategy of Decision Policy Evaluation as a Social Process.* New York: Free Press.

Beyen, J. W. 1968. *Het spel en de knikkers: een kroniek van vijftig jaren.* Rotterdam: Donker.

Biel, A., and H. Montgomery. 1989. "Scenario Analysis and Energy Politics: The Disclosure of Causal Structure in Decision-Making." In H. Montgomery and O. Svenson, eds., *Process and Structure in Human Decision-Making,* 243–260. Chichester: Wiley.

Bihl, W. 1989. *Von der Donaumonarchie zur Zweiten Republik : Daten zur Österreichischen Geschichte seit 1867.* Wien, Köln: Böhlau Verlag.

Bonham, M. G., and M. J. Shapiro. 1986. "Mapping Structures of Thought." In I. N. Gallhofer, W. E. Saris, and M. Melman, eds., *Different Text Analysis Procedures for the Study of Decision-Making,* 29–51. Amsterdam: Sociometric Research Foundation.

Botz, G. 1976. *Die Eingliederung Österreichs in das Deutsche Reich: Planung und*

Verwirklichung des politisch-administrativen Anschlusses (1938–1940). Wien: Europaverlag.

Brady, L. P. 1975. "Explaining Foreign Policy Using Transitory Qualities of Situations." Paper presented at the Amercian Political Science Association, Los Angeles, September 2–5.

———. 1982. "Goal Properties of Foreign Policy Activities." In P. Callahan, L. P. Brady, and M. G. Hermann, eds., *Describing Foreign Policy Behavior,* 137–152. Beverly Hills, London: Sage.

Brecher, M. 1972. *The Foreign Policy System of Israel: Setting, Images, Process.* London: Oxford University Press.

———. 1974. *Decisions in Israel's Foreign Policy.* New Haven: Yale University Press.

———. 1977. "Toward a Theory of International Crisis Behavior." *International Studies Quarterly* 21 (2): 39–74.

Brecher, M., and B. Geist. 1980. *Decisions in Crisis: Israel, 1967 and 1973.* Berkeley: University of California Press.

Brecher, M., B. Steinberg, and J. Stein. 1969. "Foreign Policy Behavior." *Journal of Conflict Resolution* 13: 75–101.

Callahan, P., L. P. Brady, and M. G. Hermann, eds. 1982. *Describing Foreign Policy Behavior.* Beverly Hills, London: Sage.

Chang, L., and P. Kornbluh. 1992. *The Cuban Missile Crisis, 1962: A National Security Documents Reader.* New York: Free Press.

De Beus, J. G. 1978. *Morgen bij het aanbreken van de dag.* Rotterdam: Donker.

De Jong, J. J. P. 1988. *Diplomatie en Strijd: het Nederlands Beleid tegenover de Indonesische Revolutie 1945–1947.* Meppel, Amsterdam: Boom.

De Pijper, W. M., and W. E. Saris. 1986. *The Formulation of Interviews Using the Program Interv.* Amsterdam: Sociometric Research Foundation.

Does, R. M., and F. J. Overweel. 1978. "Tree Structure Measures." Unpublished manuscript. Amsterdam: Sociometric Research Foundation.

Drees, W. 1963. *Zestig jaar levenservaring.* Amsterdam: Arbeiderspers.

Drooglever, P. J., and M. J. van Schouten, eds. 1981–1992. *Officiële Bescheiden betreffende de Nederlands Indonesische Betrekkingen, 1945–1950.* Vols. 1–17. 's-Gravenhage: Nijhoff.

Dunn, W. N. 1981. *Public Policy Analysis: An Introduction.* Englewoods Cliffs N. J.: Prentice Hall.

Duynstee, F. J., and J. Bosmans. 1977. *Het Kabinet Schermerhorn-Drees.* Assen, Amsterdam: Van Gorcum.

East, M. A. 1975. "Explaining Foreign Policy Behavior Using National Attributes." Paper presented at the American Political Science Association meeting. Los Angeles, September 2–5.

East, M. A., and Ch. F. Hermann. 1974. "Do Nation-Types Account for Foreign Policy Behavior ?" In J. N. Rosenau, ed., *Comparing Foreign Policies: Theories, Findings, and Methods,* 269–304. New York: Wiley.

East, M. A., S. A. Salmore, and Ch. F. Hermann, eds. 1978. *Why Nations Act: Theoretical Perspectives for Comparative Foreign Policy Studies.* Beverly Hills: Sage.

Edwards, W. 1961. "Behavioral Decision Theory." *Annual Review of Psychology* 12: 473–498.

Ericsson, K. A., and H. A. Simon. 1984. *Protocol Analysis: Verbal Reports as Data.* Cambridge, Mass.: MIT Press.

Farnham, B. 1990. "Political Cognition and Decision-Making." *Political Psychology* 11 (1): 83–111.

Fishburn, P. C. 1964. *Decision and Value Theory.* New York: Wiley.

Fulbrook, M. 1990. *A Concise History of Germany.* Cambridge: University Press.

Gallhofer, I. N.1968. *Der "Damenfrieden" von Cambrai, 1529.* Unpublished Dissertation. Vienna: National Library.

Gallhofer, I. N., and W. E. Saris. 1978. "Coder's Reliability in the Study of Decision-Making Concepts, Replications in Time and Across Topics." *Methoden en Data Nieuwsbrief van de Sociaal-Wetenschappelijke Sectie van de Vereniging voor Statistiek (MDN)* 1: 58–74.

———. 1979a. "An Analysis of the Arguments of Decision-Makers Using Decision Trees." *Quality and Quantity* 13: 411–430.

———. 1979b. "Strategy Choices of Foreign Policy Decision-Makers: The Netherlands 1914." Journal of Conflict Resolution 23 (3): 425–445.

———. 1988. "A Coding Instrument for Empirical Research of Political Decision-Making." In W. E. Saris, and I. N. Gallhofer, eds., *Sociometric Research,* vol.1, 343–370. London: Macmillan Press.

Gallhofer, I. N., W. E. Saris, and B. M. de Valk. 1978.*"Een begrippenapparaat voor de beschrijving van redeneringen van politici."* Acta Politica 3: 371–382.

Gallhofer, I. N., W. E. Saris, and M. Schellekens 1988. "People's Recognition of Political Decision Arguments." *Acta Psychologica* 68: 313–327.

Geiss, I. 1963. *Julikrise und Kriegsausbruch 1914.* Hannover: Verlag für Literatur und Zeitgeschichte.

George, A. L. 1980. *Presidential Decision-Making in Foreign Policy: the Effective Use of Information and Advice.* Boulder, Colo.: Westview Press.

Gross-Stein, J., and R. Tanter. 1980. *Rational Decision-Making: Israel's Security Choices, 1967.* Columbus: Ohio University Press.

Halperin, M. H. 1974. *Bureaucratic Politics and Foreign Policy.* Washington D.C.: Brookings Institution.

Hermann, Ch. F., ed. 1972. *International Crisis.* New York: Free Press.

Hermann, Ch. F., M. A. East, M. G. Hermann, and S. A. Salmore. 1973. *CREON: A Foreign Events Data Set.* Beverly Hills: Sage.

Hermann, M. G. 1974. "Leader Personality and Foreign Policy Behavior." In J. N. Rosenau, ed., *Comparing Foreign Policies: Theories, Findings and Methods,* 201–234. New York: Wiley.

———. 1982. "Independence/Interdependence of Action." In P. Callahan, L. P. Brady, and M. G. Hermann, eds., *Describing Foreign Policy Behavior,* 259–274. Beverly Hills, London: Sage.

Hermann, Ch. F., Ch. W. Kegley Jr., and J. N. Rosenau, eds. 1987. *New Directions in the Study of Foreign Policy.* Boston: Allen & Unwin.

Hirschfeld, H. M. 1959. *Herinneringen uit de jaren 1933–1939.* Amsterdam: Elsevier.

Holsti, O. R. 1969. *Content Analysis for the Social Sciences and Humanities.* Reading Ma.: Addison Wesley

———. 1979. "Theories of Crisis Decision-Making." In P. G. Lauren, ed., *Diplomacy: New Approaches in History, Theory and Policy,* 99–136. New York: Free Press.

Hommes, P. M. 1980. *Nederland en de Europese Eenwording.* 's-Gravenhage: Nijhoff.

Huber, O. 1982. *Entscheiden als Problemlösen.* Wien: Hans Huber.

Jonkman, J. 1977. *Memoires: Nederland en Indonesië beide vrij. Vol 2.* Assen-Amsterdam: Van Gorcum.

Keeney, R. L., and H. Raiffa. 1976. *Decisions with Multiple Objectives: Preferences and Value Tradeoffs*. New York: Wiley.

Kersten, A. 1981. *Buitenlandse Zaken in Ballingschap: Groei en verandering van een ministerie 1945–1962*. Alphen aan den Rijn: Sijthoff

Klein, P. W., and G. N. van der Plaat, eds. 1981. *Herrijzend Nederland*. 's-Gravenhage: Nijhoff.

Komjáthy, M. 1966. *Protokolle des Gemeinsamen Ministerrates der Österreichisch-Ungarischen Monarchie (1814–1918)*. Budapest: Akadémiai Kiadó.

Krippendorff, K. 1970. "Bivariate Agreement Coefficients for Reliability of Data." In E. F. Borgatta, and G. W. Bohrnstedt, eds., *Sociological Methodology*, 139–150. San Francisco: Jossey Bass.

Kuypers, G. 1980. *Beginselen van de Beleidsontwikkeling*. Muiderberg: Coutinho.

Lentner, H. 1972. "The Concept of Crisis as Viewed by the United States Department of State." In Ch. F. Hermann, ed., *International Crisis*, 112–134. New York: Free Press.

Leurdijk, J. H. 1978. *The Foreign Policy of the Netherlands*. Alphen aan den Rijn: Sijthoff.

Lindblom, Ch. E. 1959. "The Science of Muddling Through." *Public Administration Revue* 19: 79–99.

———. 1982. "Still Muddling Not Yet Through." In A. G. McGrew, and M. J. Wilson, eds., *Decision-Making Approaches and Analysis*, 125–138. Manchester: Manchester University Press.

Manning, A. F. 1978. "De buitenlandse politiek van de Nederlandse regering in Londen tot 1942." *Tijdschrift voor Geschiedenis* 91: 49–65.

Manning, A. F., and A. E. Kersten, eds. 1976–1984. *Documenten betreffende de buitenlandse politiek van Nederland, 1940–1945*. Vols. 1–4, 's-Gravenhage: Nijhoff.

Maoz, Z. 1981. "The Decision to Raid Entebbe: Decision Analysis Applied to Crisis Behavior." *Journal of Conflict Resolution* 23 (4): 677–707.

———. 1986. "Multiple Paths to Choice: An Approach for the Analysis of Foreign Policy Decisions." In I. N. Gallhofer, W. E. Saris, and M. Melman, eds., *Different Text Analysis Procedures for the Study of Decision-Making*, 69–96. Amsterdam: Sociometric Research Foundation.

———. 1990. *National Choices and International Processes*. Cambridge: Cambridge University Press.

Montgomery, H. 1983. "Decision Rules and the Search for a Dominance Structure: Towards a Process Model of Decision-Making." In P. Humphreys, O. Svenson, and A. Vári, eds., *Analysing and Aiding Decision Processes*, 343–370. Amsterdam: North Holland Publishing Company.

———. 1989. "From Cognition to Action: The Search for Dominance in Decision-Making." In H. Montgomery, and O. Svenson, eds., *Process and Structure of Human Decision-Making*, 23–50. Chichester: Wiley.

Papadakis, M., and H. Starr. 1987. "Opportunity, Willingness and Small States: the Relationship between Environment and Foreign Policy." In Ch. F. Herrmann, Ch. W. Kegley Jr., and J. N. Rosenau, eds., *New Directions in the Study of Foreign Policy*, 409–432. Boston: Allen & Unwin.

Perelman, C. and L. Olbrechts-Tyteca. 1969. *The New Rhetoric. A Treatise on Argumentation*. Notre Dame: University of Notre Dame Press.

Phillips, W. R. 1978. "Prior Behavior as an Explanation of Foreign Policy." In M. A. East, S. A. Salmore, and Ch. F. Hermann, eds., *Why Nations Act: Theoretical Perspectives for Comparative Foreign Policy Studies,* 161–172. Beverly Hills : Sage.

Pólos, L., and M. Masuch. 1995. "Political Arguments from a Logical Point of View." In F. H. van Eemeren, R. Grootendorst, J. A. Blair, and Ch. A. Willard, eds., *Reconstruction and Application: Proceedings of the Third ISSA Conference on Argumentation,* vol. 3, 436–446. Amsterdam: International Centre for the Study of Argumentation.

Raiffa, H. 1968. *Decision Analysis.* Reading, Mass.: Addison-Wesley.

Rosenau, J. N. 1966. "Pre-Theories and Theories of Foreign Policy." In R. B. Farrel, ed., *Approaches to Comparative and International Politics,* 27–92. Evanston: Northwestern University Press.

Rosenau, J. N., and G. D. Hoggard. 1974. "Testing a Pre-Theoretical Extension." In J. N. Rosenau, ed., *Comparing Foreign Policies: Theories, Findings and Methods,* 117–150. New York: Wiley.

Saris, W. E., and W. M. de Pijper. 1986. "Computer Assisted Interviewing Using Home Computers." *European Research* 14: 144–150.

Saris, W. E., and I. N. Gallhofer. 1975. "L'Application d'un modèle de décision a des données historiques." *Revue Française de Science Politique* 25 (3): 473–501.

———. 1984. "The Formulation of Real Life Decisions: A Study of Foreign Policy Decisions." *Acta Psychologica* 56: 247–265.

Savage, L. J. 1954. *The Foundations of Statistics.* New York: Wiley.

Shapiro, M. J., and M. G. Bonham. 1973. "Cognitive Process and Foreign Policy Decision-Making." *International Studies Quarterly* 17: 147–174.

Shultz, G. P. 1993. *Turmoil and Triumph: My years as Secretary of State.* New York: Scribner's Sons.

Simon, H. A. 1957a. "A Behavioral Model of Rational Choice." In H. A. Simon, *Models of Man: Social and Rational,* 135–152. New York : Wiley.

———. 1957b. *Models of Man: Social and Rational.* New York: Wiley.

Sked, A. 1992. *The Decline and Fall of the Habsburg Empire 1815–1918.* London, New York: Longman.

Smit, C. 1950. *Diplomatieke geschiedenis van Nederland, in zonderheid sedert de vestiging van het Koninkrijk.* 's-Gravenhage: Nijhoff.

———. 1962. *De liquidatie van een Imperium: Nederland en Indonesië 1945–1962.* Amsterdam: Arbeiderspers.

———. 1962. *Documenten betreffende de buitenlandse politiek van Nederland, 1848–1919.* Vol. 4. 's-Gravenhage: Nijhoff.

———. 1970. *Het dagboek van Schermerhorn. Geheim verslag van prof. dr. ir. W. Schermerhorn als voorzitter der commissie-generaal voor Nederlands-Indië, 20 september 1946 tot 7 oktober 1947.* Utrecht: Nederlands Historisch Genootschap.

———. 1972. *Nederland in de Eerste Wereldoorlog (1899–1919).* Groningen: Wolters-Noordhoff.

Snyder, R. C., H. W. Bruck, and B. Sapin. 1962. *Foreign Policy Decision-Making: An Approach to the Study of International Politics.* New York: Free Press.

Stapel, F. W. 1943. *Geschiedenis van Nederlands Indië.* Amsterdam: Meulenhoff.

Stikker, D. 1966. *Mémoires: Herinneringen uit de lange jaren waarin ik betrokken was bij de voortdurende wereldcrisis.* Rotterdam: Nigh van Ditmar.

Svenson, O. 1979. "Process Description of Decision-Making." *Organizational Behavior and Human Performance* 23: 86–112.

Svenson, O. 1989. "Eliciting and Analyzing Verbal Protocols." In H. Montgomery, and O. Svenson, eds., *Process and Structuring in Human Decision-Making,* 65–82. Chichester: Wiley.

Thorngate, W. 1980. "Efficient Decision Heuristics." *Behavioral Science* 25: 219–225.

Toulmin, S., R. Rieke, and A. Janik. 1979. *An Introduction to Reasoning.* New York: Macmillan.

Tversky, A. 1972. "Elimination by Aspects: A Theory of Choice." *Psychological Review* 79 (2): 207–232.

Tversky, A., and D. Kahnemann. 1986. "Rational Choice and the Framing of Decisions." *Journal of Business* 59 (4): 5251–5278.

Van Eemeren, F. H., R. Grootendorst, and T. Kruiger. 1984. *Argumenteren.* Groningen: Wolters-Noordhoff.

————. 1987. *Handbook of Argumentation Theory: A Critical Survey of Classical Backgrounds and Modern Studies.* Dordrecht: Foris Publications.

Van de Graaf, H., and R. Hoppe. 1989. *Een Inleiding tot Beleidswetenschap en Beleidskunde.* Muiderberg: Coutinho.

Van Kleffens, E. N. 1983. *Belevenissen,* vols. 1, 2. Alphen aan den Rijn: Sijthoff.

Vedung, E. 1982. *Political Reasoning.* Beverly Hills: Sage.

Von Neumann, J., and O. Morgenstern. 1947. *Theory of Games and Economic Behavior.* 2nd ed., Princeton N. J.: Princeton University Press.

Von Winterfeldt, D., and W. Edwards. 1986. *Decision Analysis and Behavioral Research.* Cambridge: Cambridge University Press.

Voorhoeve, J. C. 1979. *Peace Profits and Principles: A Study of Dutch Foreign Policy.* 's-Gravenhage: Nijhoff.

Ward, D. M. 1982. "Cooperation and Conflict in Foreign Policy Behavior." *International Studies Quarterly* 26 (1): 87–126.

Wilkenfeld, J., G. W. Hopple, P. J. Rossa, and S. J. Andriole. 1980. *Foreign Policy Behavior: The Interstate Behavior Analysis Model.* Beverly Hills, London: Sage

DOCUMENTS

Dutch Documents

Maintenance of neutrality during World War I
Council of Ministers. October 1 and 3, 1914. Minutes. In C. Smit , ed., *Documenten betreffende de buitenlandse politiek van Nederland,* vol. 4, no. 171, 145–160. 's-Gravenhage: Nijhoff, 1962.

Maintenance of armed forces during World War I
Council of Ministers. October 16, 1916. Appendix to the Minutes. Archives of General Affairs, record no. 147a.

Gold standard
Economic Affairs Official. April 9, 1935. Note. In H. M. Hirschfeld, *Herinneringen uit de jaren 1933–1939,* app. 4, 195–218. Amsterdam: Elsevier, 1959.
Prime Minister. April 15, 1935. Note. Ibid., app. 5, 219–226.

Revision of an economic treaty between Britain and the East Indies

Secretary-General of the Department of Colonies to the Minister of Foreign Affairs. April 12, 1933. Archives of Economic Affairs, record Dir. Handel en Nijverheid, no. 777.

Minister of Colonies to the Minister of Foreign Affairs. July 4, 1934. Letter. Ibid.

Minister of Economic Affairs. September 27, 1935. Note. Ibid.

Minister of Foreign Affairs to the Minister of Colonies. December 23, 1935. Letter. Ibid.

Minister of Colonies to the Minister of Foreign Affairs. February 10, 1936. Letter. Ibid.

Minister of Economic Affairs to the Minister of Foreign Affairs. May 13, 1936. Letter. Ibid.

Peace efforts with Hitler

Council of Ministers. July 12, 1940. Minutes. In A. F. Manning and A. E. Kersten, eds., *Documenten betreffende de Buitenlandse Politiek van Nederland,* vol. 1, no. 168, 170–172. 's-Gravenhage: Nijhoff, 1976.

Council of Ministers. July 24, 1940. Minutes. Ibid., no. 199, 214–222.

Military cooperation with the Western powers in the Far East

Deputy Secretary-General of the Department of Foreign Affairs. July 26, 1940. Note. In A. F. Manning and A. E. Kersten, eds., *Documenten betreffende de Buitenlandse Politiek van Nederland,* vol. 1, no. 219, 243–245. 's-Gravenhage: Nijhoff, 1976.

Commander-in-Chief of the Naval Forces to the Minister of Colonies. August 24, 1940. Letter. Ibid., no. 314, 366–372.

Foreign Affairs Official. August 24, 1940. Note. Archives of the Ministry of Foreign Affairs, record no. LA/GA DZ–d2, vol. 1.

Foreign Affairs Official. August 27, 1940. Note. Ibid.

Commander-in-Chief of the Naval Forces to the Chairman of the Council of Ministers. November 6, 1940. Note. In A. F. Manning and A. E. Kersten, eds., *Documenten betreffende de Buitenlandse Politiek van Nederland,* vol. 2., no. 12, 15–17. 's-Gravenhage: Nijhoff, 1977.

Dutch Chargé d'Affaires in the United States to the Deputy Secretary-General of the Ministry of Foreign Affairs. November 15, 1940. Ibid., no. 40, 46–47.

To lend Dutch gold stocks to the British for the war efforts

Council of Ministers. October 29, 1940. Minutes. In A. F. Manning and A. E. Kersten, eds., *Documenten betreffende de Buitenlandse Politiek van Nederland,* vol. 1, no. 465, 541–543. 's-Gravenhage: Nijhoff, 1976.

Undersecretary-General of the Department of Finance. November 28, 1940. Note. Ibid., no. 69, 86–88.

Secretary-General of the Department of Finance. December 1, 1940. Note. Ibid., no. 77, 103–105.

Council of Ministers. December 20, 1940. Minutes. Ibid., no. 118, 152–156.

Minister of Finance. May 23, 1941. Memorandum. Ibid., no. 431, 570–574.

Diplomatic relations with the Vatican

Deputy Secretary-General of the Ministry of Foreign Affairs. July 14, 1940. Note. In A. F. Manning and A. E. Kersten, eds., *Documenten betreffende de Buitenlandse Politiek van Nederland,* vol. 1, no. 169, 172–173. 's-Gravenhage: Nijhoff, 1976.

Minister of Foreign Affairs to the Queen, July 15, 1943. Note. Archives of the Ministry of Foreign Affairs, record LA/GA DZ–N, Vatican.

Diplomatic relations with the Soviet Union
Minister of Traffic and Waterways to the Chairman of the Council of Ministers. September 17, 1941. Note. In A. F. Manning and A. E. Kersten, eds., *Documenten betreffende de Buitenlandse Politiek van Nederland,* vol. 3, no. 273, 360–361. 's-Gravenhage: Nijhoff, 1980.
Member of the Senate to the Minister of Education. September 24, 1941. Letter. Ibid., no. 292, 384–385.
Minister of Education to the Minister of Foreign Affairs. November 24, 1941. Note. Ibid., no. 466, 615–620.
Chairman of the Council of Ministers to the Minister of Foreign Affairs. November 28, 1941. Note. Ibid., no. 486, 643–646.
Minister of Foreign Affairs to the Queen. May 5, 1942. Letter. Archives of the Ministry of Foreign Affairs, record LA/GA DZ –N1, SU.
Minister of Colonies to the Minister of Foreign Affairs. June 22, 1942. Letter. In A. F. Manning and A. E. Kersten, eds., *Documenten betreffende de Buitenlandse Politiek van Nederland,* vol. 4., no. 531, 660–661. 's-Gravenhage: Nijhoff, 1984.

Transference of the seat of the Dutch Government in exile to the East Indies
Ambassador to Rome to the Minister of Foreign Affairs. May 13, 1940. Letter. In A. F. Manning and A. E. Kersten, eds., *Documenten betreffende de Buitenlandse Politiek van Nederland,* vol. 1, no. 59, 56–57.'s-Gravenhage: Nijhoff, 1976.
Chairman of the Council of Ministers to the Queen, July 13, 1940. Letter. Ibid., no. 171, 173–176.
Chairman of the Council of Ministers to the Queen. July 19, 1940. Letter. Ibid., no. 188, 201–203.
Ambassador to Brussels to the Minister of Foreign Affairs. August 7, 1940. Letter. Ibid., no. 260, 294–295.
Dutch Governor General of the East Indies to the Minister of Overseas Territories. August 7, 1940. Phone call. *Verslag van de Parlementaire Enquête-Commissie regeringsbeleid,* vol. 1. 's-Gravenhage 1949, 2B, 229.
Minister of Foreign Affairs to the Ambassador in Brussels. August 16, 1940. Letter. In A. F. Manning and A. E. Kersten, eds., *Documenten betreffende de Buitenlandse Politiek van Nederland,* vol. 1, no. 291, 347–348. 's-Gravenhage: Nijhoff, 1976.
Governor General of the Dutch East Indies to the Chairman of the Council of Ministers. November 16, 1940. Memorandum. Ibid., vol. 2., no. 291, 47–48.
Minister of Waterways and Transport to the Chairman of the Council of Ministers. January 16, 1941. Memorandum. *Verslag van de Parlementarie Enquête-Commissie regeringsbeleid,* vol. 1, 's-Gravenhage 1949, 2B, 228.
Council of Ministers. January 17, 1941. Minutes. In A. F. Manning and A. E. Kersten, eds., *Documenten betreffende de Buitenlandse Politiek van Nederland,* vol. 2, no. 168, 211–213. 's-Gravenhage: Nijhoff, 1977.
Council of Ministers. January 18, 1941. Minutes. Ibid., no. 170, 215–220.

Participation in the United Nations
Minister of Foreign Affairs to an Ambassador. November 20, 1944. Letter. Archives of the Ministry of Foreign Affairs, record Van Kleffens, no. 3.
Ambassador to Washington to the Minister of Foreign Affairs. March 1, 1945. Letter. Archives of the Ministry of Foreign Affairs, record no. PZ/B.N.O.V. L 25, San Francisco Conference.

Minister of Foreign Affairs to the Ambassador to Washington. Letter. March 3, 1945. Archives of the Ministry of Foreign Affairs, record no. P–1.8/45.4, Dumbarton Oaks III.

Border corrections with Germany

Foreign Affairs Official. October 16, 1944. Note. Archives of the Ministry of Foreign Affairs, record no. LA/GA DZ–BI 50b.

Council of Ministers. Minutes. October 17, 1944. Archives of General Affairs, record no. 246.

Ministry of Foreign Affairs Official. September 1946. Note. Archives of the Ministry of Foreign Affairs, record no. GS 913.12 file 215, border corrections.

Minister of Foreign Affairs. September 14, 1946. Note. Ibid.

Minister of Foreign Affairs to the Ambassadors. October 2, 1946. Letter. Ibid.

Ambassador to Belgium to the Minister of Foreign Affairs. October 7, 1946. Letter. Ibid.

Ambassador to Britain to the Minister of Foreign Affairs. October 7, 1946. Letter. Ibid.

Adviser François to the Minister of Foreign Affairs. November 8, 1946. Note. Ibid.

Adviser to the Prime Minister. March 18, 1948. Note. Ibid.

Adviser of Economic Affairs to the Minister of Foreign Affairs. October 8, 1948. Note. Archives of the Ministry of Foreign Affairs, record no. GS 912.33 file 553, border corrections.

Adviser to the Minister of Foreign Affairs. October 9, 1948. Note. Ibid.

Secretary-General of the Department of Foreign Affairs. October 13, 1948. Note. Ibid.

Adviser François to the Minister of Foreign Affairs. January 14, 1949. Note. Ibid.

Ministry of Foreign Affairs. January 17, 1949. Note. Archives of the Ministry of Foreign Affairs, record no. GS 912.230 file 549, border corrections.

Western European Union / North Atlantic Treaty Organization

Minister of Foreign Affairs. March 8, 1947. Note. Archives of the Ministry of Foreign Affairs, record no. DNW, archive WEU 999.1.

Foreign Affairs Official. December 22, 1947. Note. Ibid.

Minister of Foreign Affairs to the Ambassador to Washington. January 2, 1948. Letter. Archives of the Ministry of Foreign Affairs, record no. P–1.8/48–7a.

Council of Ministers January 21, 1949. Minutes. Archives of General Affairs, record Minutes of the Council of Ministers.

Minister of Foreign Affairs to the Council of Ministers. March 11, 1949. Note. Archives of General Affairs, record Documents for the Council of Ministers, no. 446.

Ambassador to Washington to the Minister of Foreign Affairs. March 21, 1949. Letter. Archives of the Ministry of Foreign Affairs, record no. P–1.8/48.7.

Benelux

Foreign Affairs Official. April 20, 1943. Note. Archives of the Ministry of Foreign Affairs, record no. Van Kleffens VI/3.

Economic Affairs Official. June 7, 1945. Note. Archives of the Ministry of Foreign Affairs, record no. BEB 328.

Secretary-General of Economic Affairs. November 29, 1945. Note. Archives of the Ministry of Foreign Affairs, record no. 610.20, Benelux Inter-Departmental Discussion 1945.

Chairman of the Inter-Departmental Council for the Economic Policy. December 19, 1945. Note. Ibid.

Ambassador to Belgium to the Minister of Foreign Affairs. June 21, 1946. Letter. Ibid.

Economic Affairs Official. April 4, 1948. Note. Archives of the Ministry of Foreign Affairs, record no. BEB 745.
Economic Affairs Official. September 29, 1950. Note. Archives of the Ministry of Foreign Affairs, record no. BEB 744.
Secretary-General of Economic Affairs. February 24, 1953. Aide-mémoire. Archives of the Ministry of Foreign Affairs, record no. BEB 1121.
Economic Affairs Official. December 1, 1954. Note. Archives of the Ministry of Foreign Affairs, record no. BEB 1119.

European Defense Community
Chairman of the Advice Council for Foreign Affairs, August 11, 1952. Note. Archives of the Ministry of Foreign Affairs, record no. BEB 567.
Foreign Affairs Official, January 1, 1953. Note. Archives of General Affairs, record Documents for the Council, no. 486.
Council of Ministers May 3, 1955. Minutes. Archives of General Affairs, record Minutes of the Council of Ministers.
Minister of Foreign Affairs. March 24, 1955. Note. Archives of General Affairs, record Documents for the Council, no. 509.
Prime Minister. March 25, 1955. Note. Ibid.

European Political Community
Advice Commission for Participation. October 9, 1952. Note. Archives of General Affairs, record Documents for the Council, no. 483.
Minister of Foreign Affairs. January 27, 1953. Note. Archives of the Ministry of Foreign Affairs, record DGEM archive, no. 0520, file 78.
Ambassador to Britain to the Minister of Foreign Affairs. March 5, 1953. Letter. Archive of Van der Beugel, record no. 35.
Council of Ministers. April 29, 1953. Minutes. Archives of General Affairs, record Minutes of the Council of Ministers.
Foreign Affairs Official. September 7, 1953. Note. Archives of the Ministry of Foreign Affairs, record DGEM 05 EPG, vol. 2.
Minister of Agriculture to the Minister of Foreign Affairs. September 28, 1953. Letter. Archive of Van der Beugel, record no.35.
Minister of Foreign Affairs to the Minister of Agriculture. October 2, 1953. Letter. Ibid.
Minister of Agriculture to the Council of Ministers. November 11, 1953. Note. Archives of General Affairs, record Documents for the Council, no. 495.
Minister of Foreign Affairs to the Ambassador to Britain. March 11, 1955. Letter. Archive of Van der Beugel, record no. 5.

First police action in Indonesia
Commission General to the Minister of Overseas Territories. June 17, 1947. Telegram. In P. J. Drooglever and M. J. Schouten, eds., *Officiële Bescheiden betreffende de Nederlands Indonesische betrekkingen 1945–1950,* vol. 9, no. 170, 391–395. 's-Gravenhage: Nijhoff, 1981.
Lieutenant Governor General to the Minister of Overseas Territories. July 7, 1947. Telegram. Ibid., no. 291, 600–602.
Chairman of the Commission General to the Minister of Overseas Territories. July 7, 1947. Telegram. Ibid., no. 291, 600–602.
Council of Ministers. July 7, 1947. Minutes. Ibid., no. 300, 611–621.

Lieutenant Governor General to the Minister of Overseas Territories July 17, 1947. Telegram. Ibid., no. 351, 703–707.
Council of Ministers July 17, 1947. Minutes. Ibid., no. 355, 710–719.

First intervention of the Security Council in Indonesia
Lieutenant Governor General to the Minister of Overseas Territories. July 26, 1947. Telegram. In P. J. Drooglever and M. J. Schouten, eds., *Officiële Bescheiden betreffende de Nederlands Indonesische betrekkingen 1945–1950,* vol. 10, no. 46, 72–74. 's-Gravenhage: Nijhoff, 1982.
Lieutenant Governor General to the Minister of Overseas Territories. July 28, 1947. Telegram. Ibid., no. 65, 100–102.
Lieutenant Governor General to the Minister of Overseas Territories. July 28, 1947. Telegram. Archive of Van Mook record no. 90., ZG 329.
Council of Ministers. July 30, 1947. Minutes. In P. J. Drooglever and M. J. Schouten, eds., *Officiële Bescheiden betreffende de Nederlands Indonesische betrekkingen 1945–1950,* vol.10, no. 77, 115–123. 's-Gravenhage: Nijhoff, 1982.
Lieutenant Governor General to the Minister of Overseas Territories. July 31, 1947. Telegram. Ibid., no. 92, 141–144.
Chief of the Direction Far East to the Chief of the Direction of Political Affairs. August 1, 1947. Telegram. Archives of the Ministry of Foreign Affairs, record Schuurman DZG 11 GS 912.10, vol.8.
Council of Ministers. August 2, 1947. Minutes. In P. J. Drooglever and M. J. Schouten, eds., *Officiële Bescheiden bescheiden betreffende de Nederlands Indonesische betrekkingen 1945–1950.,* vol.10, no. 133, 201–208. 's-Gravenhage: Nijhoff, 1982.
Lieutenant Governor General to the Minister of Overseas Territories. August 4, 1947. Telegram. Ibid., no. 149, 223–225. 's-Gravenhage: Nijhoff, 1982.
Lieutenant Governor General to the Minister of Overseas Territories. August 6, 1947. Telegram. Ibid., no. 170, 251–252.
Chief of the Direction Far East to the Minister of Foreign Affairs. August 6, 1947. Telegram. Archives of the Ministry of Foreign Affairs, record GS 999.224, U.N., vol. 3.
Lieutenant Governor General to the Minister of Overseas Territories. August 8, 1947. Telegram. *Officiële Bescheiden betreffende de Nederlands Indonesische betrekkingen 1945–1950,* vol.10, no. 199, 294–296. July 21–August 31, 1947. 's-Gravenhage: Nijhoff, 1982.
Dutch Representative to the Security Council to the Minister of Foreign Affairs. August 8, 1947. Telegram. Ibid., no. 203, 303.
Lieutenant Governor General to the Minister of Overseas Territories. August 10. Telegram. Ibid., no. 221, 320–322.
Dutch Representative to the Security Council to the Minister of Foreign Affairs, August 11, 1947 (6.30 p.m.). Phone call. Ibid., no. 240, 357–361.
Minister of Foreign Affairs to the Dutch Representative to the Security Council. August 11, 1947 (11p.m.). Phone call. Ibid., no. 238, 355–356.
Lieutenant Governor General to the Minister of Overseas Territories. August 12, 1947. Telegram. Ibid., no. 247, 366–367.
Army Council to the Queen. August 12, 1947. Telegram. Archive of Van Mook, record no. 223.
Council of Ministers. August 13, 1947. Minutes. In P. J. Drooglever and M. J. Schouten,

eds., *Officiële Bescheiden betreffende de Nederlands Indonesische betrekkingen 1945–1950*, vol.10, no. 259, 384. 's-Gravenhage: Nijhoff, 1982.

Council of Ministers. August 14, 1947. Minutes. Ibid., no. 272, 397–407.

Prof. François to the Minister of Foreign Affairs. August 14, 1947. Note. Archives of the Ministry of Foreign Affairs, record no. GS 999.224 U.N., vol.3.

Lieutenant Governor General to the Minister of Overseas Territories. August 15, 1947. Telegram. In P. J. Drooglever and M. J. Schouten, eds., *Officiële Bescheiden betreffende de Nederlands Indonesische betrekkingen 1945–1950*, vol.10, no. 282, 426–428. 's-Gravenhage: Nijhoff, 1982.

Council of Ministers. August 15, 1947. Minutes. Ibid., no. 285, 426–428.

Council of Ministers. August 18, 1947. Minutes. Ibid., no. 315, 484–497.

Chief of the Direction Far East to the Minister of Foreign Affairs. August 25, 1947. Telegram. Ibid., no. 390, 626–627.

Minister of Public Works and Reconstruction to the Prime Minister. August 26, 1947. Letter. Ibid., no. 402, 641.

Lieutenant Governor General to the Minister of Overseas Territories. August 26, 1947. Telegram. Ibid., no. 401, 639–640.

Council of Ministers August 27, 1947. Minutes. Ibid., no. 410, 657–670.

Minister of Finance to the Prime Minister. August 29,1947. Note. Ibid., no. 428, 702–706.

Council of Ministers. September 4, 1947. Minutes. Ibid., vol.11, no. 16, 18–29.

Lieutenant Governor General to his Deputy. September 8, 1947. Telegram. Ibid., no. 30, 57.

Second police action in Indonesia

Foreign Affairs Official. February 1948. Memorandum. Archives of the Ministry of Foreign Affairs, record no. GS 999.224 VN, vol.12.

Commander-in-Chief of the Dutch troops in Indonesia to the Lieutenant Governor General. October 20, 1948. Letter. Archive of Van Mook, record no. 222.

Foreign Affairs Official. October 24, 1948. Note. Archive of the Ministry of Foreign Affairs, record Indonesia in the transition period, no. 147 (overall agreement).

Council of Ministers. October 26, 1948. Minutes. In P. J. Drooglever and M. J. Schouten, eds., *Officiële Bescheiden betreffende de Nederlands Indonesische betrekkingen 1945–1950*, vol. 15, no. 259, 515–525. 's-Gravenhage: Nijhoff, 1989.

Minister of Foreign Affairs to the Cabinet. November 10, 1948. Note. Ibid., no. 313, 639–643.

Council of Ministers. November 15, 1948. Minutes. Ibid., no. 328, 662–670.

High Representative of the Crown to the Minister of Overseas Territories. November 13, 1948. Telegrams. Ibid., no. 321 and no. 322, 650–657.

Dutch negotiators in Indonesia. November 24, 1948. Minutes of meeting. Archive of Stikker, record no. 7D, Batavia II.

Dutch authorities in Indonesia. November 25, 1948. Minutes of meeting. In P. J. Drooglever and M. J. Schouten, eds., *Officiële Bescheiden betreffende de Nederlands Indonesische betrekkingen 1945–1950*, vol. 15, no. 376, 736–741. 's-Gravenhage: Nijhoff, 1989.

Dutch negotiators in Indonesia. November 30, 1948. Minutes of meeting. Archive of Stikker, record no. 7D, Batavia II.

Council of Ministers. December 9, 1948. Minutes. In P. J. Drooglever and M. J. Schouten, eds., *Officiële Bescheiden betreffende de Nederlands Indonesische betrekkingen 1945–1950*, vol.16, no. 41, 73–82. 's-Gravenhage: Nijhoff, 1991.

Council of Ministers. December 13, 1948. Minutes. Ibid., no. 73, 114–119.
Council of Ministers. December 14, 1948. Minutes. Ibid., no. 85, 132–138, no. 88, 141–147.
High Representative of the Crown to the Minister of Overseas Territories. December 17, 1948. Ibid., no. 137, 213–214.

Second intervention of the Security Council in Indonesia
Minister of Overseas Territories. December 25, 1948. Note. Archives of the Ministry of Foreign Affairs, record no. GS 999.24 U.N., vol. 10, November–December.
High Representative of the Crown to the Minister of Overseas Territories. December 25, 1948. Telegram. In P. J. Drooglever and M. J. Schouten, eds., *Officiële Bescheiden betreffende de Nederlands Indonesische betrekkingen 1945–1950*, vol. 16, no. 265, 341–343. 's-Gravenhage: Nijhoff, 1991.
Ministry of Foreign Affairs. December 26, 1948. Comments regarding ZG 75. Archives of the Ministry of Foreign Affairs, record no. GS 912.10 U.N., vol. 13.
Dutch Delegate to the United Nations to the Minister of Foreign Affairs. December 27, 1948 (8 p.m.). Phone call. Archives of the Ministry of Foreign Affairs, record no. GS 999.24 U.N., vol. 10.
High Representative of the Crown to the Minister of Overseas Territories. December 27, 1948. Telegram. In P. J. Drooglever and M. J. Schouten, eds., *Officiële Bescheiden betreffende de Nederlands Indonesische betrekkingen 1945–1950*, vol. 16, no. 286, 363–364. 's-Gravenhage: Nijhoff, 1991.
Foreign Affairs Official to the Minister of Foreign Affairs. December 27, 1948. Note. Ibid., no. 299, 382–383.
High Representative of the Crown to the Minister of Overseas Territories. December 29, 1948. Telegram. Ibid., no. 322, 405–406.
High Representative of the Crown to the Minister of Overseas Territories. January 3, 1949. Telegram. Ibid., no. 390, 492–493.
High Representative of the Crown to the Minister of Overseas Territories. January 4, 1949. Telegram. Ibid., no. 402, 528–530.
Dutch Delegate to the Security Council to the Minister of Foreign Affairs. January 15, 1949. Telegram. Ibid., vol.17, no. 28, 56–57.
Dutch Delegate to the Security Council to the Minister of Foreign Affairs. January 22, 1949. Telegram. Ibid., no. 96, 155–156.
Council of Ministers. January 28 , 1949. Minutes. Ibid., no. 175, 263–267.
Council of Ministers. January 31 , 1949. Minutes. Ibid., no. 203, 310–317.
High Representative of the Crown to the Minister of Overseas Territories. February 2, 1949. Telegram. Archives of the Ministry of Overseas Territories, ZG 114, record no. 2, telegrams.
Council of Ministers. February 7 , 1949. Minutes. In P. J. Drooglever and M. J. Schouten, eds., *Officiële Bescheiden betreffende de Nederlands Indonesische betrekkingen 1945–1950*, vol. 17, no. 263, 439–452. 's-Gravenhage: Nijhoff, 1992.
Council of Ministers. February 10 , 1949. Minutes. Ibid., no. 283, 489–498.
Minister of Overseas Territories to the Cabinet. February 11, 1949. Note. Ibid., no. 288, 509–514.

Negotiations with Indonesia about a Union treaty
Minister of Foreign Affairs to the Council of Ministers. April 2, 1954. Note. Archives of General Affairs, record Documents for the Council of Ministers, no. 502.

Prof. François to the Council of Ministers, June 15, 1954. Note. Ibid., no. 503.
Foreign Affairs Official to the Council of Ministers. July 30, 1954. Note. Ibid., no. 504.

Rhine navigation dispute
Minister of Foreign Affairs. April 29, 1954. Note. Archives of General Affairs, record
      Documents for the Council of Ministers, no. 501.
Ministry of Traffic and Waterways Official. May 4, 1954. Note. Ibid., no. 501.
Minister of Traffic and Waterways. May 7, 1954. Note. Ibid., no. 501.
Council of Ministers, May 25, 1954. Minutes. Archives of General Affairs, record
      Minutes of the Council of Ministers.

Trade relations with the Soviet Union
Minister of Economic Affairs, December 12, 1953. Note. Archives of General Affairs,
      record Documents for the Council of Ministers, no. 496.
Direction of Foreign Economic Relations, December 17, 1953. Note. Ibid., record no.
      496.
Direction of Foreign Economic Relations, April 4, 1954. Note. Ibid., record no. 605.

Stratsbourg Plan
Foreign Affairs Official. May 8, 1952. Note. Archives of General Affairs, record
      Documents for the Council of Ministers, no. 479.
Economic Affairs Official. October 31, 1952. Note. Archives of the Ministry of Foreign
      Affairs, record BEB, no. 1036.
Foreign Affairs Official. November 14, 1952. Note. Ibid.
Economic Affairs Official. November 21, 1952. Note. Ibid., no. 1038.

Remaining documents relating to diverse topics
Minister of Finance. June 9, 1947. Note about the exchange control regulation. Archives
      of the Ministry of Foreign Affairs, record BEB, no. 1935.
Foreign Affairs Official. October 29, 1949. Note about the extension of competencies of
      the European Council. Archives of General Affairs, record Documents for the
      Council of Ministers, no. 453.
President of the Dutch Bank. November 10, 1949. Note about the multilateralization of
      the trade intercourse. November 10, 1949. Archives of the Ministry of
      Economic Affairs, record DGEM, no. 6106.
Foreign Affairs Official. February 4, 1950. Note about the recognition of the People's
      Republic of China. Ibid., no. 488.
Economic Affairs Official. March 24, 1950. Note about the settlement of economic
      relations with Italy. Archives of General Affairs, record Documents for the
      Council of Ministers, no. 584.
Minister of Defense. April 4, 1950. Note about the defense budget. Ibid., no. 458.
Minister of Foreign Affairs. April 12, 1950. Note about human rights. Ibid., no. 456.
Minister of Foreign Affairs. May 27, 1950. Note about the potential membership to the
      Security Council. Ibid., number 458.
Minister of Foreign Affairs. March 19, 1951. Note about the nationalization of Dutch
      property in Yugoslavia. Ibid., no. 466.
Minister of Foreign Affairs. April 6, 1951. Note about World Broadcasting. Ibid., no. 467.
Council of Ministers. July 7, 1951. Minutes about Greece's and Turkey's admission to
      NATO. Archives of General Affairs, record Minutes of the Council of Ministers.

Minister of Foreign Affairs. July 26, 1951. Note about the peace treaty with Japan. Archives of General Affairs, record Documents for the Council of Ministers, no. 469.

Minister of Economic Affairs. February 4, 1952 Note about financial aid for Fokker. Ibid., no. 477.

Minister of Foreign Affairs. March 25, 1952. Note about the ratification of the peace Treaty with Japan. Ibid., no. 477.

Foreign Affairs Official. June 17, 1952. Note about the seat of the administration of the European Coal and Steel Community. Archives of the Ministry of Foreign Affairs, record BEB, no. 565.

Minister of Foreign Affairs. July 10, 1952. Note about the recognition of the title of the Egyptian king. Ibid., no. 481.

Foreign Affairs Official. October 2, 1952. Note about the participation of Antillean and Surinam delegates to the General Assembly of the United Nations. Ibid., no.483.

Minister of Foreign Affairs. July 10, 1952. Note about the recognition of the title of the Egyptian king. Ibid., no. 481.

Foreign Affairs Official. April 8, 1953. Note about the implementation of the arms embargo on China. Ibid., no. 488.

Minister of Foreign Affairs. February 11, 1954. Note about the increase of payments to Indonesian war victims. Ibid., record no. 498.

Minister of Foreign Affairs. May 4, 1954. Note about a Friendship Treaty with the United States. Ibid., no. 501.

Minister of Economic Affairs. July 7, 1954. Note about the increase of financial aid to Korea. Ibid., no. 503.

Minister of Foreign Affairs, July 27, 1954. Note about his candidacy in the Economic Social Council of the United Nations. Ibid., no. 504.

Economic Affairs Official. August 5, 1954. Note about the Dutch contribution for development aid. Ibid., no 504.

Economic Affairs Official. October 14, 1954. Note on the admission of Japan to the GATT. Archives of the Ministry of Foreign Affairs, record BEB, no. 1201.

Minister of Foreign Affairs. January 1, 1955. Note about legal assistance for Indonesian infiltrators in New Guinea. Ibid., no. 508.

Delegation to the GATT. February 2, 1955. Communication to the Minister of Economic Affairs with regard to an American waiver. Ibid., no. 507.

Director of the Office of Foreign Economic Relations. February 17, 1955. Reply to the Delegation. Ibid., no. 507.

Minister of Foreign Affairs. March 3, 1955. Note about an agreement with the United States concerning patent protection. Ibid., no. 510.

Minister of Foreign Affairs. September 15, 1955. Note concerning the establishment of diplomatic relations with Afghanistan. Ibid., no. 515.

Ministers of Social- and Foreign Affairs. November 28, 1955. Note about the admittance of foreign workers. Ibid., record no. 518.

Foreign Affairs Official. September 25, 1956. Note about the admission of Spain to OEES. Archives of the Ministry of Economic Affairs, record Foreign Economic Relations (OEEC), 698.

Economic Affairs Official. July 23, 1957. Note about the participation of Spain in the OEES. Ibid.

American Documents

Stevenson, Adlai, U.N. Ambassador, to the President. October 17, 1962. Letter. In *L. Chang and P. Kornbluh, eds., The Cuban Missile Crisis, 1962: A National Security Archive Documents Reader,* New York: Free Press, 1992. no. 19, 119–120.
Dillon, Douglas, Secretary of the Treasury to the President. October 17, 1962. Memorandum. Ibid., no.18, 116–118.
Ball, George W., Undersecretary of State. October 18, 1962. Note. Ibid., no. 20, 121–122.
Executive Committee Meeting. October 19, 1962 (11:00 a.m.). Minutes. Ibid., no. 21, 123–127.
Sorensen, Theodore, Special Counsel to the President. October 20, 1962. Note. Ibid., no. 22, 133.
Central Intelligence Agency. October 20, 1962. Note. Ibid., no. 24, 134–143.
Secretary of the Treasury's group. October 25, 1962. Discussion paper. Ibid., no. 37, 168–171.

Austrian Documents

Common Council of Ministers of the Austro-Hungarian Monarchy. July 7, 1914. Minutes. In *M. Komjáthy, ed., Protokolle des Gemeinsamen Ministerrates der Österreichisch-Ungarischen Monarchie (1914–1918),* no. 1, 141–150. Budapest: Akadémiai Kiadó, 1966.
Hungarian Prime Minister to the Emperor. July 8, 1914. Letter. In *I. Geiss, ed., Julikrise und Kriegsausbruch 1914,* vol.1., no. 51, 128–131. Hannover: Verlag für Literatur und Zeitgeschichte 1963.

German Documents

Hitler, Adolf. November 10, 1937. Address to his ministers and the supreme commanders. November 10, 1938. In *Akten zur Deutschen Auswärtigen Politik 1918–1945,* Serie D (1937–1945) vol.1, no. 19, 25–32. Baden-Baden: Imprimerie Nationale, 1956.
Memorandum on Operation Green. April 22, 1938. Ibid., vol. 2, no. 133, 239–240.
State Secretary for the Foreign Minister. June 20, 1938. Memorandum. Ibid., no. 259, 420–422.
State Secretary for the Foreign Minister. August 30, 1938. Memorandum. Ibid., no. 409, 662–663.
Hitler, Adolf. August 22, 1939. Address to the supreme commanders. Ibid., vol. 7., no. 192, 167–172.

Subject Index

272

restriction of range of strategies, 66, 96, 124, 168; restriction of number of consequences, 168

Decision Rules (models, heuristics):
Addition-of-Utilities Rule, definition, 34; in case studies, 117–118, 137; determination of class of decision rules, 52–55; Dominance Rule, definition, 33–34; recognition from interviews, 142, 249– 254; Dominance Principle, definition, 152, 250; in case studies, 150, 164; Dominance structure, 144, 146, 147, 150, 231; Lexicographic Rule, definition, 37; in case studies, 66, 78, 94, 122, 137; recognition from interviews, 145–146, 253; MAUT SEU model, definition, 26–27; Minimax Rule, definition, 32; no fitting decision rule, 137–138, 144, 146, 148; prediction of expected decision rule, 136–137; recognition of expected decision rules, 144, 146, 148; Reversed Simon Rule, definition, 37– 38; in case studies, 60, 63, 65, 84– 86, 102–103, 118, 137; recognition from interviews, 146–148, 251–252; Risk-Avoidance Rules, Positive Risk-Avoidance Rule, definition, 28–29; Negative Risk-Avoidance Rule, definition, 28–29; in case studies, 60, 72, 77, 90, 100, 106, 110–112, 115, 117, 137; recognition from interviews, 143–145, 252–253; SEU model, definition, 24–26; SEU type of argument, 39, 137, 144–148, 151–152, 254; Simon's Rule, definition, 36–37; in case studies, 60, 63, 65, 74, 76, 85, 109, 137; recognition from interviews, 146–148, 250–251; rules are not explicitly mentioned, 65–66, 78, 94, 122, 126, 131, 230–231

Decision theory:
concepts, 16–17; trees, 17–19; tables, 19–22

Explanatory variables:
external actor characteristics, 172; in-

fluence of type of the other nation, prior actions of external actors on the generation and choice of strategies, 191–192, 194–195; influence of issue area, prior actions of external actors on the generation of strategies, 192–193, 198–199; influence of a decision-maker's function and prior actions of external actors on the generation and choice of strategies, 193; influence of issue area and satisfaction on the generation and choice of strategies, 197; influence of the type of other nation, reaction/initiative and satisfaction on the generation and choice of strategies, 199, 204–205; influence of crisis and issue area on the specification of the time frame of outcomes, 207–208; influence of departmental affiliation and issue area on the substance of outcomes, 209–211; influence of crisis and control over the future on the use of argumentation rules, 216, 218–219, 232–234; influence of a decision-maker's cognitive style on the use of argumentation rules, 216, 218–219, 232–234; influence of a decision maker's function on the use of argumentation rules, 216, 218–219, 232–234; influence of agreement and sequence on the use of argumentation rules, 217–219, 232–234; organizational characteristics, 172, 183–184; personal characteristics, 172, 185; situational characteristics, 172, 178–183; social context characteristics, 172, 185

Probabilities:
calculation of products, 21, 52–54; with intensities, definition, 14–15; without intensities, definition, 14–15

Propositions:
generation and choice of strategies, 191–193, 196–197, 199–200, 203, 204–206; specification of different time frames of outcomes, 208; speci-

Name Index

About the Authors

IRMTRAUD N. GALLHOFER is Senior Researcher at the Sociometric Research Foundation in Amsterdam and has been engaged for more than 20 years in research on political decision-making and text analysis. Her articles have been published in a variety of European political science and psychology journals.

WILLEM E. SARIS is Professor of Statistics and Methods at the University of Amsterdam. In addition to his work on structural equation modeling and the improvement of measurement procedures, he has published several papers on decision-making with Irmtraud Gallhofer.

ISBN 0-275-95433-1

HARDCOVER BAR CODE